Knowledge of Freedom

KNOWLEDGE OF FREEDOM

Time to Change

by

Tarthang Tulku

NYINGMA PSYCHOLOGY SERIES

Reflections of Mind
Gesture of Balance
Openness Mind
Hidden Mind of Freedom
Kum Nye Relaxation, Parts 1 and 2
Skillful Means
Knowledge of Freedom: Time to Change

Library of Congress Catalogue Card Number 84–282–52

ISBN: 0-913546-96-8
ISBN: 0-913546-95-X (pbk.)

Typeset in Fototronic Optima with Optima Semibold
Outline titles and initials. Printed and bound by
Dharma Press, Oakland, California

9 8 7 6 5 4 3 2 1

Dedicated to the Human Mind

Contents

Preface

During the more than sixteen years I have lived and worked in this country, I have engaged in a wide range of projects and interacted with people from many backgrounds and occupations. Having recourse to the wealth of technology and opportunity this society affords, I have been able to develop a publishing and printing company, found an educational institute, write several books, and build a spiritual center, along with raising a family. Many students and friends supported and worked with me on these endeavors, but none of these projects could have been accomplished without knowledge.

Months and sometimes years of preparation were devoted to each project. Much time was spent learning the intricacies of the educational and business systems of this country and in studying the technology, equipment, and materials for printing and construction. In addition, it was necessary to build a basis that would support the growth and development of the projects I hoped to accomplish. Although all of these fields were complex and unfamiliar to me, the knowledge we needed was available and with effort could be gained and applied.

In working with my students and friends, I found that our greatest challenges came not from technical problems or lack of information, but from another direction altogether. The difficulties that most hindered our efforts were self-imposed limitations that made even the most dedicated supporters of these projects vulnerable to frustration and disappointment.

From the very beginning, the nature of my work brought me into contact with people from a wide range of professions, including educators, psychologists, scientists, businessmen, shopkeepers, artists, and students of all ages. In working with so many different people over the years, I have heard both young and old express the same feelings. Many people, despite wealth, education, and success in their chosen occupations, are dissatisfied with their lives and feel a deep inner hunger that they do not know how to fill.

Looking for solutions to our specific difficulties did not seem to be the answer. It seemed far more important to question the underlying patterns of personal dissatisfaction, and to discover what was limiting achievement and enjoyment of life for so many. Perhaps inside each pattern lay the keys to a greater understanding. In discussions with many people on a great variety of subjects, from physics and psychology to business and personal aspirations and difficulties, I found that their responses touched upon universal human concerns.

Many topics surfaced in these discussions: the problems of society and the individual; attitudes towards work; definitions of happiness; motivation to achieve goals and reactions to challenges and problems; the meaning of responsibility, knowledge, and freedom. We compared the views and attitudes of different cultures, and considered the historical influences that shaped their development. We also questioned the patterns of language and discussed how language affects thought and communication. What are the difficulties of communication if we do not have shared meanings and values? How well can we communicate even within a shared language? What significance does this have for the loneliness and isolation that affect so many people? How are our attitudes towards work and life affected by our upbringing and the need to adjust to a complex way of life? How does what we learn early in life influence the way we think and work, the quality of our lives, our definitions of success and happiness?

As we explored these and many other questions, I observed general patterns to the responses. Later, I explored the implications of these patterns with the people I was working with most closely. In examining these patterns in their own lives, many gained valuable insights and provided additional perceptions that deepened our inquiries. In time, as missing details were filled in, patterns showed themselves more clearly. Gradually, whole pictures came into view through this dynamic of questioning, reflection, and response. Although the specific details might vary, the patterns that were true for one individual turned out to be true for others as well.

The people who participated in this process felt that what they had learned had already made a difference in their lives, and would be the starting point of a deeper inquiry into more satisfying ways of being and acting in the world. At their request, I agreed to prepare a series of essays for publication. The editors of Dharma Publishing collected talks given over a period of nearly three years and shaped them into the essays that appear in this volume. Over a period of many months, I reviewed their editing and added new information.

Many of the topics that appear in this book are closely related to daily life and universal human difficulties. Although each essay focuses on a different aspect of modern life, together they offer an approach that may be useful today: a direct inquiry into the human situation that encourages the questioning of all aspects of experience.

This book is only the beginning for what I hope can be a rewarding search into the nature of the human mind. There may be no limits to how far we can extend our inquiries, and no limits to our capacity for understanding ourselves and our world. In the future, I plan to carry this investigation much further, looking with greater depth into the stages of human consciousness. For now, I am grateful for the opportunity to offer these essays to a wider audience. Long ago my teachers emphasized that a basic knowledge of human nature was essential for a productive life; in the light of their words, I hope that in some small way these essays will promote peace and harmony within the hearts of those who read them, and that all who benefit from questioning their own lives will extend what they know to the peoples of the world.

Introduction

Knowledge is our birthright and our inspiration. We are a living embodiment of knowledge: It is the key to our evolutionary development and the basis of our survival. Our being had its origin in knowledge imprinted on two living cells which produced our present form. Our senses 'know' how to see, smell, and taste; our bodies know how to breathe and how to bring new life into being to continue the human heritage.

Our minds are receptacles for the knowledge of ages past. Treasuries of thought and inspiration, our minds enable us to reflect on the past and conceive dreams for the future. Knowledge grants us infinite opportunities for growth. Every moment of our experience is knowledge, a dynamic interaction of our being with the changing world around us. Our thoughts and speech are manifestations of knowledge. Even suffering is knowledge, a pointer to our problems and limitations; it shows us the need for greater understanding and motivates us to invite knowledge into our lives.

Knowledge joins us to every human being who has ever existed on this planet. Although barriers of time and place may separate us, we are never alone. We are brought together by the universal language of the human heart, which is also knowledge. All people share the same basic needs and desires. We rejoice together in times of plenty; we see in our children the hope for the future, and we grieve when this hope is taken from us.

While we share a commonality with others, each of us has a unique life story that unfolds like a great drama, forged from hopes and dreams, actions and interactions. Our every experience adds to our knowledge, and our every action is an expression of what we know. The ability to learn from our experience throughout our lives is also the gift of knowledge.

But our stories are not always happy ones. Within a single day, we might experience many of the feelings that characterize the human condition: desire and frustration, confidence and anxiety. The body that enables us to experience the heights of rapture is the same body that makes us vulnerable to pain. The mind that is so adapted for knowledge can also torment us with memories, regrets, grief, fear, and emotional distress. After more than a million years of evolution, we have yet to find the knowledge that will stabilize our happiness and set us free from suffering.

Is there something fundamentally wrong with our knowledge? In itself, knowledge is beneficial and liberating. Knowledge has made it possible for us to shape our environment and to enhance our well-being; it has enabled us to create the freest and most prosperous societies that have ever existed in the history of the world. Our knowledge increases daily, holding out the promise of extending freedom and prosperity to all the world's peoples.

Yet, while our knowledge and freedom appear to be expanding, we seem to be less at ease with ourselves than ever before. Beneath the prosperous surface of our lives, we still experience frustration and confusion, anxiety, and even despair. Within our societies, even the most fortunate among us have little hope of complete liberation from frustration and dissatisfaction.

Formal education may help us make better choices for our lives, but offers no guarantee that our choices will not lead to pain. Perhaps after many years of experience, we may develop enough wisdom to stabilize our lives, and may finally recognize where our greatest hopes for satisfaction lie. Life is our greatest teacher, but its lessons are often learned too late and at the cost of much suffering. We may have to repeat mistakes many times before we learn, and some lessons we may never learn at all. Depending on whether we learn quickly or slowly, we may have a happy or less happy life. But even if we as individuals become very wise, our happiness can be threatened by social, environmental, and international problems. After several hundred thousand years of accumulating knowledge, what we know does not insure our protection from suffering.

If we could see through the locked corridors of time and participate directly in the entire human experience, perhaps we would be able to discover the knowledge we need to live a better life. As living historians, contemporary witnesses to the unfolding of past time, we could see directly the transformations that have taken place in human consciousness. We would know how fear was overcome when humans first mastered the use of fire. We would endure the struggles for survival in the ice ages and rejoice at the development of agriculture. Our experience of life in the early centers of civilization would broaden and deepen century by century as mankind gradually spread across the continents.

The fabric of civilization would be clear in our memory: We would recall hundreds of cultures overlapping in time and space, each contributing a different color and shape to the grand pattern. How many times would we have felt triumph and defeat as civilizations rose and fell? We would have marveled at the birth of religion and philosophy, and understood the ideals for which men have lived and died. After hundreds of thousands of years of experience, we would know beyond a doubt the patterns of thought and action that lead to suffering. We would know the full meaning of our history, and be free of the need to repeat the errors of the past.

If all of us could experience such a journey, our version of the human story might be far different from the lifeless facts that now comprise our history; revitalized by our experience, the past would become living knowledge that we could apply in our lives today. Seeing the patterns underlying life in a far more comprehensive light, we might not be so willing to engage in actions that have always resulted in suffering. Perhaps, after shedding tears for countless centuries, we would grow weary of frustration, pain, and the waste of human life. Aware of the causes of suffering, we would know what was truly beneficial and how to bring it into being. With such understanding, there would be no limits on our vision for human being, and no limits on human freedom.

But we do not have this vision, and we cannot foresee the results of our actions. It is difficult to learn the lessons of the past, and convert past pain into present knowledge. Thus we have no choice but to repeat old patterns, hoping that somehow what we do will turn out differently than it did in the past. But without greater knowledge, the future is always uncertain, and our hopes may only prevent us from seeing the magnitude of our problems. The knowledge that has brought us wealth and prosperity could as easily become the means of destruction of human life or even the annihilation of life on our planet. Our happiness and our freedom, dependent on conditions that we do not fully understand and cannot control, are still insecure.

To protect our freedom of thought, word, and action, we have many guidelines and laws. But even when our freedoms are safeguarded, even in a land where the rights of the individual are honored, we have no complete freedom of choice, for we cannot choose not to suffer. No matter how far we extend our individual freedoms, our knowledge is not broad enough to make our vision of freedom a reality. Even the actions we take to expand our freedom and material prosperity seem to heighten our sense of wanting and increase the level of frustration in our lives. The pain we experience bears witness to our lack of knowledge and the limitations on our freedom.

Without greater knowledge, we cannot be certain that our actions will not bring suffering to ourselves and others. Continuing to act unknowingly in the world, we can only create more confusion and suffering in a world already overburdened with hopelessness and pain. On a national level, even well-intentioned actions can bring about the opposite of what we desire: serious imbalances in our environment and the heightening of tensions that endanger world peace and prosperity.

How can we open our field of alternatives and find the knowledge we need to gain true freedom? We want to be free to realize our full potential; we want to be free to make full use of all the opportunities life offers us; we want to be free to incorporate all that is good into our lives, and be free of all that causes suffering and pain; we want to appreciate the beauty of the world and the intimacy of communication with other human beings. Whether or not our wishes come true depends upon the range of our vision and the knowledge that informs our actions.

How can we discover what is truly meaningful and beneficial for human beings? How can we bring the full meaning of freedom alive in our hearts? Knowing that we do not yet have the knowledge we need *is in itself* knowledge that can open our minds to a new perspective on freedom.

Recognizing our need for greater knowledge, we can begin to widen our vision. Our lives, and the conditions under which we are privileged to live, offer us all the opportunity we need to create a freer, more satisfactory way of life. Our education has given us the tools for inquiry. Without depending on any dogma or complex doctrine, we can rely upon our own intelligence to open up new ways of knowing and being. We can read between the lines of the human story, looking for themes and patterns underlying problems and pain. With this broader understanding, we can look at our lives, our societies, and our world from a new perspective, more aware of the repeating patterns of human life.

Observing life, and reflecting upon our experience, we can see more clearly the relationships between what we do and the results that follow. With the growth of insight, we can learn more quickly from every kind of experience, and free ourselves of the need to respond to experience with frustration, anger, or pain. We can go even further and begin a dynamic process of observing and converting what we learn into new knowledge that we apply in our lives. If we bring all our knowledge to bear in our words and actions, we can engage each experience openly, without judgment, as an opportunity to expand what we know. As this quality of attention touches more and more of our life, experience becomes more deeply interesting and vital. When we view whatever happens to us as a manifestation of knowledge, knowledge shows itself in the results of our actions.

In opening our minds to knowledge, we can discover a new form of responsibility that would offer greater hope for happiness in our societies and in the world. Rather than being an obligation or a burden, responsibility, backed by knowledge, can be seen as the freedom to respond to our world effectively and wholeheartedly. Responding in this way, we take care of ourselves 'in time'; we have a long-range vision for our lives, and can address potential problems before they become sources of distress and affliction for ourselves or for others.

When we have the courage to face directly the problems in our lives and in society, and recognize our need for greater knowledge, we honor the freedom this society has given us and take responsibility for broadening its meaning in our own lives. Freeing ourselves of problems, we reduce the amount of suffering in the world and increase the potential for others to gain greater freedom for themselves. When we no longer have to pay with our tears for the privilege of living a human life, the knowledge we gain is truly free.

Knowledge, freedom, and responsibility are our most valuable assets, the essential ingredients for our growth and prosperity. With them our potential for growth is unlimited. Each is a catalyst for the other: Knowledge gives meaning to freedom, and our responsiveness creates an openness to new knowledge. Our freedom allows us to tap all our resources for knowledge, and gives us room and opportunity for action. Building upon this foundation, each of us could contribute to a new model of happiness and prosperity based upon the unbounded freedom of the human mind.

Whatever we learn we can share with others, for every human being shares in the difficulties that we confront in our own lives. What greater gift could we offer than relief from suffering and pain? Our children will benefit from this knowledge as well, passing on what they learn to their own children. In this way, each of us can help to uplift the vision of human destiny for generations to come. Were many people to do this, we could project an image of freedom so strongly that obstacles to peace, joy, prosperity, and love would have no place to take root. Illuminated by knowledge, our collective vision could shine like a beacon far into the future, pointing the way for an infinite expansion of all that is good for human beings.

SECTION ONE

Knowledge
in
Time

CHAPTER 1: THE HUMAN INHERITANCE

CHAPTER 2: RESPONDING TO TIME

CHAPTER 3: QUESTIONING MIND

1

The Human Inheritance

We exist in a rare moment of stability,
dependent upon a delicate balance
that could change at any time.

Like children, we find it difficult to believe in a time before the world we know took shape, a time when the house we inhabit had not been built, when its lumber was trees, its nails rock-embedded ore, its windows sand along the ocean's shore. From our perspective, the universe seems vast and eternal, the earth fixed in its orbit, the mountains and oceans changeless. Each day the sun appears in the sky, each night the moon reflects its light. The planet moves invariably through the seasonal round. Even our civilization, though constantly changing, seems to endure. Yet from a different perspective, matters might seem otherwise.

Looking at the evening sky, we may become aware of standing on a planet that is moving through space and wonder how it all began. In our mind's eye we can envision the far-flung reaches of space, empty and vast, pulsing with primordial energy. Rhythms develop, rippling with momentum and direction. As the dynamic openness of space gives rise to qualities and textures, innumerable appearances dance into being —sub-atomic, atomic, molecular—and form more complex patterns. Gaseous clouds begin to glow and spin into planets and stars.

Today it is believed that our own planet spun into existence more than four thousand million years ago. A rocky crust solidified; the atmosphere gradually developed; rains fell and oceans filled. In slow but unceasing movement, continents drifted over the oceans, joining together and splitting apart, their collisions creating giant mountain ranges.

Wind and rain leveled the peaks and ground rock into soil. The orbit of the earth and its tilt toward the sun shifted in cycles, while the magnetic poles changed back and forth, time and time again. Huge ice caps covered vast stretches of land and retreated. Islands rose from the ocean floor through volcanic action, and lakes dried to become desert. For aeons this drama took place with no living creature present.

Hundreds of millions of years ago, the first life forms emerged in the oceans, as certain molecules found a way of replicating themselves and formed simple cells. True animals, such as jellyfish, arose from many cells arranged as a simple, unstable body with barely developed sense organs. According to present knowledge, animal bodies gradually became more complex. Folded layers of cells formed tube-like worms, open at each end. Oriented along an axis, this new kind of body had more developed sensory organs and nerves clustered at one end. A mouth connected the inside of the life form to the outside world.

Based on this simple pattern, more complicated life forms arose—fish, amphibians, and reptiles, birds, and mammals—variations on a four-limbed, hollow body arranged along an axis of nerves. More complex sense organs centered around the head, interacting with the world through numerous apertures. Breath flowed rhythmically through the body, entering and emerging through the mouth and nose. Muscles and organs that developed along this channel made possible a variety of sounds that became forms of communication. Animals formed elementary social structures such as those found in schools of fish and flocks of birds.

For ages before human beings appeared, 'lower animals' ruled the earth. The Era of Fishes, when most land was beneath oceans, was followed by the Empire of the Dinosaurs, when huge reptiles roamed the forests of the world. As the dinosaurs mysteriously disappeared, mammals grew larger and eventually dominated the planet. Long before the earliest Indians established their first settlements, three-toed horses, rhinoceroses, and camels left their remains on American soil.

The earliest humans seem to have emerged more than a million years ago. Though based on the older four-limbed pattern, the bodies of these first human beings were oriented toward the environment in a new way. Their upright stance and forward-facing eyes gave their vision wide perspective and great depth. Eventually, their highly developed sense organs and flexible intelligence were matched by throats and mouths capable of making a range of complex sounds. With expressive faces, and arms and hands free to gesture, point, and grasp objects, human beings possessed unique abilities to communicate with each other. As these capabilities developed, humans passed on their knowledge from generation to generation, building their understanding of their world and molding their surroundings to accord with their wishes.

Bands of early humans spread throughout most of the world. Physically weak and defenseless compared to many animals, they survived by joining together in clans, cooperating to hunt large game and gather roots and edible vegetation. They made tools out of stone and clothed themselves in animal skins. From natural forest fires, human beings took flames and learned to keep them alive. Now they could live in colder regions, cook food, and frighten away animals. Gathering around their fires for safety and companionship, they communicated in a way no animal had before.

Perhaps emerging first as murmured sounds of comfort or cries of danger and need, the rhythms of speech grew gradually more elaborate and distinct. People began to use sounds in a new way. Remembering and repeating a sound, two people could agree upon the name that would distinguish a particular person or object.

Over a long period of time, many sensory impressions—sights, sounds, textures, tastes, and smells—were identified and linked to sounds. Symbols scratched into trees or stone or drawn upon the ground could be connected to particular sounds. By means of symbols and pictures, meaning could be conveyed in the absence of sound or the physical object.

Using their abilities to discriminate and remember, human beings observed their world and its patterns, noting similarities and relationships, and made assumptions based on their past experience. Gradually, simple concepts gave rise to more complex ways of thinking, and humans could reflect differently upon themselves and the world. People began to observe natural cycles and learned to predict their recurrence.

The awareness of our ancestors ranged beyond the knowledge needed for simple survival. Responding to the movement and beauty of their world, certain peoples expressed in symbolic drawings meanings that could not be communicated verbally. Human figures, animal forms, and other artistic shapes drawn on cave walls expressed deep inner responses to experience.

From remembered experiences, human beings began to select and recount important events. They named the unseen forces that could give life or take it, and found ways of defining their relationship to the awesome powers that lay beyond human control.

This knowledge may have come more readily to some than to others; the 'knowing ones', both feared and respected, became healers and guides, channels to powers others could not comprehend. They instructed their people in the order of the world, showing them the attitudes and actions that would harmonize with the great powers and ensure survival. Over time, knowledge was accumulated and organized, and concepts and beliefs were shaped into more abstract thought.

For hundreds of thousands of years, early humans lived in small groups as hunters and gatherers. About ten thousand years ago a revolutionary event took place—the discovery that plants could be cultivated. Domesticated strains of food crops soon followed; the plow was invented, and eventually the wheel.

As humans settled into larger communities, they developed basic technologies: pottery, basketry, the weaving of cloth, and the smelting and forging of metals. Animals were domesticated and trained as hunters, protectors, and beasts of burden, and were used as dependable sources of food and clothing. As human life grew more complex, human beings developed a fuller understanding of natural cycles as well as a more elaborate vision of their place in the world.

About five or six thousand years ago, the rhythms of human civilization shifted again. Urban civilizations took shape in the great valleys along the Nile, the Indus, the Huang-po, and the Tigris and Euphrates rivers. Urban communities evolved more complex forms of social organization. Distinct classes gradually developed—farmers, merchants, administrators, and priests—supporting the growth of technology and material wealth. Large-scale pyramids, temples, and irrigation networks that required planning and co-operation were built. New metal ores and alloys were discovered and fashioned into finer weapons, ornaments, and tools.

More frequent and varied social interactions affected the development of language. Eventually written records were kept, scratched first on clay tokens, bones, or wood, then upon tablets, and later written with ink on leaves, bark, or paper made from plants.

Over the centuries, literate and artistic cultures arose and flourished. Drawing on the achievements of the past and influenced by neighboring cultures, each civilization created its own traditions of language, art, architecture, philosophy, religion, and technology. Calendars, alphabets, and art styles were shared. As each civilization reached its peak and declined, new cultures arose in turn. The building of pyramids and ziggurats gave way to pillared temples and ornate palaces; armies of horse-drawn chariots were supplanted by mounted armored cavalries.

Some cultures endured for thousands of years; others sprang up only to be quickly overrun or absorbed by their neighbors in wars long since forgotten. Entire cultures may have disappeared, their knowledge lost to us. Great libraries, repositories of ancient wisdom, were destroyed by those who did not comprehend their value. Sometimes the vanquished absorbed their conquerors, creating a new cultural synthesis. Interacting and overlapping in time and space, cultural forms shifted through the millenia like the patterns on a kaleidoscope.

Within many cultures, bodies of oral and written knowledge grew up around the insights of great seers, thinkers, and holy men. Traditions that arose to preserve and pass on this knowledge stimulated all aspects of culture, including literature, medicine, art, and architecture. Many schools of philosophy came into being.

There were also seekers who sensed the incompleteness of human knowledge. The questions they raised challenged existing views of the human condition. The knowledge that grew out of their queries passed into established societies, where it catalyzed new insights and bursts of creativity, enriching and broadening human understanding.

Many of the world's great civilizations were eventually linked together, as adventurous explorers and merchants found routes between sea coasts and across deserts. The knowledge of movable type and paper-making spread from China to Europe and the Middle East. The Arabs, borrowing Indian numerals, developed algebra and trigonometry. Knowledge traditions from Asia were carried along trade routes toward the west, while western traditions found their way east.

As practical knowledge grew, raising the standard of living for many cultures, demands for goods and resources also increased, encouraging the search for trade routes to more and more distant lands. Growing contact between cultures encouraged the diffusion of knowledge and the spread of religious and cultural values, sometimes transforming or destroying whole societies.

In Asia, Turks, Arabs, and Mongols established vast empires whose influence spread even into Europe and Africa, altering the patterns of culture they encountered. As the knowledge held by the Greeks disappeared in the West, it was kept alive in the Middle East; later, its return to Europe sparked a renaissance. As Europeans began actively exploring the rest of the world, many civilizations in Asia began to feel the impact of a different way of life. In the Americas, the Indian cultures and the ancient Aztec and Inca civilizations crumbled under the European conquest.

During the eighteenth century the sciences and technologies that had arisen out of the renaissance in the West began to change the face of the world. One invention followed another in rapid succession: the steam engine, the threshing machine, the cotton gin, and the early telegraph; the cylinder printing press, the electromagnetic motor, the reaping machine, and the telephone. Soon the discovery of cells, bacteria, and x-rays changed the world of medicine. In this century, quantum theory, relativity theory, and the splitting of the atom have opened a new era of nuclear technology and revolutionized our concepts of time and space.

Century after century, human culture has built upon itself. The lightning that started the forest fires where early man stole his first flames was later tapped for proof of electricity. Solid-wheeled carts inspired spoked-wheeled chariots, and eventually railroad trains and automobiles. Levers, pulleys, axles, and gears have been refined and powered in turn by horses and oxen, steam, electricity, and gasoline. Now more powerful fuels propel airplanes that cruise at supersonic speeds and rockets that travel through outer space, exploring the planets our ancestors could only admire in the night sky.

Mankind's earliest exclamations of 'Ah!' and 'Oh!' have given birth to great libraries of books; our first efforts at writing with sticks on pieces of clay have matured into electronic carvings on magnetic discs. Vast communications networks linked by satellites orbiting twenty thousand miles above the earth transmit signals worldwide. Emerging from the use of stone tools, cooking fire, water jugs, and animal skins, human civilization has spiraled into a realm unimaginable to our ancestors.

Although our modern technological societies draw upon at least ten thousand years of civilization and hundreds of thousands, perhaps millions of years of human prehistory, on a cosmic timescale, all that has occurred to human beings on our earth has unfolded in less than an instant. Our planet and the sun that nourishes it were brought into being by a conjunction of conditions that we do not fully understand. Elements created in unknown parts of the universe gathered together, stabilizing in a dynamic balance to form the features of our world. In time, they gave rise to a special strand of molecules capable of coding for living cells. In a process that still seems miraculous, the earth became filled with innumerable forms of life. Among these, we are the most recent and possibly the most intelligent.

Despite our sense of permanence on this earth, we exist in a rare moment of stability, dependent upon a delicate balance that could change at any time. Like guests who come to visit, the forces that have created our world and brought us into being may not stay the night.

Although we cannot know the duration of our time, in this present moment we have a precious opportunity to participate fully in life and realize the destiny of human being. Human creativity and intelligence have brought forth an unimaginable variety of forms that have carried us far from our earliest beginnings; now we are capable of drawing upon the full legacy of human experience.

How can we best build upon what has been given us by nature and by the efforts of those who have gone before us? What future shall we fashion for ourselves and for those who follow after us? What wisdom will inform our actions? What vision will guide and inspire us to preserve all that is good for human beings and for our earth, and to set aside all that is destructive?

If the cultures of the world were linked together in friendship and peace, sharing knowledge, technologies, and resources to uplift all human beings, what limit would there be to the benefits that could be realized? Drawing upon the full power of human intelligence, we can seek out the root causes of difficulties between individuals, cultures, and nations, and discover the knowledge we need to create the best future possible for all the world's peoples.

2

Responding to Time

Where is our present knowledge rooted,
if not in patterns of thought
so deeply ingrained that they may be
imprinted in our consciousness and genes?

As human beings, we can choose our way of being in the world. We have consciousness; we are capable of responding creatively to our surroundings. Our experience, shaped into knowledge by our rational minds, can be transmitted to our descendants. Because we have these capabilities, we have the potential for liberating ourselves from conditions that limit many other forms of life. But how well do we understand our potential? Do we know the whole context of human life?

Our lives unfold in time: Our time is our energy and our life. All that is knowable is intimately connected to time. But the nature of time itself remains mysterious. We do not know when human beings began to think about time, or consider how their actions in the present might affect their survival or their well-being in the future. At some point, observing the cycles of natural phenomena, our ancestors learned to measure what they could not comprehend. In dividing time into hours, years, centuries, and aeons, they arranged events in a linear progression, carving out an area in which human thought and action assumed central importance.

Anchored to a fixed point of reference that we term the present, we reach back in time to understand our history and look ahead to anticipate the future. Who would now question this concept of time, which frames the context of our experience? Yet within our framework of past, present, and future, how complete is our knowledge, and how well is it serving our needs?

From our vantage point in the present, we have pieced together what we know of our past. Exploring the sites of early habitations and excavating the earth, we sift through great gaps in time for clues to our origins. We study ancient literary, cultural, and religious traditions that have persisted to the present day; we examine historical records that document the rise and fall of literate civilizations.

But the thread of dynamic meaning that could bind our facts together and give them relevance to our living experience seems beyond our reach. For all our efforts, the story of our past remains fragmentary; our interpretations of history are based on incomplete information. Oral and religious traditions take their full meaning from vanished cultural contexts for which we may have lost the keys. Perhaps our ancestors relied on ways of knowing that we no longer trust; perhaps their concepts and values were rooted in belief systems that have no relevance to our present experience. Written records may be distorted through bias, limited knowledge, and lapses in human observation.

Although full understanding of our past does not now seem possible, we may still be tied to the past in ways that blind us to its power. Where is our present knowledge rooted, if not in patterns of thought so deeply ingrained that they may be imprinted in our consciousness and genes? The past lives on in our thoughts and speech, and in our way of knowing the world around us.

Where did our language come from, our concepts, and our ways of interpreting our experience—memories, associations, assumptions, evaluations, and judgments? Our minds as well as our bodies are linked to our ancestors in a continuum that traces back to the earliest human beings. Although we cannot trace their origins or conceive of other ways of knowing, mental patterns rooted in the past structure our present experience, conditioning our way of being in the world.

We may be viewing our present through eyes more ancient than we realize. Our eyes may now be seeing what our patterning conditions us to see; our minds may be resolving discrepancies in our experience with thoughts and concepts we unquestioningly accept as truth. Like the blurred double image on a photograph of a moving object, our picture of ourselves and our world may not entirely accord with the realities we are experiencing.

Depending upon thoughts and concepts as the only reliable approach to knowledge, we can only interpret what we see in terms of the past. No matter how much information we store in computers or libraries, we are unlikely to create anything really new. Bound to the past, we can only evolve endless variations of patterns established long ago, and pass them on to future generations to perpetuate. With each repetition, these patterns grow more complex, allowing fewer opportunities to discover alternative courses of action.

What we do in our time will either accelerate this narrowing of our alternatives or will open up new possibilities for the future. What patterns will we imprint upon time? What currents will we set in motion, and how will they be reflected in the future? What reverberations from the past will condition the effect of our actions: Will chaos result, or harmony? Whether our actions increase confusion or create a healthier environment for all life depends upon whether our knowledge is comprehensive and the vision that directs it is clear.

Because our present approach to knowledge has brought us great material prosperity and expanded our knowledge of the physical world, it enjoys a special position. We tend to trust it as the only certain way to understand ourselves and our world. But generations before us have lived as we do, conditioned to the same patterns of thought and action. Following their dreams, they thought they were growing a beautiful garden for their descendants to enjoy. Yet when we look around us, we are not entirely satisfied with the results. Weeds keep sprouting; we identify them and cut them down, but new varieties appear. We cannot always see them for what they are or predict how they will mature.

Meanwhile we are casting seeds from last year's plants into the ground, creating the conditions for the future. Yet the climate is changing, and the composition of the soil alters with each season. Is there a way to distinguish before we plant them which seeds will produce lasting beauty, and which will add to our future difficulties?

Although it seems that we cannot predict our future, our intentionality has great power. Our collective will, shaped by the past, projects our dreams into the future, while the force of our desires pulls them into being. Eventually time will return to us the fruits of our actions, conditioned by all that has gone before.

Now we seem to be walking backward into the future, interpreting all we do with views and concepts rooted in the past. In the present we are busy and preoccupied, our minds distracted by anticipations and memories. We trust that somehow we will not stumble, or that what we do today will somehow turn out all right tomorrow. What prevents us from turning around and waking up to the present, tapping the dynamic energy of time directly to free ourselves from bondage to the past? Then we might see more clearly the potentialities we are creating for the future.

Perhaps deep in our hearts we fear that in seeing the present clearly, we will have to confront the full implications of our actions, and face the one certain reality of human life directly: In fifty years, a month, or possibly the next instant, our lives will come to an end. The knowledge of our mortality is our unique human gift. Yet we reject the inevitability of death. We turn away from our one most reliable piece of knowledge and will ourselves into ignorance, choosing a lifetime of uncertainty over a direct encounter with what we know.

Fear drives us back to the past, binding us firmly to thoughts and patterns that are familiar and secure. But we know our security is an illusion. However we try to manipulate time, dividing its dynamic continuum into past, present, and future, saving, planning, and spending it as we choose, ultimately we know we have no control. Time will always be the victor. In avoiding a confrontation with time, we cannot engage its momentum and wake up to what is happening here and now.

If we avoid the implications of time, we cannot know the full context of human life. We know we will die, but we do not know death itself, or what lies beyond its boundaries. Could we somehow see beyond the brief span of our lives? Could we know directly the time before we were born, or the time after our senses will cease to function?

Perhaps in turning around and directly confronting the inevitability of death, acknowledging our fears and uncertainties, we would gain a key that might unlock the mysteries of time and reveal a passage to greater knowledge. What new dimensions of meaning might we discover if we could free ourselves from fear and awaken the full resources of our consciousness?

The key to greater understanding of time lies as close to us as our own being. Our bodies are finely attuned to time; our senses respond to all that happens in our surroundings. Our experience is a direct interaction with the present moment; only our interpretations may be inaccurate. If there were a way to relax our hold on judgments and preconceptions, we could look with fresh eyes on what is happening here and now. Once we can see our present directly, without illusions, we can direct our future with real wisdom. Knowing the extent of the uncertainties we face, we could find a way to greater knowledge, and create the potentiality for a more secure future for all forms of life.

3

Questioning Mind

To begin to know something new,
we first must realize that
there is something we do not know.

Our ability to go beyond the boundaries of the known is one of our most precious resources. Whenever we question the familiar, we open the gates to knowledge and catch glimpses of expansive vistas. Poised on the edge of wonder that turns us toward the unknown and unexpected, the questioning mind is alert and open, receptive to new meanings.

Questions that are deeply meaningful strike an inner chord that attunes our mind and senses to a wider scope of possibilities. Such questions are like the questions we have as children before we learn what we can question and what we cannot.

Although questioning is essentially a move out of the known into the realm of the unknown, we are often encouraged to ask only questions for which there are already answers. As children we ask fundamental questions such as "Where did I come from?"

"Why does the world exist?" "Where do I go after I die?" Perhaps our questions arouse delight but go unanswered, or the answers are more confusing than the questions; unsatisfied, we continue to ask "Why?" What conclusions can we come to when we encounter a vague sense of discomfort from the adults around us, who may even doubt the reliability of the answers they give us? What do we feel when the answer is simply "That's the way it is"? Yet even thoughtful responses may not silence our wonderings. Is our persistence childish? Are our questions unimportant?

Eventually most of us come to believe that the most worthwhile or important questions are either beyond us personally or are ultimately unanswerable. We tell ourselves that fundamental questions about life and death raise such complex philosophical, scientific, or religious issues that only professionals are qualified to deal with them. But fundamental questions are basically simple ones, and they address issues that are important to every human being. It is therefore most fruitful to continue to look at these questions closely and consider their meaning for our own lives.

Answers to questions about where we came from, who we are, our destiny, the meaning of life, and the causes of the events that shape the course of our lives form the foundation of our existence. These answers are the seemingly self-evident, unquestionable truths at the basis of all our understanding. But how often do we consider that the conclusions we accept have been reached without full participation on our part?

Perhaps long ago basic assumptions were made to explain how human beings live and act in the world.

Faced with a vast unknown, people created points of reference to make sense of their world and find their place and purpose among all that existed. What shaped the directionality of their consciousness? What if different reference points had formed the basis of the earliest conclusions? Would we see ourselves differently? Or our world? Would human experience be other than it is if our understanding of ourselves were different?

Of what value are such questions? Once we have learned the fundamental agreements that shape our familiar reality, we feel we 'know the way things are'; after we have made this assumption, we usually do not investigate much further. By accepting provisional answers as conclusive, we close off the possibility of deeper knowing. We trap ourselves in a vast unknown realm that we do not even know is unknown. Paradoxically, it will remain unknown as long as we already 'know' it. To begin to know something new, we must first realize that there is something we do not know.

As individuals we may question whatever we wish. If we begin by assuming that all the most important questions have already been answered or cannot be answered, we lose interest in opening our own investigations. But what do we really know that was not taught to us by someone else, or is not in some way dependent on what we have accepted as true? Would we not prefer to base our lives on our own knowledge?

Building our own basis for knowing invites us to step into the unknown and begin a process of inquiry that has infinite potential for expansion. But looking toward the realm of the unknown, we may sense a vague anxiety that makes us hesitate to look too closely. We may prefer the solid ground of the known and familiar. Yet how do we know the ground we stand on is actually solid if we do not investigate it? Perhaps if we are willing to inquire, we can find the way to a new understanding that would offer more lasting security.

Our human history and our individual experience teach us that the boundary between the known and the unknown is capable of shifting, depending in part on how closely we look and how deeply we question. A question for which someone else may have an answer might lead us to a new perspective that would reshape our familiar knowledge. Aspects of the known world as well as our ordinary experiences, when examined closely, can open up surprising new worlds for investigation. Truly vital questions seem to have many layers of answers, each of which extends our understanding. The key to discovery lies in accepting no answer as final; within all we know, many new possibilities await discovery. Like children, we can persist in asking another "why."

Open inquiry is the basis of all our freedoms. We are accustomed to inquiring of others; but why not begin to inquire of ourselves? Questions we ask ourselves have an evocative quality that calls for response; those that seem most unanswerable keep the gates of our minds open the longest. In this openness, we might find new insights into the significance of being human. Protecting ourselves from dogmas, limiting assumptions, and outworn ideas of all kinds, we move closer to realizing the freedom of a fully awakened human mind.

SECTION TWO

Knowledge Today

CHAPTER 4:
ALTERNATIVES TO DISSATISFACTION

CHAPTER 5:
ACCELERATION OF CHANGE

CHAPTER 6: FREEDOM AND PROSPERITY

4

Alternatives to Dissatisfaction

For all their unhappiness,
few people seem to question
the basic patterns of their lives.

Life in modern societies seems to resemble a view of the Golden Gate Bridge, a symbol of prosperity known throughout the world. The structure is beautiful from a distance, but maintaining it is a full-time job for crews of painters whose work is never finished: By the time they repaint the entire bridge, the section painted first needs another coat. Viewed close up, the shades of color vary, and the result is never quite satisfactory.

Despite centuries of effort directed toward increasing our material well-being, we do not seem to be achieving the happiness, security, and peace of mind that bring lasting satisfaction to human life. Today life seems more pressured and in many ways harder than it was in the past. Seeing changes occur with such speed, we may wonder how future generations will be able to manage. "What is our world coming to?"

Whatever our propensities or beliefs, we cannot escape a growing awareness of dissatisfaction. When we look around us, we see few signs of real happiness. Even the wealthy have problems with boredom and are unable to find lasting satisfaction in possessions or in acting upon their desires. Success in society or in a career does not necessarily bring contentment; a life of striving and competition often produces complex problems and, in the end, great weariness.

High ideals and expectations are often lost in discouragement as years go by without goals seeming any closer. How many people spend thirty or even forty years without accomplishing what they set out to achieve? Everywhere people are anxious for the security of their loved ones, their possessions, or their jobs. In the richest countries of the world, at all levels of society, regardless of status or wealth, emotional pain and frustration are on the rise. Our way of life is not bringing us the satisfaction it promises.

Some young people who feel strongly motivated to achieve success—as well as some people in less wealthy countries—find this difficult to believe. Riding the crest of energy and ambition, urged on by parents who feel wealth or status would solve most problems, they may not notice the difficulties and dulling routines in their parents' lives. Or perhaps they think they can avoid making the same mistakes.

Others find themselves lost, disconnected from the past and ill at ease in the present. Disillusioned with the lifestyles and values of those around them, many feel they must search on their own for a sense of direction and purpose. But when they become involved in work and family, their new responsibilities demand their time and energy, and they too can easily find themselves caught up in patterns similar to the ones they had wished to avoid.

Each day brings new opportunities, but which choice will lead where we want to go? Though we anticipate great pleasures, we often end up with frustration instead. The very things that bring us happiness—our friends, our children, our jobs, our leisure—may become sources of pain.

Friends can tire of us, or move away; where we once felt joy in thinking of them, we may be left with a feeling of loss. In the same way, our enjoyment of our children will turn to pain if they get into trouble or fall ill. The satisfaction we gain from our jobs may dissipate over the years, leaving us bored, or full of regret for what we could not accomplish. Or our work may remain interesting but pressured, and difficult to enjoy over time. Even during leisure hours we may feel forced to have a good time, or find our time evaporating in activities we do not really enjoy. It seems that eventually, something always blocks our satisfaction.

Perhaps our attempts to find satisfaction are actually leading us into frustrations. It may be that we are trying to take care of ourselves without knowing our real needs. If we fed an infant nothing but sugared water, the baby might like it and cry for more, but inside he would still be hungry and dissatisfied. Not knowing his needs, we might continue giving him what he seemed to enjoy; his demands would grow more insistent, and our efforts more desperate, until at last he starved for lack of the right nourishment.

There may be alternatives that would offer a more secure, healthier, and fulfilling basis for our lives—but where can we find such alternatives? The models of our society are based on the rich and successful, those who have achieved power, fame, or made a name for themselves in a profession. But even they have no protection from anxiety and frustration, and the need to maintain their position may cause them more emotional stress than we could ever imagine. Where can we find examples of human beings who have maintained inner balance and strength through all the stages of their lives?

There seem to be few exemplars for us to follow. Everyone around us feels emotional pain, regrets lost opportunities, or wishes the quality of life were better. Yet for all their unhappiness, few people seem to question the basic patterns they are following and pursue this questioning to the point of real change.

Most of us have already tried altering our circumstances to find a better way to live. Changing relationships, jobs, or environments provides some temporary relief, but the same pattern of difficulties often arises again—only the outer circumstances have changed.

Lacking any clear alternatives, most of us still keep going on, no matter how discouraged we become. But while we can force painful memories out of our minds, pain accumulates deep within, poisoning our lives by degrees. The older we become, the more difficult it can be to support the illusion of satisfaction.

Eventually, at the end of our lives, we will have to face our own situation directly. But then we may lack the energy and the drive to wake up to a deeper understanding. Now, while we have the opportunity to change, is the time to look closely at what is happening in our own lives, in society, and in our world environment. For real understanding, we have to uncover the repeating patterns that rob us of time and energy. If we remember that our time is short and very precious, and that we alone can take responsibility for our lives, we can find the knowledge we need to protect ourselves from pain now, and from far greater suffering in the future.

We need to look closely at what we are doing and ask whether our actions are likely to bring us the satisfaction we seek. Are our attitudes and personal philosophies in harmony with what we really want? Perhaps we can find an entirely new way to live—not by changing our occupations, but by changing the views and attitudes that prevent us from enjoying our lives and benefiting others. With a more awakened vision, we can discern the difference between lasting and temporary satisfaction.

When we see clearly, we will have knowledge. Knowledge is honest; it counters all forms of avoidance and self-deception, and strengthens our ability to cut through the web of problems that beset our lives. Knowledge touches our deepest feelings and imparts a sense of power and confidence that no one can take away from us. Grounded in knowledge, we can establish clearer priorities and awaken a new sense of purpose for our lives.

5

Acceleration of Change

*The increasing pace of change itself
may be a symptom of larger imbalances
of which we are not aware.*

In earlier times, ideas and technological advances entered the world slowly. Major innovations occurred roughly five hundred years apart, and concepts and ideas changed very gradually. Stressful periods of significant change were followed by long intervals of stability and balance, when people had time to fully experience, reflect upon, and evaluate events. Shifts in social values tended to come slowly.

Within the past two centuries the pace of change has dramatically increased, and in recent times major changes have occurred with incredible speed. The United States rose to power in less than two hundred years, while whole new forms of government and technology have developed only in the past century.

The rate of change is now so fast that there seems to be little sense of order and direction in our societies. We are traveling so quickly that we have no time to consider whether we might be losing valuable aspects of our past; we have no time to question if what we are carrying into the future has enduring value.

Earlier in this century, shared values provided more stability. Many people spent their entire lives among neighbors they had known since childhood. Parents could pass on their knowledge with confidence, knowing that the values that had served them well would also support their children. In the decades of social change that followed, the generations were still linked by a basic continuity of attitudes and views. As younger people moved from the towns to the cities, taking up new professions and establishing smaller families, they usually brought with them the moral and ethical values of their families.

In the past forty years the gap in shared skills and values between generations has widened dramatically, and new gaps are opening between persons even closer in age. Fads and fashions have always come and gone erratically, but now we are seeing far deeper changes occurring with enormous speed. Many older people can hardly relate to the moral values and attitudes underlying new lifestyles and actions. Values seem to be constantly changing.

Today the stream of events brings exciting new opportunities and pleasures, but pressure to keep up the pace continually intensifies. It is possible that the rate of change may be passing beyond our control. We now live in a whirl of new products, entertainments, and information. Fascination with the new and different, and the feeling that new is necessarily better, lead us to automatically replace the old with the new.

Consumer goods go out of date so quickly that it is more convenient to buy a new model than to repair the old. No sooner have we learned how to use the latest technology than we are told it is obsolete, since it cannot perform functions we did not even know we were missing.

Change naturally creates pressure to adapt, and the accelerated rate of change has increased this pressure by allowing us less and less time to respond to what is happening. We struggle to keep up with the competition, with changes in lifestyle or fashion, with advances in our fields. As societies we can hardly keep up with ourselves. Having produced vast new technologies and complex networks connecting people with products, we now must pour our energy into maintenance. We must update our machinery, repair our roads, revise our educational programs, and renovate our expanding cities.

Only a few decades ago many people felt confident that hard work would be rewarded, and that there was room at the top for those who strived to achieve. It was possible to take charge of one's own life and make a place for oneself whatever the condition of the world as a whole. If parents could not realize all of their dreams, they still had faith that their labor would open up greater opportunities for their children.

Today we cannot be so certain that we will reap the full rewards of our efforts. Our skills and training may not sustain us throughout our productive years; many of us may end our working lives short of our goals. It is becoming clear that our children may not be able to enjoy a more comfortable, secure way of life than our own.

The uncertainty we feel about the future subjects us to levels of stress unknown to previous generations. On personal, national, and international levels we have little control over events that could affect our lives at any moment. Many feel anxious and helpless, knowing that the dangers to our world are increasing as the rate of change accelerates. Even now stress is seriously affecting the human heart, body, and mind; physical, emotional, and mental problems are increasing in variety and intensity, and are beginning to reach epidemic proportions.

A sense of instability extends far beyond our own cultural sphere, arousing uncertainties about the future direction of nations and the world. Political, military, and economic policies shift so frequently it is difficult to assess their implications. Worldwide competition for resources, manufacturing, and trade heightens as new nations become industrialized.

We have the wealth, knowledge, and powerful instruments to work more good in the world than ever before; world leaders in particular have an unprecedented opportunity to channel the energy of millions of people in the direction of peace and prosperity. We clearly have enormous power to alter the course of events. On the other hand, our power may prove no more secure than the flame of a candle in the wind. Without greater knowledge, we are powerless against the dynamic forces of time, which can easily turn our knowledge against us.

When we are unable to recognize and use the opportunities we have 'in time', time will sweep opportunity out of our grasp and catch us in its wake. Weighted down with problems, we may find ourselves pushed into hasty decisions and actions that could have serious repercussions.

Now that the nations of the world are linked together through elaborate communication networks and delicate balances of economic, political, and military power, ripples of change travel rapidly across the entire globe. Whereas knowledge of the downfall of an empire might once have taken years to spread across a continent, today the effects of the smallest alteration in the precarious balances we depend on for our safety and well-being are felt around the world within hours.

Traditionally, nations, cultures, and individuals have avoided threats to their security by building barriers between themselves and the outside world. Today there is no refuge, no safe place to live in isolation from an ever more bewildering complex of problems. Aggression anywhere threatens to set off a chain reaction that could involve the entire world.

Negative forces already set in motion, repeatedly reinforced by our present actions, may be becoming too powerful for human control. Individuals who are themselves unbalanced and neurotic have little protection from negative influences and little control over their responses. If such persons attain positions of power anywhere in the world, they can easily become open channels for desires and hatreds that have been accumulating for hundreds of years. The confusion that allows hatred and desire to overwhelm our human sensibilities may be our greatest enemy, and a danger to which all of us are vulnerable.

The increasing pace of change itself may be a symptom of larger imbalances of which we are not aware, perhaps even reflecting chaotic forces at work in the universe itself. Unseen destructive forces may be building, like the underground stresses that precipitate earthquakes. What we do in our time might have more profound reverberations than we realize.

Before we can understand the full significance of human actions and their effects on society, on the world, and possibly on a far larger scale, we need to appreciate the interconnections among all aspects of our world. Only through greater knowledge can we balance the destructive forces in the world and within our minds.

Perhaps we can turn to our earth, our parent and our home, as a great teacher. The salt water in our bodies reminds us that the seas gave us life. The growth of the human embryo, repeating in its development the evolution of life on our planet, teaches us that we share a bond with everything that lives.

In all the universe, we know of nothing more beautiful than our planet. No one desires to accelerate the forces that could leave our world barren and humanity homeless. If we can acknowledge our interrelationship with all forms of life and appreciate the lineage we carry within our bodies and minds, we may find the resources we need to protect ourselves and our world. Strengthened by our inner resources, we can counter the gathering momentum of negativities and choose a new direction for the future.

6

Freedom and Prosperity

*It seems that the more we know,
the more we need to know.*

The concept of progress has changed over the centuries, keeping pace with the technology that has brought us the wealth of goods and comforts we enjoy today. Several hundred years ago, the notion of progress carried religious and philosophical overtones closely related to the idea of the perfectibility of man. As scientific knowledge accumulated and was joined to new social ideas, the focus of progress shifted towards improving material and social conditions. Although this change in emphasis has weakened the association between progress and spiritual growth, the idea of progress still touches deep yearnings and aspirations.

The contemporary concept of progress has captured the imagination of modern man and become a guiding force in our civilization. New understandings of freedom, justice, and human rights have created a vision of increasing liberty and prosperity as our natural birthright. This dream has aroused the desires and hopes of millions of people and inspired sweeping social change. Social change has, in turn, been strongly supported by the rapid advances in science and technology, aspects of modern life that testify to the power of human intellect and support the image of man as arbiter of his own destiny. Rich in ideas and expertise, our culture stimulates our ingenuity to accomplish anything imaginable, from exploring the ocean depths to settling the reaches of space.

Our willingness to share our increasing knowledge with cultures around the world has strengthened our feeling of being a part of one human family, as well as our desire to be of benefit to the whole of human society. Our broadening vision, combined with our increasing commitment to freedom throughout the world, seems to bear witness to genuine progress in our society.

Looking around us today, we can see tremendous advances made in the past century alone. Our technology has brought us great prosperity, and the modern dedication to freedom and to individual rights has created the most open societies that the world has ever known. In many countries, freedom of speech, freedom of thought, and freedom of belief are now all protected by law.

Yet our difficulties seem to keep pace with our advances. The world's problems in many ways seem more far-reaching and more complex than in the past. We face interlocking environmental imbalances and complicated societal and economic issues. Every advance we make seems to carry with it new difficulties that we have not been able to predict. The pesticides that have brought us higher crop productivity now cause concern for our health; the drugs used to treat one disease are found to be hazards in their own right; institutions and laws intended to benefit the elderly, the poor, the handicapped, and the mentally ill may actually contribute to the suffering we are trying to alleviate. The list of problems seems endless. Our problem-solving process itself seems to be generating problems.

We now seem to be capable of altering balances in nature, in our societies, and in ourselves. Our technology is powerful enough to change the very conditions upon which life on this planet depends. In removing basic substances from the ground and redistributing them throughout the world, are we creating imbalances within our planet that could have far-reaching implications? Will the composition of our atmosphere be altered in ways that will have unforeseen effects on ocean levels, crops, or human life? What is happening to the world-wide economic balance as nations vie for control of resources?

Up to this point we have relied upon our political and legal systems and upon our technological expertise to find solutions to any problems that may arise. If one energy source is running out, we assume we can find another; if we create pollution with our technology, we turn again to technology to devise ways of cleaning it up. If injustices are created by benefiting one group, we expect our law-makers to enact more comprehensive laws. The very abundance of solutions we have put forth in the past gives us confidence in our ability to find more solutions in the future. But can we continue doing this indefinitely?

The more sophisticated and complex our problem-solving becomes, the broader and less predictable its effects. Our knowledge cannot seem to catch up with its own results. It seems that the more we know, the more we need to know; the more we accomplish, the more we need to do. Now that we have, for example, artificial life-support systems, genetic engineering, and earth-orbiting satellites, we are faced with new legal and ethical problems related to the use of this technology. In setting up the procedures to guarantee each individual the right to protect his interests, we seem to have set in motion a wave of distrust and defensiveness that was never intended. Now minor disagreements become full-blown controversies that embroil us in litigation, crowding our courts and slowing the process of justice.

Somehow in espousing freedom and aiming at prosperity for all, we have brought mixed blessings upon ourselves. In our frustration, we may feel that there are hidden forces at work, undermining our very ideals and efforts. Yet our guiding principles seem true, just, and noble; it would be unthinkable to trade our way of life for that of less free societies or less developed nations.

Much of our modern progress and prosperity would have been impossible without the inspiration of technology together with the free enterprise system and the principle of competition; they have given individuals the opportunity to exercise their intelligence and creativity in the fulfillment of their dreams.

The free enterprise system challenges people to do their best to produce better products and services and to improve the conditions of life. This system has served us well, creating such prosperity that it has become a model throughout the world.

Yet free enterprise has an unattractive side that expresses itself in increasingly self-oriented and irresponsible action. In the name of personal rights, many people interpret 'free enterprise' as license to serve selfish goals, and consider knowledge as a personal possession that can be bought and sold at the discretion of the 'owner'. Though we attempt to regulate abuses of knowledge, many questions remain: Do a few individuals have the right to profit from knowledge at the expense of the welfare of others? What is the dividing line between the 'greater good' of society as a whole and the inconvenience or harm of a few? If the right to apply knowledge for gain must be restricted, precisely how far can restrictions go without intruding on individual freedoms?

Interpreting knowledge and freedom selfishly creates the conditions for both individual and global conflicts. If individuals and groups pursue their own special interests exclusively, their vision may become dangerously narrow. This seems to be happening today. As competitive pressures heighten worldwide, we have little time to consider the effects of our actions. Ideas and advances in technology are implemented quickly, often with little thought for what future problems they might cause. In our completely interconnected modern world, whatever we do will affect others. Yet in order to gain a competitive edge, we may settle for expedient short-sighted actions that do not consider the needs of society as a whole.

If we compete successfully, our prosperity attracts competitors we did not have when we were less successful. Competition grows more intense; the pressure to keep up the pace intensifies, for competition itself does not seem to have a natural stopping point. The same western societies that have promoted the ideals of progress and competition are now economically threatened by other nations who admire and desire this prosperity and so have begun to compete in their own right. Once competition has escalated, success can be counterproductive: When one is imitated, one can also be surpassed.

One of the most distressing side-effects of our material success is the insecurity it fosters in our lives. Our technology now advances so rapidly that companies need to 'update' their equipment and procedures over and over again in order to remain competitive. New research is being done in so many fields that few people can feel on top of their chosen specialty without constant study. Many of us today cannot rely upon one set of skills to sustain us throughout our working lives.

The competitive atmosphere that challenges us to do our best and brings us much of our success also fosters a sense of separation among people, provoking envy, fear, and an unwillingness to cooperate or share. The insecurity and pressure it creates contribute to personal and social problems. Under increasing stress, we may turn more readily to alcohol and drugs; people today seem to succumb more easily to emotional imbalances, anxiety, and depression. Those in high-pressure situations often feel the quality of their lives is decreasing even as they advance in their careers. Individuals who have been unable to match the competition may be caught up in feelings of failure that spiral down into despair. Others who are unwilling to participate competitively become discouraged from making valuable contributions to society.

The side-effects of many of our social and political freedoms seem perhaps even more baffling, for freedom is the cornerstone of our way of life. The Constitution guaranteed freedom of thought and religion to everyone; the principle of the separation of church and state removed questions of individual morality and ethics from the sphere of government to insure that these freedoms would never be lost. Basic ethical and moral standards were incorporated into civil law, while the responsibility for instruction in morality and ethics was left to the family, the schools, and to religion.

This system worked for generations. But in recent decades, the schools have been pressured to draw back from matters that seem to impinge on personal freedom. The family is in flux. Parents have less time to devote to their children, and many people have loosened their ties to religion. A gap in moral and ethical instruction has opened up that we cannot close without arousing much controversy.

As a society, we have lost touch with a widely shared moral standard that would provide individual and social stability. We have a seemingly endless array of moral choices. New attitudes toward social roles of men and women have made a wide range of behaviors, ethics, and lifestyles available. But we must search on our own for what has meaning and value for our own lives. This has left us in a quandary: Individuals have many choices, but where can they gain the knowledge and understanding to make meaningful choices for their own lives? We do not want religion or government to dictate moral and ethical choices to us, but without a coherent moral and ethical consensus, it is easy to doubt the wisdom of our choices and difficult to build a basis of trust with others. As a result, many people feel a lack of stability and commitment in their lives.

Lacking moral consensus, society seems to be fragmenting into smaller and smaller groups, each with its own views, tastes, interests, and demands. As a group divides into smaller units, the support and balance provided by the larger group is lost. Now that the older generation, for example, has lost its place within the family, we face the problem of support for the elderly. Institutions are created, but this solution creates its own problems—psychological, social, and financial. At the same time, the smaller family has lost the wisdom and experience of its older members and the sense of continuity with the past, increasing the sense of rootlessness and confusion in our societies.

With our sense of community in decline, and moral and ethical values in flux, violence is increasing on the streets and even within families. Our sense of inner restraint and our respect for law in the context of a larger society is eroding, and we are coming to rely more heavily on external forms of restraint.

When we cannot trust the stability or intentions of others, what freedom actually remains to us? We live in fear on the streets and in our homes; we lock our doors, instill fear in our children, and arm ourselves. In the name of our own personal freedom, we may feel compelled to demand stronger laws. But this approach is not completely satisfactory. Even now we do not have all the prisons we need to carry out sentences passed under existing laws. And few of us would be happy living in a society where security and stability depended solely upon increased restrictions and ever harsher enforcement of the law.

Although on one level our choices seem nearly unlimited, in the freest, most prosperous societies in the world, we seem to have few real choices open to us. How can we guarantee our own right to free speech without subjecting our children to confusing or harmful propaganda? Can we make moral choices for others without sacrificing our own freedom of choice? How can we even begin to address pollution of the environment when we cannot get to work without using a car or mass transit?

The kind of large-scale, interlocking problems we face today are difficult even to think about carefully and unemotionally. Confronted with situations in which we have no control, we feel helpless and anxious. How can we respond effectively? Surely we cannot ignore the ominous possibilities for our future, or the responsibility we have to protect the welfare of our children's adult lives.

The potential for increasing difficulties and confusion extends beyond our families and communities to include the entire world. As more developed societies offer aid to developing nations and provide technological assistance for their industries, we are seeing the early symptoms of potentially serious problems. Less wealthy nations are accumulating debts in order to modernize, and are purchasing technology that can be used not only for peaceful means but also for aggression. Such changes threaten the welfare and stability of these traditional cultures as well as the balance of world power.

While the wish for world prosperity is universally shared, is it actually possible for all societies in the world to enjoy the same level of material wealth? Has the world sufficient resources to sustain billions of people attempting to live as we do? How would the economies of the now prosperous nations fare in a vastly more competitive world? Even now, hostilities and tensions seem to increase in tandem with the demand for goods and resources.

In cultures where human beings still struggle for survival, the values of modern societies raise expectations for a higher standard of living. If power passes into the hands of a prosperous few, the greater part of the population can be left with a heightened sense of deprivation and injustice that sets the stage for unrest and violent revolution.

What will happen if envy of the material benefits enjoyed by industrialized societies increases the sense of separation among the people of the world? Will we face even greater frustration and danger, group polarized against group, the old against the young, race against race, nation against nation? If we have to compete for resources to protect our security, or even to survive, will we increase the level of anger and aggression in our world, and create the conditions for anarchy that would endanger the whole human race?

In the face of such widespread potential difficulties, the need for fuller knowledge has never been greater. Although we draw upon all the knowledge at our command, and try to foresee the consequences of our actions, our predictions are seldom accurate or comprehensive enough to take all factors into account. Our information and our theories seem somehow incomplete. We often obtain not only something different from what we desire, but the opposite of what we desire. Like the sorcerer's apprentice, we seem to be at the mercy of our own partial knowledge. What would we need to do to obtain pure and unmixed benefits from our efforts to enhance freedom and prosperity?

There may be alternative approaches and actions that we have not explored, new possibilities that could free us from the destructive side-effects that now follow us like a shadow. Each of us individually can question what is happening to our world and to ourselves, asking whether what we are getting is worth the price. Perhaps there are concepts and values that are not serving us well, which we could redefine or set aside. Perhaps the time has come to reconsider progress in terms of inner as well as external well-being, and reflect on what builds lasting meaning and value in an individual human life.

Where can we look for a measure of good that would offer the greatest hope for uplifting human being? Upon what basis can we shape a new vision for human value and freedom? How high can we set our goals for human happiness? Surely we can expand our definition of freedom. Perhaps the only factor holding us back is a lack of confidence in our ability to counter the negative forces that impede our progress. Can we devote our time and energy to finding a new dimension of knowledge that will free us from limitations and be an unending source of hope and inspiration?

There are many treasures in this society that could support a far more peaceful, harmonious, and satisfying way of life. We have great wealth and tremendous technical expertise. Educational systems, communication systems, and vast service networks already exist. How will we use these tools? What knowledge will guide us? Will self-interest prevail, or will we use our resources to achieve a higher purpose?

Perhaps we can discover a deeper meaning to the freedom and individualism that have inspired so much of our success, and put them into practice within our own minds. If we could examine how our present patterns of thought and action jeopardize the very qualities we most value, we might open our hearts and minds to a more comprehensive knowledge.

With greater knowledge, we could well afford to abandon short-sighted goals and view prosperity in an entirely new light. Inspired by a broader vision of freedom and well-being, we could awaken to new possibilities for unlimited human progress.

SECTION THREE

Invitation to Knowledge

CHAPTER 7:
OPPORTUNITY FOR CHANGE

CHAPTER 8: KNOWLEDGE AND SELF

CHAPTER 9:

BREAKING THROUGH THE KNOWN

7

Opportunity for Change

*No problem that affects us as human beings
is so beyond our comprehension
that we cannot look at it
and question why it is happening.*

Most of us feel fairly well-informed about the problems of modern life. We read newspapers and magazines; television takes us to the scene of the latest disasters and crises; daily we hear about international tensions, terrorism, and increasing crime. Accounts of disasters and suffering arouse an odd kind of fascination: They are real, yet remote; repelling, yet stimulating. We listen and read, concerned about individual and social problems.

As events come and go, today's news supplants the old, and the details of yesterday's crises fade from memory. Image after image, fact after fact crowd our minds, evoking impressions and emotions, but allowing us little time for reflection on the broader implications of what is happening in our societies and in the world.

We may be overwhelmed by the conflicting facts, interpretations, and opinions that accumulate around every important issue, and feel that many issues today present us with insurmountable complexities. Yet at other times, the causes of problems may seem so obvious and their solutions so simple that we wonder why someone cannot fix them.

Despite differences of view and opinion, most of us probably feel apprehensive about many of the same things and are reacting in many of the same ways. Reflecting upon the disturbing trends in society, knowing they could affect our lives at any moment, is disconcerting. We may conclude that the problems proliferating in the world today are the inevitable price of progress, and resign ourselves to a kind of disapproving toleration. We may ascribe the cause to innate human greed or society's intrinsic inhumanity; reminding ourselves that human beings have always been this way, we may excuse ourselves from examining current problems more deeply, and gradually sink into cynicism or pessimism. Knowing that the problems are extensive and complex, we may be tempted to ignore them altogether; already pressured by more immediate concerns in our daily lives, we may sense that what we see may only increase our frustration. Perhaps we prefer to concentrate on the positive aspects of life.

But we cannot completely ignore our social and international situations. Long after events fade from memory, their emotional overtones stay with us, heightening underlying tensions. We feel unsafe in the streets or in our own homes; we are anxious for our children and for the future. Yet we do not know how to connect our concern with effective action. It seems as if we have little choice but to accept whatever happens.

When our concern penetrates more deeply, and we want to take action, what can we do? Most of us have limited access to information and lack the background to analyze any one situation in depth. Even experts do not agree; their opinions may be swayed by personal prejudice or alignment with special interests. Often those closest to the problems may acknowledge that there are no easy solutions, and end by offering no clear course of action.

Sometimes a specific problem may seem clearly defined and too pressing to ignore, so we rouse ourselves to action, protesting injustices or demanding changes from groups or national leaders. As we take a strong position on one side of an issue, we try to affect the outcome by imposing our will and raising our voices. Those on the other side of the issue do the same. But this approach seems to produce only limited results. While our intelligence and energy are drawn into a conflict of wills, opportunities to change situations often diminish; in the heat of opposing passions, the problem gains momentum, just as a child grows more unruly while his parents argue about his discipline.

There have been times when it seemed that good intentions backed with passion and commitment were all we had to rely on to force changes we saw must be made. But were our knowledge and methods sufficient to ensure the results we wished, without entangling us in further difficulties? We may be repeating an approach that brought about changes in the past, but we might question whether those changes were accompanied by changes in underlying views. Entrenched attitudes do not change easily; in forcing the appearance of change without changing the human heart and mind, we may be heightening tensions that pass unnoticed for a time, but create reservoirs of resentment that could backlash if conditions were ripe. Perhaps we have to look more deeply into the underlying causes of our problems to find alternative means of solving them.

Part of our difficulty seems to grow out of our hopes: We hope that good intentions will bring about a good result; we hope that we are improving the human condition. In allowing ourselves to be distracted by hope, we do not see clearly the forces at work in the present. The underlying patterns of our problems elude us. We experiment with solutions to isolated problems, but are unable to predict the outcome of our actions. How then can we take responsibility for the future our actions are creating? Yet without taking responsibility, we have no real control; we drift with the current, hoping it will not lead to a waterfall—or believing that somehow we will break free at the last moment by a strenuous new leap of ingenuity.

In the West, as individuals and as societies, we have a responsibility for the future that extends beyond our own concerns. Less developed nations consider the model established in western societies as the key to wealth, security, and human happiness. Few countries have not felt the influence of modern technological societies, and the pressure to modernize is intense.

Educated classes around the world are adopting the languages that give them access to western science and technology, and enable them to communicate internationally. Western civilization is now setting the pace, and the world will follow where it leads.

Many people may not be aware that the spread of western science and technology throughout the world is precipitating rapid changes in traditional values and lifestyles, upsetting the balance of entire cultures. Occupations that gave millions a place in society, however humble, are being displaced by new methods and technology that leave many with no employment or position. The sense of inherent human worth and self-respect, which once could be maintained even in the face of poverty, is being lost as human value is coming to depend more exclusively on wealth and power.

As hopes for a better life are increasingly invested in material well-being, cultures that have emphasized spiritual values are losing contact with their religious traditions. Knowledge of alternative ways for finding meaning in life is disappearing, while the limited benefits of material prosperity reach only a few of the world's peoples. If modern patterns of living are established worldwide, and faith in a materialistic approach completely supplants religious traditions, we may lose valuable opportunities to consider other ways of being in the world.

We may be losing something very precious. Throughout history, widely divergent views and attitudes, even profound cultural differences, have been catalysts for new insights. While unfamiliar ideas are often unsettling, they can also create openings for new knowledge that can have long-range benefits for the entire world.

In following only one model for future societies, we may be locking ourselves into one way of thinking and acting. A greater uniformity of values, language, and culture might reduce prejudice and misunderstanding, but it will also diminish possibilities for creativity, fresh ideas, and the reevaluation of established patterns. When hostilities arise that commonality of culture cannot resolve, concepts from different traditions might provide valuable perspectives that could inspire new and creative solutions.

In these dangerous times, it seems very important—for everyone's sake—that our actions be guided by a concern for all of the world's peoples. Otherwise, the developed societies may lead the whole world into deeper suffering. What may now appear to be good ideas and expedient solutions could result in serious disruptions in the future. While we may avoid such difficulties in our lifetimes, generations who follow will have to cope with an increasingly troubled world.

The problems facing the world can appear overwhelming, but no problem that affects us as human beings is so beyond our comprehension that we cannot look at it and question why it is occurring. As human beings, we have the privilege and responsibility to ask basic questions about our destiny. It may be that the questions we have grown used to asking have themselves become too complex. Simpler, more fundamental questions may actually serve us better.

Perhaps by asking such questions, we can begin to relieve our minds of outworn assumptions and expose the roots of the problems shared by all peoples.

Seeing our problems more directly, we can clear away confusion and become aware of the urgent need for a new kind of knowledge. Often the very awareness that an emergency exists can stimulate our minds to their greatest power and clarity, simultaneously broadening and focusing our vision, and waking us up to a greater range of alternatives. Asleep, we relinquish any hope of creating the future we desire. Awake, we have an opportunity to discover within ourselves new sources of understanding that may benefit us now and protect our future more effectively.

Each time we accept responsibility for what happens in our lives, our receptivity to deeper understanding increases. Our openness to knowledge draws greater knowledge to us. As our understanding deepens, our confidence in knowledge grows stronger, and we are able to widen our sphere of responsibility. Eventually, our sense of responsibility broadens naturally to include the welfare of all beings.

Even the actions of one individual who wholeheartedly addresses the problems in his or her own life can be reflected in society and beyond, into the world. Just as a single light attracts attention on a dark night, action informed by knowledge attracts and awakens others, inspiring emulation.

Those who have positions of leadership have a unique opportunity to make a great impact on the world. Though they hold power only briefly, the consequences of their actions can endure far into the future. In supporting broader understanding of the strengths and weaknesses of both modern and traditional cultures and in encouraging intensive research into the nature of human knowledge, they could help alleviate individual and social problems and lay the foundation for the discovery of the root causes of frustration and dissatisfaction. The knowledge gained would offer greater hope for bettering the human condition worldwide, fostering mutual appreciation among all peoples and cultures. A natural balance based on a wider vision of human being could provide a more stable foundation for peace than any 'balance of power' among a few dominant nations.

There have been times in the past when unusual individuals acted from a higher knowledge for the benefit of the world. Recalling their examples, we can inspire ourselves to question the direction of our lives and find within ourselves the knowledge to transform destructive attitudes and actions into a positive force for world peace. To sustain motivation, we can imprint the headlines we read upon our minds, and visualize a world where all peoples could lead meaningful lives free of anxiety and pain.

8

Knowledge and Self

*Could we be entirely free from
reliance on 'the self who knows'?*

Our way of knowing and acting in our world, continually reinforced by our cultural conditioning,
has established a complex interlocking system. Everything—language, educational systems, economies,
commerce, politics, and social institutions—is dependent upon everything else. Underlying this great
superstructure are our concepts, beliefs, assumptions, values, and attitudes, which are linked together
like an underground network of pipelines connecting cities across a vast continent.

But the pipes are old, and too narrow for the
pressures they must bear. Leaks are erupting; while we
try to repair the leaks one by one, adjusting to each
crisis, we are continually extending the network itself.
Because the original pipes are deeply buried and we
do not know how they are interconnected, we have
no way to thoroughly examine the entire system.
Despite the uncertainties and cost, we seem com-

mitted to our present course of action. We cannot even conceive of a new pattern that would serve our needs better.

Because we see no viable alternatives, we shy away from the evidence that our problems are proliferating, threatening the welfare of the individual and society alike. We may like to point out proofs of the success of our way of life; we take pride in the material and social benefits our society enjoys. But we cannot completely ignore the symptoms of what seems to be a deep underlying distress.

Although some people today tend to blame technology for our difficulties and seek solutions in returning to a simpler way of life, the knowledge that has given us so much that is useful is not inherently destructive. Our problems do not seem to be rooted in technology, but in our inability to balance this knowledge with a wider vision of human life.

Throughout history human beings have adopted many ways of knowing in order to orient themselves to their world and derive meaning from existence. Today we tend to consider older views that conflict with our own as remnants of a more naive stage of human consciousness. But in embracing our own underlying attitudes to knowledge without question, we fail to appreciate the value of other perspectives that could widen our vision. The knowledge we consider 'new' consists primarily of scientific breakthroughs that will change our perspective on the physical world, or give us new insights into social or psychological realities. But no matter how earth-shaking these discoveries seem to be, they do not affect our basic approach to knowledge.

Unless we see the limitations of our understanding and take steps to overcome them, what we do now may bring us the opposite of what we want. Is the price in loss of peace of mind and enjoyment of life worth the benefits we are gaining? Might the costs come to exceed the benefits? If so many people in our societies are dissatisfied, unable to appreciate the opportunities and beauty of our way of life, what is the purpose of our knowledge? Ultimately, the full price of acting without a broader understanding of the implications of our actions may include the surrender of the human heart and mind to a way of life that perpetuates not only frustration, but also hopelessness and despair.

Today, our many forms of knowledge all derive from a view of human being as separate from the environing world. This view comes naturally to us, for it is rooted in our basic perceptual patterns and is reinforced by the integrating and deductive processes of the rational mind. We divide our world into self and other, and establish ourselves as agents acting upon and responding to situations. By this we commit ourselves to a view grounded in separation. We stand outside what is knowable, finding meaning through the range of human perception, the capacities of the senses, and the interpretation of the observer. We have no direct knowledge, for we make ourselves separate from knowledge, and become the 'one who knows'. Knowledge itself becomes another object we possess.

The observer considers his position as do-er and know-er to be central to experience. If there is no one to know, how could there be knowing? If there is no one to act, how could there be action? This way of understanding weighted toward a self who *must* respond to and act upon the world leads us to react to and evaluate every situation from a fixed point of view: ourselves. Thus, while we see ourselves as using knowledge, it may be more accurate to say that what we know is using us: We are drawn into responding to all that occurs around us.

From the viewpoint of the separate self, it is very difficult to 'let be', resting in pure observation, without thinking of what we can do as a result of what we are observing. Every situation is an invitation to create another one we view as more desirable. Succeeding situations also have possibilities for improvement, so we repeat the cycle again and again. We act, evaluate, and act again, elaborating upon what we have done before.

In relating to our world as a problem to be acted upon, we predispose ourselves toward dissatisfaction. Our minds easily look past the positive aspects of any situation and focus upon what seems to be missing or problematic. Because we value this incisive critical ability, we tend to emphasize it in our educational processes and view it as a hallmark of intelligence. But in reinforcing this approach, we may not notice that we run the danger of training ourselves into a perpetual state of discontent, punctuated only by waves of pleasure or pain, with the prospect of happiness just out of reach.

This discontent can feed a deep inner frustration, for we never seem to 'get' satisfaction. Our actions can bring us, at best, only temporary pleasure. We may spend our whole life trying to solve the problems and feed the 'needs' of this 'self', without ever stopping to question why, with all this effort, we have little real satisfaction and experience so much emotional pain.

As the doer and problem-solver, we are restless in the present, busy worrying about or anticipating the future; distracted, we cannot see clearly the tendencies in motion here and now. Events appear isolated and disconnected; they seem to move faster and faster, crowding in on us, giving us less and less space to reflect meaningfully upon what is happening. We feel forced to respond, but our responses are 'second hand', never new, always based on memories or shadows of desires. Our opportunities to learn from our experience and bring new understanding to our responses continually diminish.

It seems we can only repeat patterns that have led us into difficulties in the past. This duplication is inherently enervating and wasteful, dulling to the human spirit. Rather than opening to opportunities that enrich our experience, life tends to grow more narrow and restrictive. Bound to the same understanding, we are also bound to the same actions and results. Thus we tend to respond in predictable ways, like a dog who joins in when he hears another dog barking.

Accustomed to reacting to every situation, we heighten internal agitation, which manifests as excitement. Tense and off-balance, we reach outside of ourselves in anticipation, ready to react ever more quickly to whatever happens. In an excited, highly reactive state, we cannot apply well the knowledge and experience we have, and may actually increase pressures and problems for ourselves or others. No matter how good our intentions, we make mistakes.

Obliged to react before we have full knowledge of what we are doing, we cannot connect our actions with the results that follow, particularly if the results do not show up at once. Problems appear to arise as isolated incidents, for we cannot see their interconnections. Thus it can be difficult to learn from mistakes and gain the full benefit of our experience.

When our minds are highly attuned to quick responses, we look and feel alert and quick-witted, but this feeling of alertness is based on tension and can be deceptive: Under pressure, our intelligence and perspective can easily be misdirected and distorted. It is very difficult to determine whether we are responding from a basis of real knowledge or from a need to protect our position.

If our own view of ourselves or our position is at stake, we might not notice how emotional agitation is leading our minds, marshaling the force of our thoughts and logical processes, and focusing them on what we perceive as a serious problem or danger. When we are threatened we can feel very certain that we are acting from high motivation and ideals; our words sound confident and reasonable, and emotional power gives them the ring of conviction.

Once we have taken a position and stated it clearly, we can convince ourselves and others that it is true. As we gather support for our logic and view, our vision narrows, limiting us to a position that appears to be our only alternative. Channeled in only one direction, our energy goes into maintaining and defending this position ever more one-pointedly until we become locked into a course of action that we view as inevitable. Seeing no alternatives, we act strongly and decisively with little regard for the results.

When this cycle reaches a high pitch of tension, we may feel we have to make whatever sacrifices are necessary to maintain our position. This view is very powerful; it fuses all of our dedication, moral strength, and faith to a single objective. Those around us respond to this strength of feeling; some are attracted to support us, but others react just as strongly by taking the opposite view. Once this happens, the conditions for gridlock are established. Both sides then have no choice but to follow a course of action that works against the best interests of all.

If we look at our own experience honestly, we can remember times in our lives when we felt we had no alternatives, and acted in ways that went against our conscience, perhaps even against our own welfare. Perhaps we felt forced into doing something we really did not want to do. Looking back on those experiences, we may wonder why it had to be that way. What if we had spoken and acted differently? Was the issue really that important? Surely there must have been other possibilities that would have led to more sat- isfying results or caused less disruption in our lives. Yet at the time we felt very confident that we were doing the only right thing.

Times of great tension inevitably arise not only in our personal lives but in our societies and the larger world as well. Groups and nations alike are vulnerable today to cycles of tension and reactiveness that could lead us into great danger. In the past, when tensions were heightened, incidents occurred that seemed triv- ial in retrospect, but were viewed at the time as jus- tifications for aggression. The polarities that now exist between the superpowers of the world have created the potential for reactive responses that could lock us into destructive actions, with far-reaching conse- quences for the future.

N ow, more than ever before, it is important for us to reconsider our present attitudes toward knowledge and work toward more comprehensive and effective methods of addressing our problems. When we see the hidden dangers in a self-oriented view, and realize how it can distort our perspective in potentially self-destructive ways, we have an opportunity to consider other possibilities. To the degree that we can tap a new knowledge and imprint it deep in our memory, we can shape the outcome of the crises we face as individuals and as societies.

When we can relax our hold on self-centered positions, we lessen the pressure that intensifies reactive tendencies. Then there is more allowance for clarity and a greater receptivity to new knowledge. Thinking through each situation with a more awakened quality of mind, we can protect ourselves better from emotional reactions and gain a new perspective on knowledge.

Allowing more room for appreciation in our lives, we can see situations not so much as problems to be acted upon, but as opportunities for inquiry and learning. This attitude gives us space to observe the scope of our situation more clearly and to discover more effective ways of responding. When we begin to free ourselves from the *need* to react, even emergency situations can stimulate a new clarity and depth of vision that invite new insights and creative actions.

We could further widen our view by considering how much we ourselves have benefited from the efforts of many who came before us. Built up over hundreds of thousands of years, the world's store of knowledge is a rich resource, the heritage of every human being. In our language, our upbringing, and in our education, we have drawn upon this knowledge. All that we have learned from our life experience is also knowledge, and we express our understanding in everything we do. Each moment, each situation is an opportunity to reflect on our experience and use it to extend the knowledge we embody. The more we extend our knowledge, the more we can free ourselves from the need to repeat situations that cause pain to ourselves and others. With every insight we grow in understanding; we help ourselves, and we contribute to knowledge that carries the potential for benefiting future generations.

Considering that knowledge, liberated from our wish to possess it, is unselfish and giving, like life itself, we might be able to touch upon a fuller understanding of what is truly valuable for human life. Could we be entirely free from reliance on the 'self who knows'? Rather than depending on 'being aware of' things, an actor always pressured to react, might we be able to investigate an awareness that is not bound to the agent, an awareness closer to the pure nature of knowledge? If we pursued these questions, we might find there are no limitations to what we can know.

9

Breaking Through the Known

Questioning and being aware:
These are the most precious teachers.
They dwell in the heart of every human being
who begins to awaken to the waste
and danger of an unexamined life.

The energy that activates the universe manifests in shifting patterns of forms: Energy becomes form and form energy in complex interactions so closely entwined that human eyes cannot perceive the incessant flow of change. Each form arises from what has gone before, in a continuous stream of becoming. No beginning is wholly new; no ending is a complete termination. Only the sense organs of sentient beings, specialized for a limited scale and dimension, structure discrete forms from the continual stream of becoming.

The forms we view as solid are in reality spacious and teeming with energy, constantly participating in the creative play of the universe. From the farthest nebulae to the most minute particles of our own bodies, nothing in our world is static—not stars, not mountains, not living beings. The air we breathe, the water we drink, the earth we stand upon are all in dynamic movement, responding to an inner timing.

As human beings, we are all children of time, shaped by factors in constant flux, and grown to adulthood through a continual series of transformations. Cells we were born with have been replaced many times over. Our bodies and their constituent parts are never still, while our consciousness, feelings, perceptions, and cognitions continually respond to the energies that shift and flow around us. Each action, each thought, each moment of our existence is the expression of thousands, perhaps millions of subtle movements and interactions.

When we participate so intimately in the unceasing movement of all that is, where is there a fixed point of reference? Yet long ago, human beings, exercising their ability to discriminate and judge, formed a concept of themselves as separate observers somehow apart from the world 'out there'. Living within this concept, forgetful that we ourselves created it, we have learned to stand back and comment on the world, evaluating our experiences as good or bad, desiring some objects and experiences, while avoiding others.

The separate, independent, and single 'knower' who stands apart from his surroundings forms the basis of our view of ourselves and our world, and permeates the fabric of our existence. In the past, human consciousness may have been more flexible, open to other views and concepts. But over the centuries we have come increasingly to depend on the viewpoint of the independent knower, crowding out other approaches to knowledge.

Pursuing the way of the observer, we have developed more and more sensitive instruments to heighten the capabilities of the senses. We have refined our logical faculties and tried to purge our minds of personal prejudice to purify our knowledge from subjectivity, thus insuring an objective point of view.

Objective knowledge gained with such care certainly seems far more reliable than knowledge based on unexamined assumptions or blind belief. It lets us move with precision from specific facts to general hypotheses or from premises to specific facts; it allows us to make observations, develop and test theories, and then evaluate and interpret results.

Even so, the theories and results, the questions we ask, as well as the facts we derive from observation, are all shaped by our subjective thoughts, concepts, associations, memories, past knowledge, experience, and the particular quirks of the inquiring mind. The distinction between self and object is itself a concept, continually concretized in our linguistic patterns. Even refined symbolic logic and mathematics, which bypass conventional language and move closer to objectivity, are still grounded in many fundamental and unquestioned premises.

Despite our efforts at detachment, human consciousness participates in our 'objective' knowledge. And this consciousness itself has never been subjected to a thorough scrutiny. Our knowledge is not objective in the absolute sense; instead, it is only the purest form of subjective knowledge we are able to achieve.

This knowledge we consider objective can relate to the world only as external to the knower; it cannot convey immediate knowledge of the forces that pattern all that exists, including our bodies and minds. We can describe the appearance of reality, but cannot know reality directly. Without complete knowledge of what we, the 'knowers', are, we can never understand how we are distorting our view of reality; we can never arrive at pure objectivity. It thus seems critically important that we learn more about the nature of human consciousness.

But if our objective knowledge is only able to relate to the world as external to the knower, can we use its methods to know our consciousness? Committed to separating the knower from what is knowable, we have to conclude that we cannot know our own consciousness, because we cannot separate ourselves from it to define and measure it. Once we take this position, we have to believe that certain things are ultimately unknowable. Then we give priority to what we can know, and relegate the 'unknowable' to the realm of speculation. Within this view, we can never be certain of the true nature and potentialities of human consciousness. Yet all of our logic is rooted in the patternings of a mind we consider unknowable; this logic itself, however, cannot be validated without greater knowledge of the human mind.

Clearly, in order to gain truly objective knowledge of the dynamic forces that govern both the structure of the physical world and the workings of our minds, we need to know our consciousness. But how can we gain this knowledge? It may not be so impossible as it seems. Perhaps we have given up too soon, convinced by our own logic that our findings can never be conclusive.

Our whole approach to knowledge may be based upon an assumption of separation that is not organic to our consciousness. To discover more comprehensive knowledge of human consciousness, we may need to penetrate such basic assumptions and develop an approach suited to a new orientation toward knowledge. How can we encourage breakthroughs that could reveal new approaches to reality? Although we can manipulate and process information, analyze our findings, and perceive relationships we consider significant, we seem unable to evoke at will our capacities for reaching beyond the confines of what is known. We acknowledge the quality of vision that we term genius, but tend to view it as an unpredictable aberration rather than as a natural expression of human awareness. Perhaps by changing this view, and defining genius as intrinsic to human being, we might find better ways of cultivating this potential.

We know that individuals can break free from mental and emotional habits to introduce new knowledge into the world. Inspiration gave rise to the great spiritual and philosophical traditions; within the context of science, a few independent thinkers, relying on intuition or a sense of aesthetic harmony, have been able to mold scientific terms and mathematical symbols to express their insights, communicating profoundly different ideas that greatly expanded our understanding of physical laws and relationships.

Communication of such new ideas has always been tenuous, depending upon carefully thought-out connections to accepted knowledge. When the times did not favor the ideas, or the concepts allowing connections to be made were lacking, brilliant insights went unrecognized for generations, sometimes for centuries. Perhaps many times the connection to accepted knowledge was not made at all, to what loss for the world we cannot comprehend.

In moments of wonder and great humility, human beings through the ages have felt a different awareness emerge naturally within the more familiar ways of viewing themselves and their world. Perhaps many of us have known quiet moments when time seemed to stand still, and for a brief interval ordinary preoccupations faded into an overpowering appreciation of everything that is.

Insight drawn from such moments of silent communion with our innermost being, when our sense of separation is silenced by awe, has inspired creative breakthroughs and forms the heart of the world's great religions. But time and time again the part of ourselves that insists upon separation has arisen like a reflex, obscuring our immediate awareness of the present moment. As inspiration begins to falter, we return to the small world of the separate self; then we become self-conscious and doubt the significance of our own experience.

The evidence suggests that we may have powerful untapped resources for understanding ourselves and our world. Yet we seem very comfortable with our current ways of knowing and interpreting the physical world and our own experience. Our world is governed by rationality; even our moods and emotions are linked through reasons to our thoughts and concepts.

We build our knowledge carefully, through observation and inference, taking one step at a time. If we do not understand the reason for something now, we assume we will in the future, when our methods of observation are perfected. While a few gaps exist here and there, we can fill them with theories or interpretations, connecting one fact or experience to the next, as if we were stringing a necklace of beads.

But what if, in reality, there is no string in the necklace? What if the string is only a construct devised by the human mind? Have we fully explored the structure that orders all of our different theories and explanations? Can we feel confident in our knowledge without questioning the self that evaluates and judges or the conceptual patterns that unify our formulations? If we did not rely exclusively upon conceptual knowledge, might we find other possibilities for expanding our knowledge, rather than moving linearly from fact to fact and concept to concept?

The view of ourselves as separate from the world we know is now almost universally shared. It has gone largely unchallenged for centuries. What if we could break this pattern and begin to see ourselves and our world in a new light? Much as we explore the mythologies of cultures past, might we be able to step outside the assumptions that constrict our understanding and explore the way we interact in the world? Are there other forms of knowledge that would serve us more effectively? Suppose, for example, we could apply what physics has learned about the dynamics of energy and matter to human beings themselves. Would this give us new ways to awaken the potential of human consciousness?

Perhaps we need not accept ourselves so readily as separate from our world, as bystanders to our own experience, limited to judging and interpreting what is happening around us. Now we can overcome this sense of separation only by accident, relying on rare moments of inspiration to penetrate our conceptual barriers. But if we can query the self that is separate from its world, we may tap the wellspring of a deeper and broader way of knowing. Looking directly at our own experience, we can find reliable pathways to our awareness and trace our knowledge back to its roots.

Questioning and being aware: these are the most precious teachers. They dwell in the heart of every human being who begins to awaken to the waste and danger of an unexamined life. In taking responsibility for our lives and backing up that decision with action, we take the first step toward greater understanding of the nature of human being.

SECTION FOUR

Knowledge
of
Experience

CHAPTER 10: TIME AND CHANGE

CHAPTER 11: BIRTH AND YOUTH

CHAPTER 12: YEARS OF OUR PRIME

CHAPTER 13: THE WANING OF OUR LIVES

10

Time and Change

*Deep in our minds, change reminds us
of our mortality and our limitations.*

Wherever we look we see change. Even what seems unalterable in the world around us is in flux in ways that we cannot directly observe. Change is perhaps the central fact of our existence. We live subject to the passage of time and bend our efforts to taming its momentum, searching out ways to control the course of events or to turn them to our advantage. As changes occur, we scan their implications: "Is this good for me? Do I like it? Will it hurt me?" We want to be happy and to hold on to what makes us happy. We want to feel good about ourselves, to engage in activities that bring us pleasure and avoid those that cause discomfort. We spend our whole lives experiencing and reacting to changes, trying to exert control in the face of impermanence.

At the same time, change can open our minds to new ways of viewing ourselves and our relationship to the world, and renew our pleasure in living. We can appreciate the beauty of a flower, a human expression, or a sunset because it contrasts with our ordinary experience; we observe in it a rare and momentary state of perfection, which we value because we know it will be different in the next moment. Aware of the constant flow of time, we treasure moments that can be captured and lifted outside time through memory, vision, or art. Would we appreciate beauty if we inhabited an unchanging world? How would we know we were happy if we could not contrast happiness with unhappiness? Our appreciation of experience is closely linked to our awareness of contrast and change.

As long as changes accord with what we know or bring unexpected joy, they renew our confidence and sense of vitality. As we plan, organize, and direct our activities, we can respond to change as a stimulus and challenge. When we are confident and filled with a sense of well-being, change manifests as growth and progress. We can put aside unpleasant occurrences as minor irritations, and forget them in the momentum of achieving what we want.

But we do not seem to be able to appreciate all changes equally. Even the changes we choose for ourselves disturb our accustomed way of thinking and living, and create physical and emotional stress. When we marry, move to a new home, or start a new job, excitement produces tension in our bodies and minds. In any new situation, we can easily become apprehensive.

When we are confronted with changes we do not want, the effect is even stronger and can be deeply unsettling. Positive aspects of unwanted changes are difficult for us to see. We fear we will come up against something we cannot handle that will cause us pain. Faced with opportunities to leave painful or even destructive relationships or working situations, we may find ourselves clinging to the familiar rather than risking new and unknown demands on our inner resources.

Perhaps change is too threatening to face directly. We know that we cannot always make changes accord with our wishes. Change is impersonal and uncompromising—it may not conform to our expectations. It is also irreversible: Except in fantasy, we cannot turn back the clock and relive portions of our lives to manipulate the outcome of events to our liking.

Whatever illusions of permanence we create in our lives, the passage of time will end them. Eventually change will separate us from all we cherish, even our own bodies. In the moment of death, what will be the meaning of the passions, the joys, the sufferings we have experienced—the reality we have dealt with all our lives? Whatever we consider important now may appear quite differently to us as we near the end of our known form of existence. We would like to think that we are in control of our lives, but it seems more accurate to say that time, and the changes it brings, are in control of us.

Deep in our minds, change reminds us of our mortality and our limitations. The echo of this reminder resonates deep within us whenever we find ourselves unable to control or to anticipate the flow of events. Ultimately, human beings, aware that all life ends in death, are not comfortable living in a world of constant change. The transience that underlies all our experience tinges our happiness with sorrow, our confidence with uncertainty, and all of our pleasures with pain.

11

Birth and Youth

*During these early years,
we pattern ways of relating to the world
that may sustain us for a lifetime.*

We begin our lives as a single living cell, ignorant of events that preceded the union of sperm and egg within our mother's body. Yet this cell contains within it, like an architectural plan, the genetic instructions and timing mechanisms that will determine the physical structure of our body and the ultimate limits of our lifespan.

Our early months are spent in darkness and total dependency. Throughout this early development, we are intimately joined to another human body, sharing the experiences of another human being. How are we affected by the shifting blood pressures, the hormonal and chemical changes, the emotional tones of the body in which we reside? In what subtle ways might we take on our mother's predispositions and even memories?

Completely isolated and helpless, with consciousness and senses just stirring into life, we absorb what comes through the walls of the womb without protest or consent; we cannot choose to be born or not to be born, or determine the circumstances of our birth.

Ignorant of our history, not knowing our own nature, possessing senses but deprived of most sensory stimulation, we reside in a dark enclosed space. How does a human consciousness react to such a situation? What feelings arise within us? What do we experience at the moment of birth, when we are suddenly dislodged from the only security we have known, compressed and constricted by powerful forces, and thrust into a foreign world of light, sound, and open space? Lungs expand to sustain our first breaths, stretching muscles and tissues never used before; for the first time we know hardness and cold, and awaken to our existence as a truly separate being.

But what comfort is our independence when we have needs and are helpless to satisfy them? We cry out—for what? We might say an infant cries out for contact, warmth, and nourishment; but what needs go uncommunicated, what longings remain even when we are warm and well-fed? What frustrations and anxieties do our parents experience after they have given all they can, and still the need continues? How do their attitudes affect our earliest months?

Infants want, but do not seem to know what they want. How could they, when they cannot make comparisons or imagine possible satisfactions? This blind wanting, without purpose or object, seems a strange kind of frustration to our adult minds. How unsettling, this unspoken longing that seems to arise from nowhere in a consciousness just awakening to the timing of human affairs.

Such longings seem closely intertwined with the fears that haunt our childhood. Separation from our parents is distressing; we seem to crave approval, attention, and security; we recoil from strange people and objects, and require frequent reassurances. Are we conscious in these earliest years of our helpless dependency? How can we feel secure when we have so little choice in what happens to us? Whether our parents offer us love, resentment, or anger, we can only cling to what we know; we cannot conceive of what might be better for our lives.

When we cry, we may be given things that we enjoy holding, looking at, and tasting. Objects seem to relieve the discomfort of need, and we begin to associate them with satisfaction or happiness. We learn to say yes and no, and try to assert our desires, but often we find that our wishes are ignored and our choices are limited.

Each day we alternate many times between happiness and frustration, security and anxiety. A sense of need persists: During the day we can find comfort in the midst of people and perhaps friendly pets; but what nameless fears arise in the night, filling our dreams with strange, terrifying beasts? Why do these feelings rise up when we are alone in the dark, when darkness was our earliest home?

Soon we learn how to please others. We learn their guidelines for behavior, language, and values, as well as more effective means of winning approval. During these early years, we develop patterns of relating to the world that may sustain us for a lifetime. We are curious; we reach out and grasp; we want to satisfy desires instantly. What strategies do we devise to get what we want when wanting grows intense?

Eventually we discover that parents can feel guilty, and we learn to play on their feelings: not so difficult to get what we want, when we know how. Still, we are often left feeling dissatisfied or disappointed. Do we really know what we want?

We become more skillful at manipulating those around us, but there are limits to what we can do before adult displeasure stops us. If our parents are angered, we fear the void suddenly opened between us. If they suffer in silent exasperation, we sense the rejection and become anxious. What if they do not seem to care what we do? We must make them take notice and respond, regardless of the consequences.

Wherever we turn, it seems we eventually face conflict. Externally, restraints are imposed; internally, needs multiply faster than our bodies can cope with them, and we become frustrated with our own exhaustion. So much happens so quickly; our minds are flooded with sensory stimulations and emotional reactions, while there is little we can really understand.

Even as children, we have a means of escape: We can conjure up a fantasy world and live in our own secret realm. Here we have power and control; here there are no conflicts we cannot overcome, no difficulties too frightening to understand. Adults may intrude, but we can hide behind the play situations we have created and lock out fear and pain. Why would we willingly leave this realm where everything is orderly, warm, and secure, for the 'real' world, so chaotic and uncontrollable?

When we begin school, our world grows suddenly wider. All at once we are more 'grown up', though we have no choice but to take what comes. Perhaps our thoughts run something like this: "I like school . . . I like my new friends, but some of the ones I like won't play with me. They laugh at me. I'll show them. My teacher wants me to be smarter—like him—or do everything right—like her. Why do I have to do what they say?"

We begin to notice others in new ways—we feel we are 'special', but precisely how are we special? We compare ourselves with others, noticing differences in appearance, size, clothes, possessions, and skills. How do we 'measure up'? Do our differences make us 'better' or 'worse' than the others: Do we talk differently, or say things that make others laugh at us? Do our habits attract attention? How do others feel about us? Who is more important to please: our teachers or our classmates? Over the next few years, whether we like our situation or not, whether we enjoy our experiences or dread each day, we adjust, we socialize, and we fit in as best we can. We have to.

Soon we find ourselves changing in ways that arouse new feelings and thoughts about ourselves and others. Somehow we seem to become more self-conscious, more sensitive to criticism and ridicule. Everything seems different, and we don't really know why. The atmosphere is more competitive—we feel the need to excel in something, to carve out a place of our own. We may find ourselves emphasizing activities in which we excel while downgrading those that threaten our self-confidence.

When we do well, we feel exhilarated, although we may worry about whether we will be able to come through when the pressure increases. We feel the pangs of not being wanted when we are among the last to be chosen for a team; we may feel ashamed or bewildered when we lose in a contest of intellectual skills. Feelings of failure can be devastating, and we withdraw more quickly from situations where we have felt hurt before. But now we know we have to hide our feelings; if others sense we are vulnerable, they might hurt us more. When others are hurt or left out, we may turn away in embarrassment and fear, or join the group in ridiculing their pain.

Now we are more aware that we are growing up. We take ourselves more seriously, imagining how we would like to be. We are more sensitive to how things 'should be'; we want to belong, and to do things right. We begin to notice inconsistencies in our parents—do they measure up to our ideals? Soon we feel conflicting loyalties between parents with whom we identify and the role models we admire. A growing feeling of discomfort may suddenly crystallize into the realization that we have no certain sense of who we are.

During the confusion of our adolescent years, we feel more venturesome and independent of adults, but much more vulnerable to the opinions of our friends. Everyone seems to be looking at us. What are they seeing? What should we look like, act like? So we copy: this person's way of speaking, that person's mannerisms, the right things to say, the right things to do. We copy the characteristics of friends

we admire, people who have achieved fame and success, wealth, or power, characters in novels, movies, or
television. Experimenting with appearances, ways of
speaking and dressing, we try on different personalities. We want desperately to express ourselves, to be
at once unique and yet the same as our friends.

Our friends become our mirrors: By observing their
reactions to us, we try to figure out how to look, how
to act, how to be. We discover that dressing and acting
in certain ways make us accepted as a person. Our
relationship to the group—whether we feel part of it
or alienated from it—gives us a sense of identity. Our
developing talents and capabilities give us new feelings of confidence. But instead of disappearing, the
sources of our insecurity have only grown more
complex.

Our time is becoming more structured, and we
have less time to ourselves. Pressures and demands of
parents, teachers, and friends are often conflicting; it
is hard to satisfy the requirements that come at us from
all sides—school, social life, sports, new desires, new
standards of behavior, and plans for the future. Inner
conflicts are growing more intense, arousing strong
emotional reactions; we are torn between pressures
to act and make more grown-up decisions that force
our attention outward and feelings of inadequacy that
make us want to withdraw.

We spend a lot of time worrying about ourselves:
"Why do I feel so awkward? No one else seems to feel
this way; everyone else seems so confident. What if
they see how lonely and unsure of myself I feel? They
seem to do everything right—why can't I be more like
them? Why do I have to be me? But who am I?"

We start to think about growing up and assuming adult responsibilities, vacillating between a desire to be independent and a desire to be taken care of. Our attitudes toward our parents change dramatically, and we begin breaking away from their control: "Why won't you let me run my own life?" "As long as you live in this house, you have to follow our rules." In this process of rebellion, we may develop negative feelings toward our parents that can take years to resolve.

New energy flows through our bodies erratically—we experience bursts of excitement and new physical desires. We change physically, and we are disturbed if our development differs from what seems most desirable; our emotions flash unpredictably from elation to depression, while new desires, hopes, and interests occupy our minds. Feelings of panic overwhelm us without warning—we are changing whether we want to or not, and we are not sure what we are becoming.

Fantasies and internal dialogues fill our minds, reinforcing or criticizing this or that image of ourselves as we search for some stable identity. We want to find ourselves, as if we were somehow lost, as if there were some thread in this tangle of events and emotions that would lead to our real selves. Who can show us where to look? We want guidance, but we are afraid to open ourselves to others while we feel so vulnerable and uncertain. Slowly, painfully, we piece together the personalities that will shape our adult lives.

Gradually we become more assured in our social relationships. We identify with groups of our peers; we find a particular talent or skill that seems to express our uniqueness. If we are lucky, the skills we have chosen to develop may lead us forward toward a job or career. But what if none of the available choices seems to fit with who we feel we are?

If we have a strong sense of direction, upon what is it based? Have we been taught to think independently about goals and purposes that are healthy for our own lives? How well do we understand what is involved in a job or profession? Perhaps we are influenced by the values of friends or the expectations of parents; perhaps we feel lost. What is the meaning of our choices? We may imagine we can change our minds later; yet inevitably we are opening up some opportunities and closing off others. "I know what I'm doing. I'm independent now. I'm an adult, aren't I?"

We may know what we do not want: If the lives of our parents or other adults seem confining, we may be determined that ours will be different. But where can we look for better examples, and how can we know which models offer a healthier way of life? We find ourselves caught in uncertainty and indecision, perhaps torn between obligations to parents, economic realities, and our personal wishes. Anxieties compete with powerful fantasies, hopes, and images of success.

Unable to decide for ourselves, we may try to fulfill our parents' expectations. Or perhaps we settle into comfortable patterns that require few changes. We may take whatever opportunities arise and hold a series of jobs, prolonging a sense of freedom and independence by avoiding work that demands a commitment. Or we may never have the illusion of choice and have to find what work we can.

Now that we have become adults, significant romantic relationships are often expected and anticipated by our families. If we are in love, marriage and family may seem a logical step or a refuge from the many insecurities we face. Though we may feel our lives are opening before us as we step into 'the real world', our options begin to diminish; our lives become intertwined with the lives of others, and responsibilities accumulate.

Whether we hold back, reluctant to give up dependency on parents or childhood friends, or set out with definite goals and purposes, we must make our own way. Whether we feel the excitement of challenge or the pangs of self-doubt and anxiety, this is our time to live our own lives.

12

Years of Our Prime

If we stop for a moment, step out of our roles,
and reexamine our purposes and achievements,
what have we really accomplished?

How stimulating our early adult years can be, when we feel we are exercising our minds and bodies to the fullest! Still, we are faced with some hard choices. Once we are on our own, we may feel a welcome sense of independence, but we may also find that it is not always easy to get what we want. Establishing a living situation may be more complicated and expensive than we had thought. If we take our parents' lifestyle for granted, we may find we need far more money than we are able to earn. The salary that seemed impressive at the outset suddenly seems much too small; perhaps we find ourselves committed to debts that limit our ability to do the things we want. "What am I doing? Is it always going to be this way? Do I want more responsibility? Do I need different skills or more education to get what I want out of life? Do I want to spend years of my life struggling to make ends meet in order to have what I want? Where will I get the money?"

Things that interest us often show little promise for future employment; we may have to compromise our interests with an eye to the job market and our financial situation. If we have the chance to pursue the subjects that excite us, we may discover that we must devote long years to preparation before we can hope to master them. We are faced with the need to weigh our desires for more immediate gratification against the value of achieving long-range goals.

Even if we are living what looks like a carefree lifestyle, we are often keenly aware of time and of financial pressures. The future is much on our minds as we compete for jobs or recommendations that will open the doors to the job we want, to professional training, or perhaps graduate school. We are already sizing up our possibilities, comparing ourselves with people already established in our chosen field, considering how we might come to the attention of those who can help us succeed. We may feel we are being manipulated by the established system, and need to manipulate others in turn.

As we pursue our individual goals, we may feel lonely and restless, even if we have friends. We usually want one special person to confide in, or fall in love with, someone who can satisfy our longings for comfort and caring. Perhaps we do find someone for whom our feelings are deep and sincere. But misunderstandings may occur, and feelings of loneliness return. One partner may decide to make changes, leaving the other feeling hurt and rejected. We may drift in and out of a series of relationships that seem to fill a need, but which also haunt us as a potential source of emotional distress.

How long do we go on, not taking the time to reflect on the causes of our unhappiness? Again and again, we blame others for our problems, without looking at the fears of helplessness and isolation, at the cycles of need, desire, and frustration that propel us to begin and end relationships with lovers and friends. We know their love may not last, we know our own feelings may change, but we insist on trying to fit our lives to our fantasies.

In our daydreams, we look to the future, when everything will be better. Our apprenticeship to life will be over, and our real life will begin: "I'll have enough income to be independent and to do what I really want to do with my free time. I'll go places and do things with someone who really understands me." But in the meantime the pressures to perform increase, and we wonder: "Is this really what I want to do with my life? Did I make the wrong choice? Am I missing out on something better? Maybe I should consider other possibilities."

If we feel unsure of what we want, we may find ourselves floating along, occupying our time with fantasies or entertainments, somehow unable to connect our dreams to reality. Our plans are short-term, or else so vague we do not know how to implement them. Boredom seems to be our worst enemy, or perhaps loneliness. We feel lost and bewildered; why can't we 'get it together'?

We may deliberately avoid making commitments to jobs and professions, or resist forming close relationships. We may pride ourselves on our independence, and feel we can enjoy the rewards offered by society without the responsibilities that threaten our freedom. Are we holding back from fears of failure or inadequacy, or from a fear that others might gain power over us? "That's ridiculous—I'm doing what I want to. I just refuse to get caught up. Nothing is worth sacrificing my freedom." We may stand back from society and criticize its negative side without being willing to contribute any positive energy to change the situation. "After all, nothing can be changed—things have always been this way. Why should I waste my time?"

Most of us accept the roles society offers us—social pressures and financial needs catch up with us, and we settle down. We wish to succeed, and begin to apply ourselves to our work with vigor. Rewards may come—recognition, advancement, raises, prestige—confirming our success. Our confidence grows, and we feel more secure, able to control our lives and have what we want. We learn how to make people like us and how to win their support. If we begin to stagnate in one job, we can find another.

Soon we may decide to raise a family. We may never think about why we're doing it—everyone expects it. Perhaps we anticipate a sense of fulfillment in seeing our children grow, and in helping them shape their future. Of course, we knew children would complicate our lives, but we did not anticipate the worries that never end: Are they safe, are they happy, are they in good company? What interests are they developing, what values, what attitudes? Will they succeed in school, will they find jobs? Are we adequate as parents? What mistakes are we making? If they are disabled, grow seriously ill, or die, the anguish may be almost more than we can bear.

As we advance in life, material needs expand rapidly. We buy cars, we purchase homes and fill them with furnishings. We open businesses and buy equipment. Identifying with our possessions, we worry that we might lose them; our feelings of insecurity will not go away. We continue to add to our possessions: There is always something just beyond our reach that we can have. Looking around at all we own, we can tell ourselves that we are getting somewhere at last: "Of course I worry sometimes—doesn't everyone? Of course I have disappointments—what's life without a little trouble?"

While we are young and getting what we desire, joy and sorrow, elation and depression, love and anger color our lives with rich, compelling emotional tones. Physical discomforts come and go, and can be alleviated easily. Emotional stress can be diminished through tranquilizers or alcohol, and the haze and cloudiness they bring to our lives may seem a small price to pay for relief; at least we can keep going: "It can't hurt—everyone does it."

As the years go by, we weave an ever more intricate web of relations between ourselves and others, binding ourselves with obligations and responsibilities, involving ourselves in others' emotions, problems, and needs. We strive to live up to our roles: worker, business partner, professional, lover, mate, or parent. Perhaps we pride ourselves on our ability to play many roles simultaneously, and become adept at shifting among different language patterns, attitudes, and gestures.

When actions and events unfold as we expect, we feel confident and in control; when we feel our control slipping, or challenges come from those close to us, we tense with anxiety. Although we may become skilled at putting on a good front even to ourselves, at heart we sense our confidence is not genuine. We shrink reflexively from situations and even thoughts that threaten to reveal weaknesses we suspect but cannot acknowledge.

No matter how competent and confident we feel during the busy parts of the day, when we are alone, with nothing to stimulate our senses, we often feel uneasy. Our minds leap from thought to thought like a monkey from tree to tree. Our bodies grow restless and uncomfortable. Again and again we are impelled to do something—listen to the radio, watch television, read, talk to friends, go somewhere—to relieve a sense of boredom and dissatisfaction or escape the thoughts that come when we are alone.

How little it takes to make us feel pressured! If something goes against us at work, or our employers or families make unusual demands upon us, immediately our nerves are on edge and our bodies tense; stress gnaws at our stomachs and makes our heads ache. We may carry on, ignoring or rationalizing tension, or masking its discomforts with medication, but in time the pressure takes its toll. We may find ourselves needing more sleep, feeling dull or ill, less able to rise to challenges we once welcomed.

We can walk out of unpleasant situations, we can change our jobs, our mates, our families, our surroundings, but can we change our mental environment? We may try to resolve our conflicting thoughts, but the inner dialogues continue; we cannot escape the driving insistency of our own thoughts. Even when we need to concentrate, our internal conversations often give us no peace. Meaningless replays of situations that have left us hurt or angry cycle over and over. Can we choose not to feel hurt, not to be depressed, not to feel lonely or anxious? Are we ever free of ourselves?

If we acknowledge our anxieties and fears and wish to reconsider our situation, we may encounter the insecurities of our mates, our children, our parents; if we confide in our friends and fellow workers, we risk ridicule, loss of support and friendship, even the security of our jobs. We can complain—everyone complains, so we can feel comfortable with those who share our grumblings. We may express our worries through humor or sarcasm, but it is difficult to open our hearts completely for fear of appearing weak. Perhaps we cannot find words to express what we feel, or perhaps we have tried to communicate and found ourselves misunderstood or our confidences betrayed.

What happens when someone suggests we have a problem? That touches other feelings, and we dissemble: "I don't have problems, really; it's not so bad as all that. Actually I'm pretty well off." Anyone would feel the same in our situation.

If we feel the need for advice, we may find it less threatening to talk with someone more remote from our daily lives, to find a group or individual to support or advise us. But how do we unravel the web of anxieties that oppresses us; how do we communicate the longings and needs we feel? Although we may gain insight into our problems and be reassured that we are not alone, our anxieties are like unwelcome acquaintances we cannot bring ourselves to confront directly—they always come back. Most of us manage to keep our anxieties under some sort of control, but if we let them have their way, they may move in with us, leaving us no peace at all.

If this does happen, we may lose all interest in our usual activities and approach our work with reluctance or even dread. Just as our careers are reaching their peak, we may feel lethargic and unresponsive, unable to match the competition, 'burned out' in our prime. If we turn to less stressful work, we may face the different pressure of boredom and feelings of inadequacy.

These are the years we anticipated with so much relish in our youth. How exciting and pleasurable they can be when our vitality remains high, and our sense of value and worth is confirmed by our families, our accomplishments, or the growth of skills and expertise. We feel busy and contented—there are still so many things to enjoy, and so much more we can anticipate doing in the future. We may have our ups and downs, but our lives seem basically under control and satisfying.

We may truly be enjoying the momentum of our lives. But if, in the midst of our enjoyment and success, we stop to evaluate the meaning and purpose of our activity, do we find we would rather not examine our lives too closely? How do we feel about the choices we have made—in relationships, professions, lifestyles? Would we do some things differently if we had another chance?

If our stereotyped roles dropped away, what would be left? What are we apart from all this? Are our lives an expression of our creativity? Are our relationships with others personally satisfying? Are we spending most of our time fulfilling obligations and expectations, or are we working consciously toward substantial goals?

Nearly half of our life has now passed; are we building a basis for real value? When we look back upon this period twenty years from now, how will we remember it? Will we feel we used our time to its best advantage? If we stop for a moment, step out of our roles, and reexamine our purposes and achievements, what have we really accomplished?

13

The Waning of Our Lives

*Where have we learned what death is,
or how to face it unafraid?*

In time our energies begin to decline. Life seems to pause and shift, like a high-performance car dropping into a lower gear. We may sense a lessening of desires or subtle changes in our perception and taste; perhaps we tire a little more easily and find ourselves thinking more about our health. Accustomed things may seem a little flatter and duller than before, or we may notice the first signs of physical weakness or symptoms of beginning disability.

Quite suddenly we may see in our reflections unmistakable signs of aging and awaken with a shock to the realization that our lives may well be more than half over. Changes we had only partially acknowledged can no longer be ignored. Our children have grown and have their own values and lifestyles. We may have drifted apart from husbands, wives, or lovers: Are they bored with us now that we are older and less attractive? Have different interests separated us? We may feel threatened by the aging or disability of parents, concerned for their health and safety, or afraid of the responsibility for their care. Death may have touched us through family, friends, or fellow workers.

Now we know time is passing, and we feel the implication of change more sharply than ever before. We can no longer avoid acknowledging the inevitability of death; we know there will be no choice in the end but to give up all we have worked to achieve. The shock of this realization may shake our confidence and force us to reevaluate our lives.

If we have achieved what we set out to do, we may find that our feelings of satisfaction are not so great as we had expected them to be. If we have not achieved our goals, the chances of doing so are becoming more remote. We may sense a gap opening in our lives that we are unprepared to face.

When we were younger and faced a long corridor of time, postponed dreams or activities could become sources of pleasant anticipation. If we missed one opportunity, we could expect another to arise. Now unfulfilled wishes are disappointments, sources of pain. Our sense of time has changed, recasting our lives in a totally new perspective: Our best time is over; our future will always be uncertain. We do not know how much time is left. Have we realized the rewards we expected in our youth? What returns are we getting for the investment of decades of our lives in education and hard work?

The crises of reflection and indecision are often buried in new rounds of activity. Now that we feel time's pressure, our energy may have a more driven quality; we have to keep moving, thinking, planning, doing. Questioned, we tend to be defensive. What about the security of our jobs? "Of course my position is secure. I have more experience than younger people, and experience is worth more than money can buy." But are we sure? We may have achieved a certain status and be very good at what we do, but with younger, more energetic people eager to take our place, can we continue to advance or even sustain our position?

What about our marriage—is it secure? "Of course. We've been together too long to change now." Is there something more we want out of life? "That's absurd. I'm happy with what I have, and I'm proud of what I've achieved." And so we may not be inclined to make changes in our lives. Having already invested so much effort in the roles we have established, we may feel obligated to continue them. We may not wish to take the risk of disrupting our lives or face the pain of others who are depending upon us. Everything is all right—it has to be. What other choice is there? At worst, there are consolations: If our jobs are not well-paying, at least we can manage; if we cannot achieve more, at least we have seniority and some measure of prestige; if our work is not challenging, at least we can perform it easily and have more time for ourselves.

But disturbing thoughts keep coming back. Time is running out—have we accomplished our dreams? If we feel dissatisfied or insecure, what actions can we take? We can try to find a new job, go into business for ourselves, or even change professions; we can seek rejuvenation through younger lovers or mates, or by adopting a younger, freer lifestyle. We can reshape our image through diet and exercise, or try dressing more youthfully. If we wish, we can attempt to recover the excitement and vitality of our adolescent years and go through the whole cycle again. But how long can we maintain the illusion of youth and vitality when we know our energy is not what it was, and we grow ever more vulnerable to the inevitable effects of time?

We may seek renewal through our children, urging them to implement our values in their lives, to achieve what we could not, while hoping they will avoid repeating our mistakes. Our growing loneliness and sense of unfulfilled needs may lead us to involve ourselves compulsively in their lives, and our sense of worth may become dependent upon how well they fulfill our expectations.

As we approach the end of our working lives, we may feel an unexpected upsurge of new anxieties. What sense of purpose can we substitute for our work? Will we be remembered once we are gone? Have our co-workers appreciated our efforts? Has our work been worthwhile?

Once we are retired and work no longer provides direction for our lives, we may find new interests that give us hope for the future. Freed from family responsibilities, we may have a new sense of ease, a final chance to travel and do things we had postponed for so long. We can relax and enjoy our friends more, now that we know better than to expect too much from ourselves or from others. "This is the way life is. It's not so bad really." We don't have to dwell on unpleasant thoughts or worry about what may happen.

We can laugh at ourselves more readily and joke about the idealism and expectations of our youth. But behind the humor lies a certain sadness and regret; if only we could be young again, know what we know now, and have the same opportunities as we did then.

Now our vitality fails us more easily; our senses are noticeably duller. We may miss the feeling of accomplishment and importance we once felt in our jobs, and be less inclined to engage in social activities. Even our simplified routines may not bring us the pleasures we had anticipated. The times when we feel empty and depleted come closer together, and there are few peak events left to look forward to. We feel longings and desires, but lack the opportunities and vitality to satisfy them.

The stimulation that sustained us has diminished; the companionship of fellow workers is lost; even our friends have little energy for us. Our presence may be disruptive to the lives of our spouses and children, and we may not have the drive to establish new ways of occupying our time. Perhaps a lack of income makes us feel impoverished, vulnerable to illness, unwanted by the society that our labor has sustained.

Thoughts of death arise more frequently; whether we dwell on them or repress them, they recur, arousing discomfort and fear. We may make preparations by drafting wills and arranging for the disposition of our bodies; we may decide that suicide is preferable to lingering pain and disability, and derive comfort from the thought that we can at least control the circumstances of our deaths. But we tend to keep the reality of death at a distance, unwilling to let ourselves consider too closely what dying really involves.

By our seventies or eighties, we may have little left to anticipate; although we know we must maintain a sense of purpose, it becomes more difficult to derive meaning from our daily lives. The prospect of death is too painful—how can one look forward to that? Many of our friends are sick or have died; telephone calls or mail are likely to bring unwelcome news.

When will our loved ones grow ill or die? Where will we find the strength to watch their suffering? Will we be left alone? What pains will we have to endure, what humiliations of old age? Will we become crippled and helpless, returning, like children, to a state of increasing dependency? Will we spend our last years in a nursing home, cared for by strangers? Or will we be a burden to our families? Who might take advantage of us, hurt us, rob us, when we are so weak and vulnerable?

We try so hard to hold on to our self-confidence, our feelings of worth and dignity, our independence— but how long can we maintain them? Who will reassure us when we are terrified and alone? Who will listen and care about what we feel now? Where have we learned what death is, or how to face it unafraid?

Fearful of death, we fight back such thoughts and cling to life even if we must live in constant physical pain or endure great emotional suffering. In our need we may grasp at the lives of our children or other loved ones or withdraw into the bleakness of isolation. Memories recycle in our minds, and we may find ourselves repeating the same stories to anyone who will listen; but the flavor of the experience is no longer the same. Even our memories may only be fantasies of how we wish it had been.

As we slip into dependency, our minds become dull and confused, our senses too sluggish to respond to stimulation. But our consciousness is alive; our desires still exist, although they must go unsatisfied. Now that we cannot keep up our own defenses, we may see clearly the pretense and self-deception in others, and know that we, too, in following these same patterns, have cheated ourselves of much happiness. Somehow it seemed so important to play roles and games when we could not see them for what they were; yet in retrospect, they seem empty and unreal.

Later, buried in hazy memories of a dim past, we no longer recognize even friends or family. With the sinking of vital energy, we return to an infantile state, perhaps still crying out in our need, helpless and unaware of our surroundings. At last we lapse into total forgetfulness, completely and finally alone.

SECTION FIVE

Awakening Knowledge

CHAPTER 14: STRATEGIES FOR LIVING

CHAPTER 15: YEARNING FOR FULFILLMENT

14

Strategies for Living

*What intimacy, what closeness,
what caring can we expect
when we all conceal our real being?*

At every stage in life, we are vulnerable to unhappiness and pain. Time passes, bringing changes we cannot control, and we ourselves change in ways that we could not have foreseen or prefer not to acknowledge. To insulate ourselves from changes that are threatening, most of us adopt a style of living, a strategy that seems to promise protection, satisfaction, and meaning. There are many such strategies, but the main ones can be seen in certain lifestyles: an easy-going lifestyle, an aggressive striving lifestyle, and the lifestyles of restraint, complaint, and daydreaming. We may combine different approaches during our lives as attitudes and interests change, or even switch among them, depending upon our associates and surroundings.

Many people who have grown to maturity in affluent societies fall readily into the easy-going life strategy. Approaching life as an opportunity for personal enjoyment, we may try to take all that is pleasurable in life and brush off any unpleasantness. To avoid exposing ourselves to the pain of disappointment and loss, we may take few risks and content ourselves with whatever pleasures life offers. We may follow our impulses and desires without much concern for the results of our actions, trying to make life into an eternal holiday.

Uncommitted, we can be free from responsibility and care, living in the moment, waiting for something to turn up. Pleasures come our way, and we enjoy. When activities and associations become tiresome or demand a commitment we do not wish to make, we can drop them and move on. We may even know that we are casting away our time, our lives, as though they had no value. This feeling can provide an odd sort of satisfaction; perhaps we resent the demands that society and others place upon us, and this is our way of demonstrating that we are in control.

As long as we have the energy and income to support our lifestyle, or require little to support our needs, we may have no motivation to look more closely at what is happening to our consciousness. All around us we see others striving, risking ulcers or heart attacks to get somewhere in life. How futile the usual treadmill seems when life can be so easy and enjoyable with hardly any effort. We may even sense a spiritual dimension to our attitude; nothing really disturbs us —we are at peace with the world.

As this approach to life becomes habitual, energy and interest begin to wane. Few pastimes really seem worth the effort, and people drift in and out of our lives. There are still moments of pleasure, but in retrospect our experiences may seem vague and bland. Life takes on a bleak quality of sameness, with few contrasts to arouse our responses. Somehow even our memory seems to lose its sharpness. But we may never question why we feel so lethargic, or why our senses seem to have grown so dull.

As we grow older, we may find it hard to arouse ourselves to make even minor decisions. Discomfort and pain that we once shrugged off occur more often, and we have to make greater efforts to maintain our easy-going self-image. If we try to reverse the patterns we have established, our minds and bodies may have grown too dull to respond intelligently.

Gradually we appreciate less and less of our lives. As we feel our vitality lessen, we become more distrustful of people and changes that occur around us. Whom can we trust not to upset or betray us when we have formed no lasting bonds? When things go against us, we can no longer dismiss them so casually, and we reflect more often on the unfairness of life. Because we lack the resources to respond effectively to pain, our emotions can easily override our reason and back us into a dark corner of despair. When life experiences become overwhelmingly painful, we may even choose to end our lives prematurely: the final gesture of avoiding realities we have never trained ourselves to confront.

Most of us do not follow this path to its end: Something in the human spirit seems to rebel against prolonged passivity, however much we value the times when we can set aside responsibilities. Perhaps we sense the waste and danger inherent in placing ourselves at the mercy of random events, and do not wish to relinquish so much control over the direction of our lives.

A more aggressive life strategy can emerge from our tendency to reach out for experience, for stimulation and feelings of accomplishment and worth. We yearn for something to happen, something that will evoke a response so we can feel vital and alive. Isn't this what makes life worthwhile?

When our desires are strong, we may pursue our goals aggressively, confident that our efforts will be rewarded. We learn to take pleasure in the sense of well-being that arises from applying our energy effectively and overcoming all obstacles in our path. We feel confident in our worth and ability; we become good at what we do and gain approval from those we admire or respect.

Accepting each new situation as a challenge, we can take advantage of opportunities. Growing success may give us the power to direct the efforts of others, and we increase our striving. Our attention becomes focused on success; personal indulgence takes little of our time. Most of our pleasure in life depends upon continuing the momentum we have established, and we may drive ourselves compulsively to greater and greater heights of achievement.

When pleasure in life comes only from striving and getting, where can we find a resting place? The driving force of desire grows ever more intense; each goal attained tends to increase our appetite. Eventually whatever we acquire or accomplish is merely a symbol of our progress and worth. At each new peak of achievement, we may stop to enjoy the benefits of success, but inactivity soon makes us restless. The excitement now lies in the pursuit itself, and the pace must be continued.

Our lives move quickly and become more complex. We seldom take time to assess the effects of our actions upon others, or even pay them much attention, although from time to time we may experience feelings of guilt or resentment at their claims on our time. Our reactions speed up. We feel decisive and clear-minded, confident and in charge of our lives. But these feelings may be masking a growing short-sightedness; we become less willing to listen to advice and may easily make errors of judgment that set us up for serious difficulties.

Should we tire and wish to slow down, the pressures accumulating inside us give us no peace. We find ourselves enmeshed in nets of expectations and responsibilities that oblige us to continue. Eventually, errors in judgment catch up with us, or circumstances arise that we cannot turn to our advantage. With our sense of dignity and self-worth vested in escalating success, how do we feel when our momentum is blocked? Perhaps our first feeling is confusion. When we perceive that we are really locked in, confusion gives way to frustration and anger.

If nothing relieves the pressures, we are left with a deeper frustration that sows the seeds of self-doubt and despair. We have let down those who depend upon us; we have failed. Our guilt may be nearly unbearable; even if others offer their support, our own values lead us to reject ourselves. What resources have we developed to face the pain of self-doubt and humiliation? Or did we think such moments would not come?

Our predispositions and upbringing may condition us instead to a life strategy of restraint. Possibly from an early age we have learned to equate strength with self-control; perhaps our childhood circumstances led us to develop ways of keeping our reactions and emotions under tight control.

Over time we learn to hold our desires and aggressive impulses in check, maintaining balance no matter what happens around us. Our self-mastery can become a source of pride and well-being, a hallmark of breeding and dignity that suits our perception of ourselves, and allows us to respond intelligently to situations that promise to work to our advantage. Suffering and disappointment glance off us, as though we were surrounded by a protective shield.

But repressed impulses and reactions do not go away. Outwardly, we present a calm face to the world, while internally, unfulfilled desires and unacknowledged pain are intensifying. We must constantly be on guard lest our control slip, and others notice our weaknesses and vulnerability. Our defenses against our own impulses and feelings become so habitual that we deceive even ourselves. If we are determined not to be angry, we convince ourselves that we have no anger. Our emotions surface subtly, in ways that do not contradict our self-image.

Our actions become careful and measured. When something unexpected happens, we tense, cutting off our natural responses before we can consciously identify what we are experiencing. In building barriers between our feelings and our intellect, we also develop shells that shield us from the feelings and emotions of others, especially those who are closest to us. When we need to protect ourselves so carefully from our own impulses, how can we be open and compassionate with others?

Encased in our self-image, we assume the role of observer or mediator, never descending into the fray. Never fully engaged, we watch even our own actions with mild interest, as if we were a stranger for whom we need not be responsible. We may assume the role of martyr to a world that cannot understand us, viewing complaints that we are cold or uncaring as confirmations of our virtue and superiority. No one really understands how sensitive we are, or how nobly we endure our loneliness.

Freezing our feelings and emotions behind a mask of self-control, we become ever more rigid and unresponsive to change. We avoid situations that arouse emotions, warding off feelings that threaten to break through our outer shell. We may sense a growing isolation and blame others for not appreciating or understanding the qualities of restraint that we have so carefully developed. But however much we may try to console ourselves that we have found a superior way to live, we still feel lonely and misunderstood.

How can we break out of this pattern without exposing our weakness? What can we do with our fear of our own feelings and of the people or events that could break through our barriers? How much emotional energy have we repressed? And where can we find ourselves in the inner labyrinth we have built?

Awareness of the pervasive dissatisfaction of life may lead us to a life strategy of complaint. When we are young, our expectations are high, and we hope for the best life has to offer. But there are many small disappointments, and reality does not seem to measure up to our image of what it could be. "That wasn't the way it should have been," we say to ourselves, comparing the reality with the imagined ideal. "That wasn't good enough." A little proud of being difficult to please, we may think of ourselves as idealistic and somehow superior.

We do not realize that our tendency to focus on the negative blinds us to the positive aspects of our experience. Our complaining is not the positive approach we think it is, but is rather a force of negativity that draws negativity to us. Complaining appears to offer a convenient safety valve, a way to relieve our discomfort and to feel close to others. "It's a relief to be able to talk to someone about this." But as we grow older, our attention to what is wrong grows more pronounced. No matter where we are or who we are with, we cannot be satisfied for long.

Perhaps the problem is the people we live or work with, or the food we eat, or the place we live, or the kind of work we do. We may change jobs or mates, or move to a different city, but it makes no difference: Soon we are repeating, "This isn't the way it should be." We may criticize ourselves for failing to live up to our expectations, undermining our own confidence and ability to achieve our goals. We experience a feeling of agitation that rarely goes away. Wanting something, but not sure what, we measure our life against a standard it can never meet.

Our tendency to pinpoint the negative and ignore the positive is discouraging to others. With our husbands or wives and with our children, we may falter in our efforts to create warmth and trust. Perhaps we turn our attention to the world around us, developing exciting, even brilliant analyses of the problems confronting society. Playing the role of social critic with friends creates a feeling of camaraderie that conceals the lack of deeper closeness and intimacy.

Our ability to identify problems and criticize situations may gain us a reputation for incisiveness that leads to promotion and an established position in our field. But as we come to rely increasingly on our critical ability, we may not realize that it has become a way to protect ourselves; we ourselves may be the target of much criticism from those injured by our sharpness. Yet we do not realize that we have sparked this negativity, and feel deeply wounded and resentful when it turns back upon us. After all, we are in the right, aren't we?

As we grow older, we may wonder why we have so few friends and supporters. Have we done something wrong? Our habitual explanations come with facility: "She was so weak," or "He let me down." As we think further about what is missing from our lives, we may blame ourselves, adding deep regret to our frustration and pain.

In moments of clarity, we may realize that we have cut ourselves off from much of the beauty and joy of life. But try as we may to appreciate what we have, we cannot heal the wanting deep inside. Disappointment follows disappointment as our mates, our children, our work, our possessions all fail to match our expectations.

As we grow older, we may become bitter with disappointment. Unable to forgive ourselves and others for shortcomings, feeling unappreciated, yet wondering if somehow we ourselves are to blame, we may live out our days in loneliness and pain.

Coupled with awareness of injustices in the world, a complaining stance may develop into a life strategy of opposition. Whether the object of our criticism is government, the economic structure, the family, or society, we may embrace a specific theory of change as the key to a better world. Our interpretations of the causes of present conditions and our program for action seem so genuine that we have no hesitation about devoting our lives to this cause. Supported by an intellectual framework that makes sense of our lives and offers us hope, we develop a strong belief that our purpose is right and just.

We know that we must act decisively. Our work lies with people like ourselves who can be convinced to see things our way, even if they do not share our degree of conviction. We may try to listen to objections and questions, but generally we need not listen carefully, for whatever the opposing view, our theory provides an answer.

There may be times in our lives when our approach produces results we consider good. At other times, when conditions go against us, we remain convinced that time will bear out the rightness of our views. We may not notice the effort it takes to maintain our view under all circumstances. Caught up in interpreting everything that happens as an affirmation of our theories, we tend to reject the present in favor of a distant future.

We may even feel guilty if we find ourselves enjoying a pleasant moment or appreciating the standard of living provided by modern society. Or if the price we pay for following our ideals is present discomfort and frustration, "That's all right—it's worth it. This is the time to agitate for change."

As time goes on, our capacity for enjoyment grows less and less, and we may find it increasingly difficult to persuade others to our view. Are we getting out of touch? Feelings of loneliness may lead us to strengthen our relationships with others who believe as we do.

Whether we have some measure of success or not, without exposure to questions and differing attitudes, our views become more rigid. Since they require more energy to hold in place, we have less energy available for action. Lack of support for our views—and our life's purpose—may create bitterness or paranoia that drains us further. In setting ourselves ever more strongly against our society and culture, we may be plagued by guilt and conflict we have no way to acknowledge. Could we look at the pain we have brought upon ourselves without calling into question the rightness of our views?

Young people moved by injustice may not look to us for guidance as we had hoped and expected. After all, have we learned to act effectively in the world? Does our way of being offer a real alternative to the patterns we have spent our lives criticizing, or are we caught unawares in unacknowledged patterns of our own? Have we developed the knowledge, energy, persistence, and trustworthiness to lead others in a new direction, or have we invested our life energy in a dream that we cannot make a reality?

If we see few opportunities for happiness in the flow of events around us, or if the ordinariness of our lives makes us restless and uncomfortable, we can always turn to a life strategy where daydreaming becomes a central source of satisfaction.

Many children engage in daydreaming and fantasy play, enjoying the game of pretending they are someone else. As we grow older, we may find fantasy much more nourishing than the real world, which seems dull by comparison. We may dream of how our lives would be if only things were somehow different: "If only I could be a certain way, then my life would be worthwhile." Our sense of ourselves becomes connected with our fantasy images, even if we know they are imaginary. These images come to represent our 'real self' for us: This is how we would like to be; these are the qualities we would like to have.

Perhaps we model our fantasies on famous people or fictional characters whose lives seem much more exciting and real than our own. We can enjoy their experiences vicariously or dream of what we would do if we too were famous, irresistible, or rich. Of course, we know we are being unrealistic. What do we really know of the frustrations, worries, and fears of the rich and famous? But still we prefer to dream, creating an imaginary world where events unfold as we would want them to.

Our inner images are a shifting amalgam of qualities we add to and subtract from through the years. Creating these 'characters' can provide us with hours of entertainment. We can imagine ourselves in various roles and invent other characters to interact with. What adventures we have! They would make wonderful stories, but we just don't have the energy to write them down; our imagination seems to draw all our energy into its realm. And yet we are satisfied with our imagination; it responds to our every desire, it offers us no resistance, and gives us whatever pleasure we need.

Our 'real self' seems somehow locked inside this ordinary life that we do not really wish to live. If things were only a little different, we would be clever, courageous, beautiful, and talented. We would have the appreciation, love, and admiration of everyone around us. Then we would show our real potential! Our aspirations and ideals can be bonded so tightly to these fantasy images that it becomes very difficult to accomplish anything substantial in our lives. We prefer to dream rather than take any action to bring our ideals into being. In our dream, we are already complete and perfect; the reality might require effort and discipline, and we might have to struggle with confusion and fear.

Since we cannot express our 'real self', we may be reluctant to relate to other people—it is so discouraging to always end up just being our 'ordinary self'. We tend to cut ourselves off from outside activities and from others, and give more and more time to daydreaming. Our urge to dream may become so compulsive that we will rearrange our schedule to give ourselves more time to spend alone.

Sometimes instead of imagining 'heroes and heroines,' we may become completely caught up in interesting or imaginative ideas. We read and think and wonder—but somehow we have difficulty connecting these ideas to our lives or producing any creative work. We may feel inspired and excited, but when it comes to hard work, we drift off, looking for 'inspiration'.

On the surface our lives may be working well, and we may form stable relationships or take steady jobs. Since we find most of our nourishment within our dream realm, we do not expect much from the outside world. We just play along. But as daydreaming begins to permeate our consciousness, it undercuts our ability to respond fully to the present. By withdrawing our attention from the reality of our lives, we deepen our sense of stagnation and boredom, driving ourselves still further into an illusory existence. Out of touch with who we really are, we forfeit any opportunity to understand and change our lives.

When we look at such strategies carefully, it seems clear that they are not deliberately adopted after a thoughtful examination of their pitfalls and strengths. Who would consciously fashion their life as such a strategy? Perhaps we copied these stances from our parents or others close to us, taking up these positions before we could examine their probable results. Have we unwittingly patched together our approach to life, our whole personality, from outside sources who copied in turn from other sources? Could it be that our whole approach to life is a copy of an often recopied copy?

Accepting a preformed image to protect us from change and to fill the roles and expectations of others is like wearing someone else's ill-fitting clothes; we cannot be fully at ease, either with ourselves or in the company of others. But despite the discomfort and dis-ease, it is possible to become trapped by our roles, living out our lives in a self-deception we eventually lose the power to break.

The postures we adopt take a great amount of energy to sustain and give us little in return. We lose contact with who we are, and have difficultly sustaining a sense of meaning and progression in our lives. When we near death, the energy invested in maintaining roles and appearances will slip away, and we will face the reality of what we have done to ourselves more directly.

As we reflect on the stances we assume, we might consider that everyone else may be living in the same way. What intimacy, what closeness, what caring can we expect when we all conceal our real being in these ways?

15

Yearning for Fulfillment

*We can train ourselves
to search within and to question
the source of our deepest yearnings.*

Even in happy moments, surrounded by friends and family, we may feel somehow wistful and alone. Although we may be physically comfortable and have no pressing worries, we become aware of a vague yearning. It seems to emanate from the depths of our being, arousing a gentle aching sensation that lingers and then dissolves.

Sometimes a sound or smell touches something within, evoking this feeling like a half-forgotten memory. But when we reach out for the experience, it has gone—all that remains is an open space, a gap where something once seemed to be, but is no longer. We may find ourselves gazing vacantly at nothing in particular, listening to silence, feeling at once foolish and yet aware of a sweet sadness, a gentle pain that fades and slips away, eluding definition.

Although our lives are busy, moments do come when we feel something is missing. Somehow there is a mysterious space inside us that hungers to be filled. Perhaps we have been looking a long time for something that would fill this space and bring us a sense of completeness. We may anticipate happiness through our work or a circle of friends, or through wealth, fame, power, or prestige. Perhaps we want someone to love, someone who will comfort us, share our dreams, and understand our hopes and fears.

We may have found that someone, and now know our happiness would be complete if we had children and were a real family. Or else our children are young and demanding, and we yearn for a few moments to ourselves. When they are grown, leaving home to lead their own lives, we may wish they were young again and not so eager to leave us. Opportunities, people, possessions parade through our lives, but the longing keeps returning.

Looking for fulfillment, we sample different life-styles, relationships, and types of work, seeking a special joy or meaningful avenue of commitment. But just when our plans and goals seem to be within reach, we may find ourselves drawing back, avoiding a sense of completion. Yet we may not comprehend what we are doing, or understand why we are left with feelings of dissatisfaction. We turn to something else, searching for new frontiers to conquer, something or someone more attractive. Finding a new goal, we reawaken the sense of longing that sustains our interest.

In searching for fulfillment, we may actually train ourselves for longing. Reaching out to touch and relish the sensation of desire is our basic exercise. We nourish ourselves on desire and the anticipation of what we will attain, have, and do. What we seek may be highly valued in our society, such as professional knowledge, business expertise, or a manual skill; or it may be simple pleasures—social occasions, holidays, the prospect of travel or romance. But the yearning itself is a more important source of pleasure than anything we could obtain; we relish that sweet anticipation that tells us we are progressing toward our goals or getting something tangible to possess and enjoy.

From our earliest years to the present, we have become accustomed to the sweetness of wishing and the subtle sadness that often accompanies getting what we want. Our romantic ideals, our daydreams, the yearnings celebrated in literature and song validate and encourage longing. Pathos and sentimentality are easily aroused and confused with deep appreciation or love; we feel ourselves sensitive and alive when actually we are steeped in emotional agitation. Others can play on these emotions for their own private gain, exciting our longings further by stimulating deep emotional hungers.

If we want to prolong the sweetness our deep yearning arouses, we can focus upon things that seem unattainable—the ideal mate, unlimited wealth and power, even world peace. We can search all our lives for something we suspect we can never have. But even though we are striving for the unattainable, there must always be hope that our dreams will come true. What would life mean without hope to give us something to look forward to, some reason to continue living?

There are times in our lives when hope wears thin, when our minds tell us our dreams are empty, and our hearts are no longer so easily uplifted by anticipation. What is there left to hope for then? When we turn in our hopelessness to face what our lives truly are rather than what we imagine they could be, will we be encouraged by what we see? Will we have done anything inherently useful and satisfying? When we have no choice but to look inside ourselves for strength, what will we find? Will the emptiness and waste be unbearable, driving us into depression or back into fantasies and compulsive activities? Fed on aspirations and longing, is our consciousness strong enough to cope with hopelessness, grief, and loss?

We may turn to religion to satisfy our longings or for comfort in times of need. But our religious impulse may not be deep enough to heal our sense of emptiness and isolation; the same anxieties and fears may reappear. Or our faith may not be firm enough— we may be troubled by unresolved doubts, or our intellect may compel us to reject traditional beliefs that do not seem relevant to our lives and times.

And so we may attempt to be our own teacher, searching here and there for knowledge that will help us through the difficult times. We may find a new idea or approach that seems beneficial—it 'fills a need'. But rather than letting our new knowledge transform our lives, we adjust our new knowledge to our old way of living and end up with nothing really new.

Skill in living our lives, like athletic or occupational skills, has to be developed through practice. At present we are trained only for appreciating a portion of our lives, only for touching experiences that will satisfy us temporarily. Everything we know supports looking outside of ourselves for fulfillment: our language, the way we think about ourselves and our surroundings, the concepts we have formed, and the social conditioning that teaches us what we need and how to get what we want.

More subtly, we train ourselves to equate the joy of living with the excitement of anticipation. When anticipation fails to excite us, we nourish ourselves with memories or with dreams of what could have been. When we need strength, yearning is all we know; in our need our hearts may burst from yearning, but we get back only emptiness and fear.

We do not have to depend upon circumstances or other people for fulfillment, or settle for the sweet sadness of longing as a substitute for lasting happiness. We can train ourselves to search within, questioning the source of our deepest yearnings. Letting go of all preconceptions, we can ask ourselves what is really important to our lives, what is it that will sustain us through all forms of adversity. The times when we feel most restless and lonely are valuable opportunities to make friends with ourselves, to find within our own hearts a new depth of understanding.

When pain arises, or fear, we do not have to cover them up by seeking company or distractions. We can face them directly and question their source within our own minds. What is the cause of this pain? What within us is feeling threatened or fearful? Is it really necessary to respond to these feelings? It might be possible to say: "No! This time I will not respond. This time I will simply observe what is happening." In doing this, we reverse our accustomed patterns. We take the first step toward self-knowledge, beginning a path that can liberate us from yearning and loneliness.

If we rely upon our own resources and encourage ourselves to persevere in our efforts, we can learn to guide our lives with clarity and wisdom. When we can see more clearly what has lasting value, we can replace longing with genuine appreciation and nourish our hearts and minds with meaningful action. In later years, our consciousness will reward us for the nourishment we have given it, protecting us from unnecessary suffering and sustaining us with lasting confidence and inner strength.

As an artist allows hand and brush to be directed by an inner vision, we can be guided by knowledge of our own value and take full advantage of the opportunities a human life offers. Supported by the inner riches we have developed within ourselves, we can live secure, free from anxiety, fear, and loneliness.

16

Pursuit of Happiness

*How strong is our motivation
to discover the knowledge we need
to give greater meaning to our lives?*

Our lives seem naturally oriented toward the pursuit of happiness—we cannot even imagine not pursuing it. Although we all have different images and ideas about what would make us happy, we all wish for satisfaction. With so much effort and intelligence bent on finding happiness, why are so many hours of our lives spent in frustration and anxiety? We all have wonderful moments that are deeply satisfying, but we cannot seem to hold on to lasting happiness.

Our lives seem to run on their own, slipping past like episodes in a dream. When we look back, how fast the years have gone. The next twenty years could well pass as quickly, and all we will have is a few memories. In the meantime, we continue to eat, work, amuse ourselves for a few hours, and sleep.

The surface patterns of our lives display endless colorful variations, but if we look under the surface, beyond specific instances, the underlying patterns seldom change. We repeat the same actions, the same words, the same cycles of excitement and depression, the same renewals of hope, the same periods of anxiety. We try to maintain a sense of purpose, but are we sure of our direction? Is this the life we anticipated when we were young and full of hope? Is this the way we want to live the rest of our lives?

Most of us have raised such questions at some time or another, but we put them out of our minds before they make us too depressed. If we do begin to reflect on what to do, how easily we give up at the first indication that things may not be exactly as we have thought! We may turn back at the very moment when we are about to penetrate the boundaries of our familiar realm and gain some knowledge of what lies beyond. Discouraged and disappointed, we may resign ourselves to our lives as they are, and make the best of what we have.

A story is told of an ancient traveler who once passed through a small village. Although most of the villagers were too preoccupied with their chores to pay him much attention, a young boy not yet old enough to be at work was happy to listen to the stranger's tales. With growing awe he listened as the traveler described the grandeur of a distant city, its walls rimmed with temples capped with towers of gold. There, suffering of any kind was unknown; all of its citizens enjoyed great riches and lived in peace.

As the boy listened to the stranger's description, he saw with new eyes the routine and squalor of village life, and determined to do what he could to change it. He would go to the city, learn of its ways, and return to share his knowledge with the villagers. Although the boy had never before left his village, he set out at once in the direction the traveler indicated.

All day he walked, and by nightfall he had gone far beyond his village to the foot of a mountain range that stretched as far as the eye could see. Greatly disappointed, he stopped to rest. Surely, he thought, no one has ever traveled as far as I have, yet I have found no city. The stranger seemed so certain, his vision so real; yet he must have lied, or perhaps he was mad. Now I have reached the mountains that everyone knows mark the edge of the world. If I continue any farther, I will fall off the world and die a terrible death.

The vision of the golden city vanished; the boy quickly turned back to his village, retracing his steps in the dark. As soon as he had arrived home safely, he made a solemn pledge that he would never again be deceived in the same way. He resumed the ways of his people, and soon forgot his discontent with everyday life. When he came of age, he took a wife and raised a family. In winter he would gather his children around the fire and instruct them never to heed the wild tales of strangers. And his children followed his instructions, as did their children and their children's children.

How far do we let ourselves travel in our inquiries before we give up? What knowledge guides our first few steps? How much of our lives is patterned upon assumptions we never learned to question? How strong is our motivation to discover the knowledge we would need to give greater meaning to our lives? How much are we leaving to chance, assuming that life will automatically provide what we need? Our time and energy will not last forever; unless we ask such questions of ourselves, we may spend years repeating patterns that only increase our vulnerability to frustration, anxiety, and emotional pain.

Why can't we ask more from our lives? Are we willing to spend our entire lives in actions and thoughts that follow predictable cycles, without ever fully understanding our situation? Isn't there a more satisfying way to live?

We can learn to face questions that make us uncomfortable, rather than dismissing them as irrelevant to the realities of life. We can take our lives more seriously and demand more of ourselves. Our very impatience with questions can help reveal the habits that prevent us from finding greater meaning. Observing these habits will show us what to do, what changes are really beneficial to our growth, and how to develop our own inner strength.

Now, while we have some years left to us, why not take advantage of every opportunity to discover the real value of our lives? At the very least, this search would mark a break with old patterns and quicken our interest in life; at best, we might find a wealth of wonder and wisdom that we never suspected existed. As human beings, we have the capacity to free ourselves from limiting patterns and discover the key to true and lasting satisfaction. When we look closely at our lives and have the courage to follow our questions wherever they may lead, we can find the knowledge we need.

17

Gateway to Knowledge

The sensation we call fear
can be a gateway to inner awakening.

If we wish to explore our lives and their undis-
covered possibilities, we need to be able to look
steadily at our experience, no matter what it might be.
Right at the beginning of our explorations, are we
making agreements not to look at certain areas of our
lives? Painful or negative events, ideas, or memories
can be difficult to look at directly, for no dynamic is
stronger in our lives than the push and pull of pleasure
and pain, happiness and sorrow, and our wish to experience the one and avoid the other.

Our judgments of what is good or bad, positive or
negative, are based on concepts we absorbed as children as unconsciously as we learned our language.
These judgments are so compelling that we confuse
them with direct experience of life. Yet in accepting
them without question, we will surely limit what we
can discover. For aren't there hidden drawbacks in

experiences we call pleasant, and real value in those we call undesirable? But the reflex to turn away from 'negative' experiences is so strong that we hardly have a chance to see what is there. We cannot seem to get past our fear.

The most fearsome of all experiences, the one thing hardest to face directly, is death. But can we leave this event out of account and still hope to understand the meaning of our lives? We wish we could. Pondering the inevitability of aging and death is painful. It brings us up against a despair that leaves no avenue for escape. What in life has meaning if death is the end of all our striving?

Although we know we cannot avoid it, we act as though death had little significance in the total context of our lives. We can be realistic about death only on a superficial level, resolving to deal with whatever happens when it comes. We can deflect a serious inquiry into the meaning of death even while drafting life insurance plans and wills, or arranging the details of our own funerals.

If we knew that we had the opportunity to close a profitable business deal, we would learn as much as we could about all its implications and fully prepare ourselves to benefit from its outcome. Yet when our time comes to die, as it inevitably does, we tend to be caught unawares.

Can we allow ourselves to imagine how we will feel when it is our turn to become incapacitated and helpless, or to live daily with the knowledge of imminent death? Will our present feelings of pleasure and contentment sustain us when we feel our vital energies slipping away, or when we are suffused with pain that will not abate?

If we knew that our lives were ending within a few hours, would we surrender gently? What regrets might we experience; what would we feel we had left undone? Would we have lived differently had we known earlier that at this moment our lives would be over? What advice would we give to our children or to our friends, to help them avoid feelings of regret when it came their time to die?

Then, if we were given the opportunity to continue to live, would we take our own advice, or would we repeat the same mistakes? Allowing ourselves to think about death now might change our perspective on time and help us establish priorities for our lives that would support us better in years to come.

While we are young and healthy, time is our friend; it allows us opportunity to reflect on the value of what we are doing and supports our efforts to find the knowledge we need to counter confusion and waste in our lives. Wasting time, we lose our lives, and have little choice but to accept whatever happens in our later years. But when we accept time's generosity, and use it to build a strong basis of self-understanding, the knowledge we gain will protect us from weakness and emotional distress both now and in the future. In our old age, knowledge will be a continual source of inspiration and vigor, supporting us through all forms of adversity, and sustaining our value to ourselves and to others.

Why is it so difficult to face the reality that we will age and die? Why must we avoid a direct confrontation with our fear? When we say "I am afraid of what will happen," what do we really mean? Do we ever say, "I am afraid at this very moment because I know something I do not want to know"? Could our fear actually be an incomplete kind of knowledge, fearful only because we are unwilling to accept it fully?

Perhaps, in acknowledging our fears and allowing them to well up in our hearts, we will lose only our illusions. Within our fear we might find an unexpected resting place and feel deep gratitude that at last we know what we are and where we are going.

The sensation we now call fear can be a gateway to inner awakening. Whenever we taste fear, we can suspect that we are close to knowledge we have hidden from ourselves. Whenever we approach the boundaries of our experience and begin to perceive something new, fear will arise like a shadow, concealing whatever we most need to know.

Like a good friend, fear will never leave us until we completely understand our own being. As long as we seek greater knowledge of who and what we are, we can trust fear to serve as a compass to our own awareness, a pointer showing us the way to greater knowledge.

SECTION SIX

Knowledge
of
Confusion

CHAPTER 20: NEW BEGINNINGS

CHAPTER 21: IMAGES OF OURSELVES

18

Human Education

*In letting go our belief that suffering
is a necessary part of human life,
we can take a few steps forward.*

E ach morning as we awaken, our first impression is of light; as forms and colors come into focus, we see before us, wherever we look, the colors of the rainbow—the green of plants and trees, the rich hues of wood, the golden yellow of the sun, the blue sky above. Sparkling with light, even a stone walkway becomes a realm of jewels. As though out of a hidden cornucopia, myriad shapes flow past us and textures of all kinds brush our skin. Rustling leaves and birdsong are there for the hearing. Our senses and our minds bring us these offerings again and again each day.

In every time and place throughout history, people have been lifted out of their daily routines by moments of beauty when they sensed the wonder of being alive in this world. In these special moments we may feel deeply grateful to have a body capable of such responses, a mind that can know such pleasure and joy. A treasure-house unlocked and standing open before us, the world of our human consciousness contains a wealth of wondrous possibilities. The experience of human beings in such a realm could be an endless celebration.

When we have beautiful feelings of joy and appreciation, we know that our senses, our bodies, and our minds can enjoy feelings far richer and more complete than our ordinary sensations. Although it may now seem impossible to enjoy these feelings for more than a short time, we may simply be lacking the knowledge we need to recognize and sustain the positive aspects of our experience. We have only begun to explore the relationships among mind, body, and senses; we need more comprehensive knowledge to treat body and mind as an integrated whole.

While we have much information on the physical aspects of the body, measurements for the rational capacities of the mind, and theories grounded on observation of human behavior, we know little about how body and mind interact to influence the nature of our experience. Each of the many elements that form our bodies and minds may have functions and capabilities that we do not yet understand. If we could extend our knowledge, we might be able to open wide the channels between senses and mind, and discover new dimensions of experience that we could evoke whenever we wished.

Thinking about such possibilities may touch us deeply; most of us yearn for the understanding that will allow us to live more satisfying lives. We want to enjoy more of the positive in life—we want to feel good about ourselves, our families, our country, and our future. We want to be free of boredom, frustration, and lingering anxieties. But when we consider the possibility of real change in our lives, do we *try* to succeed or do we *know* that we will succeed? If we are optimistic, is our optimism based upon strong self-confidence and certain knowledge of alternatives? Do we know that we can find more meaningful ways to live, or is our confidence, deep down, shaky and uncertain?

Perhaps we have tried to make changes before. We may have read many books that seem to offer hope of self-improvement or invested large sums of money in classes or counseling, spending months or even years trying to free ourselves from old habits and gain more satisfaction from life. When we seem to be succeeding, a welcome feeling of exhilaration buoys up our confidence, filling us with hope for a brighter future. But if we begin to suspect that the changes we make are only superficial, or if we see old patterns resurfacing in new situations, feelings of helplessness and dismay may discourage us from continuing our efforts.

After a while we may gather our energy to try again. This time we are less certain of our ability to counter negativity, more critical of ourselves or those who would help us. We are not surprised when negative patterns reassert themselves even more strongly than before. Eventually, we may secretly come to the conclusion that it is simply not possible to change deeply entrenched patterns. We may continue to 'try' to change, but deep in our hearts we have no confidence that we will succeed. Finally, we may feel that the best we can do is to acknowledge that while we would like to feel better about ourselves, we have to accept ourselves as we are.

Real confidence that we can change the underlying patterns of our lives seems to be lacking, not only in our individual experience, but also in western society and culture as a whole. Though members of a wide range of professions—including educators, physicians, scientists, psychologists, sociologists, and political scientists—are taking a critical look at the complex problems we face today, they are not promising hope of real change. They may offer some new approaches and insights, but few professionals would claim to have been successful in their efforts to provide lasting and comprehensive solutions to strongly established social or psychological problems, and many are content to redirect them in less harmful ways. It seems that we simply do not know what to do—at a fundamental level—to make things better.

We may not be aware that the belief that we have no real alternatives is itself part of our conditioning, passed on to us not only by our parents and our school system, but by all the influences in society that make up our human education: the media, art, music, literature, history, science, politics—the list of influences includes everything in our known world. Everything we see, smell, touch, taste, and hear, everything we think, every action we take, everything that happens to us in our lives forms part of our education.

Throughout our lives, we have been taught how to view and interpret our experience—what to consider 'good' and what to consider painful; what to expect in life and what to expect from ourselves.

Everything in our experience has been channeled into categories that we have been trained to accept. Now these categories seem like self-evident truths that we cannot change. It is difficult even to imagine how we could judge ourselves and our experiences differently.

Although all human beings have had to cope with the limitations of their education, today we are more pressured than ever before and have fewer opportunities to think deeply about the preconceptions and views we are applying to experience. Life is far more complex than it was even a few generations ago. Our lives unfold in the midst of distractions and stimulations; from early childhood, our natural affinity for concentration, which is the field of creativity and inspiration, has been fragmented by a deluge of sensory impressions and continual activity. We have never learned the joy of inner freedom that can arise when the mind is naturally calm and concentrated; we have no real understanding of how to protect our mental clarity. Surrounded by the world of our experience, we are bound to what we know. Within its confines, our way of knowing is simply what it is; according to the logic of our conditioning, there cannot be other possibilities—this is the way things are.

Believing that we have no other way of perceiving or knowing may therefore seem entirely natural. Carrying this view to its natural conclusion, however, leads to diminishing opportunities for creative action. The more strongly we believe that we have no alternatives, that 'we are what we are', the less confident we become that we can change our lives for the better; our weakened efforts are nearly predestined to fail. In turn, failure verifies that we were right to doubt our chances for success, undermining our confidence still more. Convinced that we are unable to control the larger forces that affect our lives, we may direct our need for control toward our mates, our children, even our own bodies, shutting down more open, spontaneous responses and constricting our field of action even further.

As our world shrinks and closes down in increasing darkness, we may come to see only two alternatives: to rebel against oppressive influences or to draw inwards. What real choices are these? Locking ourselves into a view that we have no freedom of choice, we deprive ourselves of hope and proceed inexorably to self-destruction. If our mental freedom continues to constrict, what motivation have we to continue living? Loss of freedom sets the stage for individual and social suicide; even large-scale destructive actions, such as nuclear war, could possibly occur.

We cannot pretend that alternative sources of knowledge are already available to us, or that alternative approaches to education already exist in our culture and society. If we look closely at suggestions that are intended as alternatives, we will see that they follow familiar patterns and are unlikely to lead to anything truly new. Even educational ideas that are based on a wider vision of human potential do not begin to tap the full resources of the human body and mind.

If no new alternatives to knowledge seem to be available, and if we cannot solve our problems, we are faced with the limits of what we know. Although it may seem difficult at first to look honestly at what we do not know, this is the basis of new inquiry and new possibilities.

We know we do not know our past: We do not understand where we came from, the origins of our genes, the sources of our human energy. We do not know how thoughts and emotions arise; we do not know how negative patterns take shape; we have only begun to investigate the interrelationship of mind and body; we do not know how to tap the resources of our mental energy and sustain concentration beyond a short period of time.

We do not know our future: We cannot tell what will happen to us in the next year or in the next hour; about our death and its significance we know next to nothing. What will happen to the four billion people now living on this earth? Our destiny is like a blank. In the present we are occupied with doing what we have learned to do—to consider ourselves separate from the world, from others, even from our own deepest feelings; to be concerned with images and interpretations and the actions they give rise to; to be emotional and to seek happiness in emotional highs that we cannot maintain; to be always doing, although our actions do not satisfy us for long; to be solving problems; to feel lost and helpless when life seems to go against us; to be confused and frustrated.

Looking closely at what we do not know can make us feel uneasy and uncomfortable. We can of course turn away and continue to live as we have learned how to live, going from day to day, doing all the things we know how to do. But living like this is like living on the surface of our lives. However familiar our surroundings and activities, there may come a time when we become aware of feeling uncertain and unconnected. Our lives may seem to be suspended, as if we were waiting for something to happen, although we do not quite know what. Without deeper knowledge, we cannot know what we stand for in life, who we are, and where we are going.

We do not like to acknowledge that we need greater wisdom, but when we look around us, the tears we see bear witness to what we do not know. If we could collect all the tears wept by all the people alive in the world today, how large a vessel would we need to contain them? Our tears bear witness to our suffering. We may believe that the more we suffer, the more we know, but what do we really learn from our misery? Do we learn enough to free ourselves from suffering?

Genuine suffering can touch our hearts honestly to show us our need for greater knowledge. But in order to benefit from its instruction, we need to look beyond painful experiences and transform the patterns that caused them. Of what value is our present education—in the largest sense—if it does not teach us how to do this? If it does not teach us to be free of suffering and pain?

A truly comprehensive human education would be based on a thorough investigation of the workings of our consciousness. It would involve study of all aspects of consciousness, including our predispositions and the nature of our conditioning, so we could sort out the layers of confusion that have accumulated during the stages of our development.

To rid ourselves of pretense, we would need to integrate the face we present to the world with our real feelings; we would need to learn how to resolve inner conflicts between what we are and what we feel we should be. We would also need to understand how the ego manifests, the origin and nature of desires and emotions, and how all of these factors influence our judgment. We would need to understand the nature of relaxation and concentration and learn to protect ourselves from negativity. Ideally, we would gain a sound foundation for self-understanding as part of our early education, before negative patterns were deeply entrenched.

It might eventually become possible to review our approach to education and to develop methods of orienting our children to a far more positive view of themselves, freeing them from the pain of separation, anxiety, and guilt. Future generations may have to cope with an increasingly troubled world and will need, even more than we do, a positive vision for society and for humanity, as well as the confidence and inspiration to bring this vision into being. To help them end the problems we have not resolved in our own time, we can give them the gift of knowledge that will lead to happiness and security in theirs.

Although it is far more difficult to change negative patterns later in life, it is important for us to make this effort now, both for our own sake and for the sake of others in the future. Whatever we discover in looking into our own hearts and minds could have a powerful uplifting influence on our children, our friends, and our societies. However distant the goal, all journeys begin with a single step. In letting go our belief that suffering is a necessary part of human life, we can take a few steps forward, easing pain in our time and creating the potential for eliminating it completely in the future.

Even in asking ourselves if there are other possibilities, we take a broader view of our situation; we can stop, look, and reflect before committing ourselves more fully to our familiar ways of knowing. Recognizing that, despite the events that provoke frustration or pain, it is within our own minds and hearts that suffering takes place, we can begin to assess our inner resources and learn to trust them in a new way. We can restore positive feelings and stabilize ourselves in happiness, not by avoiding pain, but by passing through it. Seeing how our minds interact with physical and emotional pain, we can train them in more healthy patterns of response. If we listen more attentively to our thoughts, our feelings, and our bodily sensations, we can relieve the tension and anxiety of everyday life and begin a process of self-education.

The motivation for self-knowledge arises from within, as a genuine response to our deepest needs. It unfolds as an inner exploration that gains momentum as we observe our patterns, see how they formed, and understand how they affect the quality of our lives. While others might offer advice or point to new possibilities, the specific forms of our patterning are uniquely our own, and only we can track them to their source. We have no precedent for this inner exploration, but this is to our advantage: We do not know what to expect.

In this inner journey, there are no right answers and no wrong answers—only the unfolding of layers of meaning that can lead us ever more deeply into self-understanding. Questioning all our most basic assumptions about who and what we are, and allowing ourselves to listen objectively to the answers that arise in our minds, we can hear in our own thoughts the responses that limit us, undermine our confidence, and define ourselves and our possibilities.

If we are willing and receptive to our own knowing, we can train ourselves to see through the false assumptions that accumulated during the stages of our conditioning, just as we could learn to see through false logic or deceptions imposed upon us by others. We can make friends with the knowing side of our consciousness and learn to use our minds as instruments for strengthening our awareness; eventually the losers will be confusion and pain. Growing more clear with each insight, the inquiring mind can illuminate its own patterning and clarify confusion, the breeding ground of negativities.

Understanding our own minds allows us to nourish our inner being with honesty and humility, attuning ourselves to a fundamental sense of beauty and order that uplifts the quality of our lives. Inspiration shines through our hearts, moving us to share what we learn with others who need help. In this way we can create the foundation for a truly humanistic education based on an understanding that can heal pain and confusion, and remove all obstacles to harmony and universal prosperity. This knowledge would benefit generations to come, supporting their efforts to create a successful life freed from all manifestations of suffering.

19

Layers of Conditioning

Now we have an adult consciousness,
capable of sorting through the layers of confusion
accumulated during our growth and conditioning.

Each of us is a unique individual, with specific
characteristics resulting from a combination of
factors: our inborn predispositions, the influences of
our parents, friends, and cultural background, and the
specific circumstances of our upbringing. Yet we also
share a common pattern of physical, mental, and
emotional development, which takes place as our
informal and formal education prepares us to live in
our society.

Many of the diverse influences in our development
are rooted in a past that we cannot fully know or
understand. Yet these factors condition the way we
learn to think, interpret, and act upon our experience;
they determine the way we view ourselves and
everything in our surroundings. While we may feel free
within the boundaries of our conditioning, we are
unable to see the nature of its limitations, and thus

are caught in repetitions of negative patterns we have not learned to question. Seeing how these patterns were constructed, and reflecting on how they influenced our development, we can gain greater understanding of their roots. What we learn we can then apply in our lives to clarify areas of confusion that limit our growth and cause us needless pain.

It is possible to look back upon our lives, seeing images of ourselves as we were at different stages. These images may come into focus as if seen through a telescope from a great distance: perhaps fuzzy images when we were very young and clearer impressions of ourselves at later ages. If we look closely at these images, we may be able to draw out memories of how we were and how we felt at different ages.

Growth to maturity involves a series of stages, each of which is nearly a world in itself, demarcated by changes in perspective and interests. Although our experience is continuous, these changes make each stage almost a stranger to the one before it. Each stage is vulnerable to specific kinds of confusion that influence the way we view ourselves and others. As our world broadens and becomes more complex, unresolved confusions tend to accumulate.

Moving through these stages, we participate in three worlds simultaneously: our own realm of feelings, thoughts, and emotions, the realm of parents and other adults, and the realm of siblings and friends. The influence exerted upon us by each realm changes as we grow to maturity, so that we must continually reinterpret and reintegrate impressions pouring into us from all three directions.

Between each period of growth there is a certain space, almost like a gap between generations. At these times our bodies and minds are undergoing significant changes—the views and patterns of behavior appropriate to one stage are dropping away, and our consciousness is waking up to a wider view of ourselves and our surroundings. These pauses are natural opportunities to set aside outworn responses and prepare ourselves mentally and emotionally for entering the next stage.

In today's modern societies, these pauses are barely noticed. From an early age, we are pressured to move quickly towards adulthood. Our own eagerness to grow up intensifies the pressures that sweep us from one stage to another. Unable to develop according to our own inner timing, we are likely to experience transition periods as sudden transformations. No sooner have we grown comfortable with the views and behaviors of one period of development than we are swept into the next.

While we think we have 'outgrown' the responses and interests of a previous stage, we carry unresolved confusions from one stage to another. This is most true of negative feelings and thoughts we have had no opportunity to understand or transform. Misunderstandings and feelings we have had to repress or have never found words to express affect each stage of growth. Unrecognized and unaddressed, these confusions lay the foundation for negative views and emotional pain that may stay with us like a shadow throughout our lives.

W e pass through at least nine stages before reaching maturity. Although our inner timing may vary, these stages are usually from birth to eighteen months; eighteen months to three years; three to five; five to ten; ten to twelve; twelve to sixteen; sixteen to eighteen; eighteen to twenty; and twenty to twenty-three. Although in our twenties we are clearly adults, even more time may pass before we are fully prepared to take our place in the mainstream of society.

Between birth to eighteen months, our minds are an open receptacle for whatever impressions touch our senses—voices, sudden noises, hot and cold, warm skin, open space. Shapes and forms appear before us, now stable, now moving slowly, now moving too fast for us to follow. Our senses are active, our minds developing their rudimentary patternings. Parental emotions and worries for our welfare surround us. Involved in our own world, but unable to distinguish between ourselves and our parents, we uncritically absorb whatever our environment presents to us. Gradually, we emerge from a state of complete helplessness.

From eighteen months to three years, we are more aware of ourselves as individuals, separate from parents and other children. At this age, we learn that we can do things and that adults will respond, yet our behavior sometimes brings us the opposite of what we want. Alternately rejected and rewarded for our behavior, not really understanding the connection between what we do and what follows, we shift back and forth between curiosity and anxiety. We have difficulty in seeing the whole context of our experience. Our developing sense of individuality impels us to assert ourselves and say no, and we discover that we can somehow 'control' what happens through language, though the full significance of this escapes us.

While struggling to make sense of our experience, we mix up what happens outside us with our own feelings: We are at once separate and yet not separate. In the midst of this confusion, we are already absorbing and experimenting with the linguistic patterns that will determine the form and organization of our thoughts. Whatever we experience and learn, including the language that connects our mental imagery with words, reinforces the sense of a separate self and is incorporated into our childhood personality.

Between three and five years, our interactions with our parents set the initial guidelines for our values and behavior. Observing our surroundings with great curiosity, we learn to relate to what we see through play. We are the center of our world. Our behavior shifts quickly as we vacillate between feelings of self-importance and the anxiety of insecurity. As we learn to become more independent and 'separate', fears of separation intensify and diversify into fear of desertion, fears of becoming lost, and unnamed fears that come in the dark. Fears for our safety are conveyed to us, though we do not quite understand them. Confusion produced from all of these fears evokes self-doubts and feelings of inadequacy that lay the foundation for jealousy and sibling rivalry.

Communication is a mixture of new-found words that convey the meanings of simple concepts and the 'baby' language that we tend to fall back on in conveying our feelings. But our communication is often ineffective. Our experience of the world differs from that of adults, and our words may have shades of meaning unknown to them. Thus we can never fully express ourselves or feel completely understood. We are used to conveying feelings without words and are attuned to the feelings of our parents; if they are angry or upset we somehow feel it, even if the face presented to us is smiling and the words are calm. Conflicting signals may be confusing, even deeply disturbing, for we have no way to understand which signal to believe.

Between five and ten years of age, our world expands, usually to include teachers, school, and large numbers of other children. We experience new pressures to socialize and conform to the expectations of others; we have to cope with a whole new complex of feelings. More self-conscious, having to reconcile our self-assertiveness with the need to fit into a group, we begin to look at others differently, comparing physical characteristics, possessions, and skills.

Aware that others are noticing us also, we worry about being accepted. When others are critical of us, we feel inadequate and alone. Faced with the need to protect ourselves from ridicule or isolation, we may learn to fight back—or assert our place by bullying others. We learn to hide our feelings, and develop new versions of manipulative patterns we began with our parents. As if we were mastering the rules of a complex game, we learn responses that will gain us approval or recognition and minimize distress or frustration.

By this time we are comfortable with language, but find that the words we use still do not communicate what we mean. Our images and language become tangled as we try to express ourselves, and adults correct us continually. Although our perceptions and feelings may not fit the words we are given, we have to somehow learn to make them do. For a time we may feel as if we were living in two different worlds, a world of private meaning and a world of language we use for others. The gap between meaning and accepted ways of expressing ourselves grows larger as we move closer to the adult world; we tend to lose touch with the meaning and wonder we once took for granted in our experience, and become more closed to the feelings which we cannot express in ways that are meaningful to us.

From the ages of ten to twelve, still shielded from adult responsibilities, we project ourselves into the adult world, imagining ourselves in various roles. We may wonder how our parents can lead such boring lives—the things we want to do are much more interesting. Gradually we are becoming aware of ourselves as individuals in a new way; we are becoming 'self' conscious. Somehow this new awareness of ourselves produces disturbing uncertainties, and we feel a stronger need to find ways in which we can excel and bolster our self-confidence. As we try to develop whatever talents we may have, our goals become more dynamic, strongly infused with ideals and impressions gathered from many sources. At the same time, we discover that our skills and 'worth' are closely related, and that both depend upon how we 'measure up' to the standards set for us. Meeting these standards may require us to hide self-doubts and feelings of inadequacy even deeper and to strive harder for approval.

Aware of our uncertainties about who we are, we begin to think about ourselves in ways we never did when we were younger. When we look back at our younger selves, we may feel we are a completely different person than we were at eight or nine. When we look ahead, we may imagine what it will be like to be a teenager, but we do not know how this metamorphosis will take place. Somehow we must find our personality or create it—we do not know which. We begin trying on different behaviors, different clothes, even different feelings. How do we decide which is right, which is 'us'? We are not sure.

Between twelve and sixteen years, our bodies and emotions undergo rapid changes that propel us into new social interactions. Social guidelines are drawn that did not exist before. Even if we do not like them, they are there; we cannot escape them. The adult world begins to intrude more insistently; our relationship with our parents changes, and pressures from teachers and friends increase. Around the age of fourteen, we find our earlier images and plans for our lives challenged by more solid realities, made more confusing by our own shifting emotions and desires. Old fears resurface, and we may become acutely aware of doubts and inadequacies; we cannot fully accept what is happening to us, but we cannot express our feelings without exposing our uncertainties.

Need for acceptance by the group encourages us to conceal our insecurity beneath artificially assumed personality traits; pretense becomes a way of life. Maintaining a confident appearance keeps us on the defensive and involves us in self-deceptions that become more concrete as we grow more expert at concealment. We can hide even from ourselves, sealing off our hurts and insecurity behind a show of self-confidence.

The more insecure and isolated we feel, the more easily we fall into negative patterns that protect our self-image, but sow the seeds for later problems. Repressed, negative feelings grow stronger. In one respect they grow diffuse and watery, bubbling up as emotions when we are thrown off balance. Hidden below our conscious awareness, they become hard and knife-edged, surfacing in sharp words or actions that catch others off guard.

When we are upset, we may feel the sharpness of our negativity like a 'stab in the heart'. This sharpness may flash out at others erratically or turn against us when we are tormented by self-doubts and guilt. We hurt others and others hurt us, often in indirect ways we cannot open up and resolve. This quality erodes trust and undermines even the closest friendships. If we do not work out these feelings, they can later erode even long-standing marriages between loving couples. At a very deep level, these negativities make it impossible for us to really trust our own thoughts and feelings. If they grow strong enough, we can lose our drive and initiative, and cease caring what happens to us or how our attitudes are affecting others.

Unresolved negativity is further concealed under positive qualities copied from those we admire. We learn to present ourselves to others as we want them to see us. Although we may learn from our experiences and grow into these positive qualities, feelings of inadequacy and self-doubt stay with us and can surface under prolonged worry or stress. Observing our parents or other adults, we may copy forms of protection that seem sophisticated and effective, and learn to express frustration in sarcasm, humor, or overt manipulations. In time, we develop a 'sixth sense' that forewarns us when we are vulnerable, so that we can instinctively respond to protect ourselves. As we mature, we may find ways of expressing negative feelings more subtly.

Around sixteen to eighteen years of age, responsibilities and obligations begin closing in. Yet we have little solid basis or inner confidence to deal with them. We feel a need for inner strength, but when we reach for it, it is not there. We are so used to misrepresenting ourselves that we have somehow become 'unreal'. We may have a feeling that we cannot trust this personality we have created, but then whom can we trust? Can we trust our own feelings and thoughts? We have hidden our feelings, so our head and heart are divided. We look but don't see, hear but don't hear, feel but don't feel. How can we have confidence in new situations and take on responsibilities for which we are psychologically and emotionally unprepared?

Around the ages of eighteen to twenty, we have to take full responsibility for our lives and establish our own means of livelihood. We are now expected to conform to standards of adult behavior, but we still carry with us many behaviors and expectations appropriate to earlier years. We may find it harder to get what we want than we had expected, or feel restrained by the demands placed upon us.

We force down our fears and self-doubts, and slowly stop asking ourselves questions we seem to have no way of answering. We consolidate our personality, incorporating all our fears and frustrations. What else can we do? Our personality is all we have to rely on. Yet new pressures heighten old insecurities, as important decisions have to be made and acted upon. Few of us have anyone we can trust to teach us how to sort out practical from impractical hopes, ideals, and decisions about our lives, or to show us the real nature of our deepening patterns of self-deception.

Engaging the practical adult world, we are raw beginners who have to learn by the painful and time-consuming process of trial and error. So we develop a public image that fits our goals, incorporating ways of speaking, dressing, moving, thinking, and acting that others equate with success. If we lack self-confidence, we absorb the values and ethics of role models as uncritically as we once absorbed the attitudes of our parents.

Between the ages of twenty-one and twenty-three, we are adapting to the full realities of the adult world while still attempting to realize our dreams. We feel pressured to achieve and must weigh our personal interests against those of family or friends. We have to learn to support ourselves and deal with a wider range of people, conforming to the obligations of career and social role. If we have not formed a clear vision of what we want to do, this can be a stressful time, and we may find ourselves lost in our choices. It may take a few years for us to find a direction; we may change our minds several times before we commit ourselves to a particular line of work.

Creating a place for ourselves is a demanding task. Whether we succeed depends upon many factors, including our ambition, desires, personality, education, health, and other circumstances over which we may have little control. We may find we have to work harder than we had expected to establish a comprehensive basis for our adult life; there is no time for examining the negative patterns we have fallen into.

By the time we are fully mature, experienced in work and personal relationships and well-adjusted to our place in society, thirty-five years may have passed. Our conditioning is now complete; we have learned how to judge and evaluate our experiences, and what to consider desirable or undesirable. The patterns we have formed, the ways we have learned to view ourselves in relationship to others, and the obligations and responsibilities we have assumed are major factors that will determine the quality of the last half of our life.

The self-image that ultimately emerges from the conditioning process is a confused composite containing aspects of all the stages we have passed through. We can see a little of this inner confusion when we notice how our minds indiscriminately cast up memories, old responses, and associations from the past. Often we have no way of knowing which level our responses are coming from: the mature adult, the adolescent, or the child.

When certain thoughts and feelings arise, we may react with particular emotions without knowing precisely why; these responses may be completely out of character, not even relevant to our adult lives. Yet such responses continually show themselves, projecting insecurities and fears that seriously weaken our inner confidence. Conflicting thoughts and feelings can paralyze us in indecision. Or perhaps thoughts from one aspect of our personality supersede another, and we have 'second thoughts'. Often these are no better than the first, and we may find ourselves switching back and forth, unable to make up our minds.

Because we have never resolved the confusion that allowed these insecurities to take root in our lives, they continue to influence us subliminally. We may find that our most disturbing feelings can be traced to the patterns of our earliest days, which were formed at a time when we were most vulnerable. Childhood fears of separation, self-blame for misinterpreted parental troubles, and feelings of helplessness can all remain well-hidden but powerful forces in our lives, predisposing us toward a negative view of ourselves.

Until we see that self-doubts from our past and old hurts have no real place in our lives, our hold on our positive qualities is likely to be tenuous. Without realizing what we are doing, we may hold back from giving our best efforts whenever we sense the possibility of criticism or failure. It may be very difficult for us to act independently, to base our lives on our own vision and integrity.

It is easier to follow established patterns. Yet our lives are very precious. Can we afford to lose more valuable time in emotional pain and self-doubts, or risk the loss of motivation because of limitations we think we cannot overcome? How much useful time are we likely to have left to us? Possibly, at thirty-five, we have thirty more years of active participation in life; after sixty-five, we cannot predict how long our vitality will last. A third of this time will be expended in sleep, which leaves us twenty years; since we will likely spend half of our waking lives feeling annoyed, frustrated, bored, or depressed, we have automatically lost another ten years.

Even if we could use the full twenty years of our waking lives productively, we have many routine tasks to perform—we need to take care of ourselves, our homes, and our families. Some time will be spent in recreation and entertainment; unpredictable events will arise to distract us from our purposes. How much total time will these activities take? Possibly another forty percent of our remaining time. This leaves us a maximum of twelve years to accomplish our goals. If we become ill, or are weighed down by negative patterns and unresolved confusion from our earlier days, even these years could vanish in frustration, burnout, or emotional upsets.

To free ourselves from these negative patterns, we can turn to self-observation, which can be the starting point of new knowledge. When we begin to observe all of our experience from a neutral, balanced viewpoint, our minds will show us their patterns, gradually opening up layer after layer of confusion that we can resolve and clarify. For this self-exploration, we need no special knowledge: only the interest and curiosity to question our patterns and to be receptive to our inner responses. Each discovery invites new questions, further steps in a direct communication with our mind. The only help we need is a patient mind willing to look objectively and reflect on its own experience. Eventually, it will be possible to let go of all forms of self-doubt and hesitation.

In looking directly at our secret fears and weaknesses, observing how they affect our reactions in situations where we feel threatened, it is helpful to remember that what appears to our conditioned minds as negative may prove to be the key to seeing through our conditioning. Our present preference for certain kinds of experience was instilled in us while our consciousness was limited and immature. But experience is not inherently negative or positive. By reversing our tendency to reject situations we view as unpleasant, we can learn from all our experience. The very persons and situations that have presented problems in our lives can become catalysts for new knowledge.

Being compassionate and patient with ourselves, we will find ways to counsel ourselves wisely. The patterns that predispose us to pain and confusion are strong: Perhaps they will come upon us far more intensely when we turn to face them directly. If we recognize that this happens as a natural manifestation of real growth, we can protect ourselves from being either frightened or discouraged. We can remind ourselves that our minds, particularly when we were very young, were very open to impressions; deep impressions may be 'protected' by feeling tones of fear that hide 'terrible secrets' from us throughout our lives. Our minds may tell us that these fears are too terrifying for us to look upon; but if we look with adult eyes at the images and thoughts that frightened us in our childhood, they will eventually lose their power and disappear like wisps of cloud in a clear sky.

Seeing and acknowledging our own negative patterns, without blame or guilt, liberates us from the burden of pretense and grounds us in a basic honesty that we can trust as a foundation for confidence and real growth. With practice, we can penetrate the roots of tendencies that cause suffering to ourselves and to others. We can learn to enhance the qualities that support a healthy human life and let go of those that cause us harm.

20

New Beginnings

*With the completion of each cycle,
we might sense our lives
progressing in a moving spiral.*

From one perspective, our lives seem to move in a straight line. We are born; we live out our lives one day after another until we reach the end of our time. We think of our own life as a series of moments strung together or as a series of actions performed by someone who is moving through a corridor of time.

But from another perspective, this line is not continuous. There seem to be gaps or spaces at certain points where new beginnings are made. We might think of our lives as progressing through stages: infancy, childhood, youth, adolescence, young adulthood, middle age, and old age. Each stage is marked by shifts that manifest as changes in our bodies and our self awareness, in our thinking, feeling, language and imagery, and in our emotional patterns.

These spaces reveal a cyclical quality to our lives different from our ordinary linear understanding. It is as though we had come full circle through one stage and were beginning again on a new level. Sometimes, in passing through these stages, we can sense physical and mental changes almost as if we were undergoing a rite of passage. Many cultures have considered the movement from one stage to another a 'rebirth' into a new world, and have marked these shifts with ritual and ceremony. From a linear point of view, we are the same person, but our way of experiencing and our understanding shifts so that from another perspective, our view of ourselves in relationship to our surroundings changes. We start over with a new orientation and discover a different world.

Accustomed to thinking of our lifetime as a single continuous thread, we seldom dwell on the significance of these subtle beginnings and endings within our lives. We may notice changes in ourselves, our children, and in people around us, but the deeper meaning of these changes escapes us. When we are young, we are impatient to grow up, and we wish to forget our earlier ways. As we grow older, we may realize that we see things differently than we used to. But we may see this as an indication that we have learned from our many life experiences, or we may shrug off this difference, saying, "I must be getting old," as though our newer way of viewing things was a distortion of the world, a sign of our diminishing vigor. Somehow it is difficult to believe that this one person, 'me', can really be so different. But if we look closely at the various 'stages' we have gone through, we might see more clearly how dramatic the changes have been.

Each shift in orientation is a distinct change in our mode of experiencing. Our sense of time, for example, changes as we move through our lives. Each shift in our sense of time in turn gives rise to new perceptions and expectations. When we are young children, we sense time as unending, perhaps not moving at all. As we grow older, we feel time stretching before us, an unimaginably long series of years that extends much farther than we can even count. Even our next birthday seems so far ahead of the present that 'next year' seems almost like 'never'. As we enter adolescence, wishing to be grown up, we begin to push time, wanting it to hurry. Now we consider ourselves as an individual passing through time, collecting experiences. We have no fear of wasting or losing time. Even though we accept the idea that our time is limited, the implications of this are lost on us; we have so much time ahead of us that time still seems unending. As an adult we begin to sense time as moving too fast, and wish we could slow it down. Now we sense time's limit; we know in our hearts our time will come to an end.

As a younger person, we imagine that when we retire we will be free of time's pressures; harassing schedules will be a thing of the past, and the chaotic days of raising a family will be over. But by the time we are in our sixties and seventies, we may not have the sense of a long stretch of time lying before us. Aware of the limit on our time, we may choose very carefully how to use the days and years left to us. We may not wish to waste our time on petty problems, on emotional dramas, or on frustration. How much of our energy has been wasted already in such ways? This period in our lives gives us a precious opportunity to move closer to the heart of our life, to what brings us meaning and value.

At each stage rhythms of energy shift, perceptions change, and different abilities come forth. When as very young children we finally learn how to talk, a whole new world opens to us; later as we learn to reason, we find another dimension to our lives we did not even know existed. As the energy of our minds and bodies changes in adolescence, we discover feelings and possibilities that we had no access to at a younger age. Everything we know and understand as children disappears—our old pleasures, our comforts, our childish views of parental authority, and most importantly, our old sense of ourself. Suddenly we are self-conscious, aware of being a 'real person', although someone unknown to ourselves. A strange and exciting world lies before us: We are on the threshold of a new life.

Entering the adult world in our twenties, we may feel we have finally stepped into 'the real world'. Again in our forties, we see the world with different eyes, and again in our sixties. As we grow older, our physical desires seem to wane naturally, making room for a less pressured way of life that gives us a freedom no younger person has. But if we do not have a clear understanding of how desire and tension operate, we may greet this change with great reluctance. Perhaps we have images of ourselves that we have not 'updated'; or we may have prejudices about older people that developed during our teenage years. As adolescents involved in our own exploding emotions, driven from excitement to excitement by our restless energy, we may have seen only boredom and stagnation in the more stable way of life of an older person.

When we move too quickly from stage to stage, the changes we are undergoing are confusing; we feel uneasy and tend to fill in the open spaces between cycles, drawing upon our old and familiar ways of understanding and coping with experience. But the old ways no longer work. Not understanding why, we may confuse ourselves in increasingly complex ways. If we understood that the beginning and end of each stage mark a complete cycle, we could bring to mind and put aside outgrown patterns that have become hindrances to further growth, and prepare ourselves to think more clearly about the opportunities the next stage is opening to us.

If we could allow ourselves to move more gently through the space between the stages, we would find ourselves in an interesting half-formed world. Pressures of one stage have dropped away, and those of the next stage have not yet swept us up. We may have lost interest in our earlier activities but not yet have found new ones; or our energy has shifted away from familiar interests but has not yet stabilized in a new pattern. In this unsettled state, we can actually be more sensitive and aware. These times can shake us out of old patterns and habits and give us a chance to wake up to new understandings.

As we look at our lives in terms of cycles and the spaces between them, we may begin to notice smaller cycles within larger ones. Together with each cycle comes a special space between the beginning and ending, a space full of possibilities.

The round of the seasons brings changes in mood and energy to all living things. Winter gives way to the newness of spring; the growth of summer is completed in the maturity of fall. Though the modern world may not take these shifts as deeply personal events, the natural responses to these ancient cycles must be deeply embedded within our bodies and minds. Most of us feel that the time of the 'New Year' offers us a fresh start, a new beginning. Some traditions set aside special times at the close of the old year to recall and evaluate the actions and results of the last twelve months, reaffirming or changing goals and guiding principles. Something in us seems to yearn for completion, renewal, and fresh beginnings.

Each month also seems naturally to have a complete pattern of its own. A moon cycle around the earth passes through clearly demarcated quarters that are reflected in the rhythms of our bodies. It may be that our mental and emotional patterns also have corresponding rhythms that we do not usually notice. Is the new moon also a time of clearing away the old and looking ahead to new beginnings?

Even a single day is a cycle to itself—in the morning we awaken from sleep, and for a moment it seems we are not yet present. Our senses reach out toward shapes, colors, thoughts. Suddenly we find ourselves again. In the evening as we go to sleep, we experience a similar process in reverse. We slowly lose the sense of our surroundings until eventually we 'ourselves' disappear from view.

Within the day there are natural shifts in mood and energy, so we may notice certain aspects of life more clearly at different times. The hours before sunrise radiate a simple clarity and a sense of freshness and new beginnings, while the midday generates a more dynamic but also a more complex quality. The evening often lends itself to reflection. Sensing the wholeness of each day, we can conclude it with a fresh appreciation for our own time and energy. As we go to sleep, we might consider that we will awaken into a completely new day. What shall we bring to this new beginning?

If we could consider the opening of each day as the beginning of a new cycle within our lives, how many hundreds of opportunities would we have to let new possibilities come into being? If we could bring a sense of completion to the end of each day, we could begin to build our self-knowledge day by day on a firm basis. As we moved through the larger cycles of our lives, each month and each year would bear the fruit of increased awareness and a deeper understanding of our own minds. Proceeding through the stages of our lives, we could welcome each new beginning as a special opportunity.

Just as the gaps between larger cycles give us opportunities to look in fresh ways at our experience, the moments of transition between smaller cycles may also be openings to new possibilities. Even within a single day we may have many such opportunities. When we feel emotional, we may sense how we 'start up' another cycle of worrying or anger. Somehow we have passed unaware through a small opening between cycles. If we reflect on this cyclical nature of emotions and thoughts, we may discover a more spacious quality to our thoughts and emotional patterns than we had previously noticed. Perhaps each moment presents us with opportunities to see more clearly what is happening, set aside what is no longer useful, and open up new beginnings. We do not have to lose valuable time in emotional cycles that give us little pleasure. With greater self-understanding, we could see how these cycles begin, and pass through them more quickly to appreciate the positive aspects of each experience.

If we were to take these opportunities for new beginnings and deepen our self-understanding with the completion of each cycle, we might sense our lives progressing in a moving spiral. Instead of repeating our past patterns in greater and greater complexity and confusion, we could ground ourselves in a conscious appreciation of the past that allows us to learn and change. Then each new cycle, though repeating certain patterns from the past, could begin on a higher level of understanding.

As we approach the end of our lives, our knowledge will continue to protect us from fear and confusion. We may discover unknown dimensions to our own minds, and open up the mysteries of time itself. Eventually, we may find a wholly new understanding of beginnings and endings that could illuminate our last days with meaning and satisfaction.

21

Images of Ourselves

Hidden within are not only our
fears and confusions, but also
our deepest feelings and aspirations.

We have many images of what we are and what we should be. Some images we project to others, and some lie closer to our hearts. The images we present to the world are seldom completely stable, but shift according to how we see ourselves in relationship to others. With children, we may project one image; with mates, another. For employees, for co-workers and friends, among men or among women, we may project still other images.

We shift among these images so readily that they are like clothes we change at will. Our wardrobe of images helps us feel confident and at ease in whatever role we are called upon to perform in life. In a sense, our images serve as a protective layer between us and the outside world.

Which of our images really express what we are? Are all of them true to ourselves, or do some seem less real than others? Do we know when we are playing a role, or do we identify with all the roles we assume? Are perhaps all of these images extensions of ourselves in some respect?

We seem to be able to juggle numerous images at once, projecting outwardly what we want to believe we are and what we wish others to see. Other qualities that we do not like in ourselves or do not want others to see we try to hide. People around us support the positive images we present to the world, for they have their own images to protect, and usually have little to gain from challenging ours. We enter into unspoken 'pacts' with others: "I won't disturb your view of yourself if you don't disturb mine." We use this 'support' to confirm to ourselves that our positive self-image is real, and we may be genuinely surprised or upset when we discover that others do not always see us as we see ourselves.

We feel much more comfortable when people validate our positive self-image by showing us respect and trust, love and appreciation. Acting on our positive views of ourselves, we can make commitments and take on responsibilities with confidence. Our confidence may be contagious, inspiring others to rely on our strength and abilities. Our responsibilities grow, along with others' appreciation and respect.

Our faith in ourselves is confirmed as we become increasingly indispensable. But what happens if suddenly things go wrong, and the praise turns to criticism and blame? In the glow of praise and self-confidence, we may have taken on more responsibility than we could handle. Can we now sustain the positive outlook we had when we began, when we felt respected and appreciated? Can we meet the challenges, using our full energy and resources, or are we lost without the confirmation of our self-importance? If our confidence is not based upon inner strength, we may feel almost forced to pull back to 'defend ourselves'.

Covering up our failures and shortcomings with reasonable explanations, we cloak ourselves in excuses in order to escape from confronting ourselves directly. Unable to penetrate the protective layer of reasons and excuses we create around ourselves, we undermine our ability to accomplish even our most cherished goals. We let things go, subverting our own efforts to take the actions that could make the crucial difference between success and failure.

Slowly, a sense of messiness, of things undone, builds up as a feeling of warm tightness; it catches us first in the stomach, then in the heart and throat, and finally in the head. Our time goes by, filled with confusing inner debates. We begin to move and think more slowly; it becomes difficult to organize our thoughts and actions, and we begin to care less about whatever we are doing. We do not plan as well as we could; we leave things out and keep making mistakes we could have avoided, then create more rationalizations to explain to ourselves and others why this is happening.

Although we may feel the force of this pattern as a palpable presence undermining our deepest feelings and aspirations, we are so used to holding the familiar sense of limitation close to our heart that we cannot let it go. Even if we want to change, we feel too weak to do anything on our own; everyone else is doing the same thing in their own way, so who will support us if we try? If we do manage to make a start, others threatened by our attempts to increase our confidence and strength may try to undermine us. Lacking the compassion and energy to wake ourselves up to a larger view of what we can be and do, we eventually allow ourselves to believe that we cannot do what we set out to accomplish.

Once we lose confidence, we can find many reasons for failing to meet obligations: "There was an unexpected difficulty—I had no way of knowing." "Someone let me down—there was nothing I could do." "I tried my best. What else can I do?" "I didn't promise anything. I only said I would try." Sensing failure, we may back out of commitments to spare ourselves further distress. "I can't overload myself or I'll get run down and never accomplish anything." "I have to take some time off before I get so aggravated that I can't do anything."

Our rationalizations sound very convincing, and once we formulate them to ourselves and then speak them aloud, we ourselves tend to believe them. When our excuses are accepted, we may feel relieved that we are not blamed. But there is a strange feeling inside that we have somehow gotten away with something or tricked someone, perhaps ourselves. Our energy has gone into self-protection instead of into our work—but what are we protecting? An image of ourself as a failure? Protecting ourselves at the expense of diminishing ourselves, we are left with a view of ourselves that causes us pain.

Even if our excuses are accepted, our failure to match our positive image may compel us to continue blaming ourselves. Our inner dialogues may try to fix the blame securely: "What a failure I am. I was a disappointment to everyone." But to get ourselves 'off the hook' we also blame the conditions that seemed to be the cause of our failure. "But I could have done better, if only . . ." Finally, we 'accept' ourselves: "It's not so bad. Everybody breaks promises. I did the best I could in the time I had."

Why do we experience such great inner turmoil? Where have our positive qualities gone? Why do we have difficulty in sustaining them?

When the qualities that make up our self-image are not stable, our sense of self-esteem is never secure. Our images may make us feel good about ourselves for a time, but when the qualities they project are not fully integrated into our being, we are always vulnerable. Eventually our tenuous hold on these qualities will become apparent, and we will find ourselves in a dilemma.

When our image of ourselves alternates between positive and negative modes depending upon the views of others or upon our own shifting attitudes, where can we find our real selves? What qualities in any of our images are stable? Can we predict how we will feel about ourselves tomorrow or even the next hour? We cannot truly trust ourselves to follow through with responsibilities and commitments; we can never be certain that we can retain the trust or love of others. Vacillating among our many images, we lose touch with who we really are, and have difficulties in developing our full potential.

If these images of ourselves are not based upon our real qualities, what are they based upon? Why do we continue to feel they represent us even when we suspect that they are not completely accurate?

These images are very closely related to the sense of self we establish during our childhood when we learn responses that will insure our acceptance, gain us approval or attention, and minimize personal distress or frustration.

As very young children we can seldom refrain from expressing our feelings directly, but as we grow older, we soon learn to modify our behavior and attitudes in terms of what others consider appropriate. We learn when we should laugh and when we should cry, when we should be serious, when we should be aggressive or submissive, when we must be polite. We learn how to mask feelings that are unacceptable to others or that produce an undesired result, and when to express thoughts and opinions at variance with what we really think and feel.

As artificial patterns of response become deeply imprinted, they complicate more genuine responses. We learn to conceal ourselves from others, to dissemble, to manipulate, to rationalize, and to excuse our actions in ways that are socially acceptable. Eventually, we come to believe our rationalizations. Honest and dishonest responses become very difficult to differentiate—we learn to lie even to ourselves.

Just as we have strong preferences for pleasant experiences and avoid unpleasant ones, we learn to focus on the aspects of ourselves that others like or that we see are regarded as desirable. We are sincere and honest; we are confident, knowledgeable, and capable . . . how could we be otherwise? Discovering that others will accept the image we project, we consciously train ourselves to manifest qualities that will guarantee success in our work and relationships.

To create a more acceptable image, we hide or deny various aspects of our consciousness we have been taught to regard as 'bad', such as jealousy, anger, and resentment. But the unwanted qualities stay with us, surfacing in disguised forms or repressed at the cost of much energy. These disowned qualities color our relationships with others in ways we cannot readily understand. If we are unable to acknowledge rage in ourselves, but find it rising into view, we can unconsciously protect our self-image by projecting this anger onto another person, whom we can then self-righteously reject.

When we persist in seeing ourselves as always good or right, any undesirable qualities we feel inside us must be blamed on something or someone else. It is easy to convince ourselves that 'evil' thoughts and actions originate from an external source; we are therefore justified in attacking or eliminating this threat to what is 'right'—in other words, ourselves or what we stand for. In extreme cases, we may see an enemy in every idea, concept, or person that disagrees with our fixed concepts; we may make groups or even whole cultures that favor different approaches to life scapegoats for our own hidden aggression.

The more successful we become in establishing and protecting our self-image, the more powerful and capable we can appear. We may become adept at intimidating others with the sheer force of our belief in ourselves. Inflated with feelings of righteousness and power, we continually defend our sense of ourselves by setting our own ideas and opinions above those of others. We may never see how rigid and willfully blind we have become.

This tendency to hide from our inner responses permeates much of our experience. Sometimes we are aware of hiding our responses, particularly when we lie to protect ourselves or deliberately try to deceive someone. But often we only half notice what we are doing, or are completely in the dark about our actual responses. If an undesirable feeling arises, we may find ourselves expressing an emotion or feeling that is actually the opposite of the one we are experiencing. In this way we can handle the unwanted feelings without having to confront them directly. Once expressed, this fabricated outer response becomes 'the real one', and we easily 'forget' our original impulse. Or perhaps we did not notice it at all. But even if we are able to completely repress our negative responses, covering them over with our positive view of ourselves, the emotions and feelings are still present, and will subtly pervade the image we manifest to others.

As children we naturally sense the real feelings beneath the images people present to us. When there is a difference between the inner feeling and the outer appearance—when anger, for example, is hidden beneath a calm, controlled surface—the conflicting signals can be very confusing. Slowly we realize that the hidden feelings we sense are best ignored, for when we touch them, sparks are generated that inflame emotions we cannot control. Or perhaps we ourselves do not wish to see this hidden side. We learn to deal exclusively with the outer feelings displayed by those around us.

We may eventually come to doubt our own perception of the 'hidden things' and learn to ignore them altogether. Our own inner feelings may still respond to the hidden side of others, but we no longer know why we feel as we do; we can only sense that something is not right.

Just as we learn to trick ourselves into ignoring what we see in others, we learn to ignore what we do not wish to see in ourselves. These rejected qualities can combine with the deep insecurity, confusion, and fears we have collected throughout our lives to form a negative self-image. Revolving around our weakest features, this negative image presents us to ourselves in the worst possible light—hateful, incompetent, stupid, dishonest, unworthy of love, weak. Such a self-image can be just as powerful as the positive image we display on the surface. Part of the power of the negative self-image derives from its partial truth—we suspect we have traits we wish were not there. But just as our public self-image of confidence is an exaggeration of our actual abilities and qualities, so our negative image is also a one-sided and inaccurate version of ourselves.

When the image we present to the world is threatened, we often find ourselves at the mercy of our negative self-image. The images of how we wish to see ourselves war with images of how we fear we 'really' are. Sometimes the negative images prove stronger, and we are driven by fear and doubt that destroy our self-confidence. Yet no matter how much pain they bring us, the negative images we fear are also a part of our familiar sense of self. They contribute to our security.

Viewing each experience through the filter of our self-images, we become alienated from ourselves. We are unable to track our real feelings through the maze of rationalizations and projections that protects our ideas of what we are. Isolated behind these barriers, we cannot help but continually deceive ourselves about our underlying motives and situation. As patterns of self-deception become deeply ingrained, we come to feel safest in superficial relationships that do not challenge our images of ourselves. Situations that might bring hidden aspects of ourselves into the open may make us fearful or hostile. Unable to be honest with ourselves or others, we are unable to give or receive real warmth or love.

Hidden within are not only our fears and confusions, but also our deepest feelings and aspirations. Yet it is difficult to open our hearts without touching upon pain and fear as well. When there are many old pains and confusions locked in our hearts, we need more than ever to believe that the images we present to others are true. It may be nearly impossible to acknowledge our own weak and negative qualities. Convincing ourselves that we are 'fine' just as we are, we may see no need to develop real inner strength and confidence.

In our blindness, we cannot see the effects of our actions on others or understand why we feel so isolated and alone. Loneliness increases our pain, which we pass on to others in many ways, perpetuating the unhappiness we feel deep inside. Trapped within these narrow views, we can spend the whole of our life defending ourselves against self-knowledge. We close off options for enriching our lives with compassion and joy, and lose opportunities to develop the real confidence that would allow us to accomplish something meaningful.

Even when we wish to strengthen our positive qualities, we may not be able to make our wishes a reality. We have many good intentions: "I really want to improve. I really want to change. If I had another chance, I would behave differently." Or "I wish I could really be confident. Next time I'll try harder." But our attempts may end in frustration. Our wishing is not enough; we do not know how to break the force of old patterns, so we fall back into them. Then we may blame ourselves even more.

Perhaps we are trying to act prematurely—before we can change our patterns we may need to know more about them. By observing our own experience and asking ourselves what is limiting our efforts to develop the qualities we desire, we can begin to deepen our understanding of these patterns. When we reflect on how long we have been trained to hide our worst qualities and remember how many others share the same difficulties, we can treat ourselves more gently. Deeper compassion will help us relinquish the fear and blame we tend to direct toward ourselves and others.

Our initial attempts to see ourselves more clearly and honestly may be confusing. All our training and conditioning have taught us to hide our undesirable qualities, to push them away, or explain them in ways that seem reasonable. Following old patterns, we may trick ourselves into not seeing what is before our eyes, automatically covering up our reactions by denying them or excusing ourselves with networks of reasons. Perhaps we are ashamed of our reactions and believe others would shame us further if we allowed them to surface; perhaps we feel they are beyond our control. But we have run a great risk in refusing to acknowledge our darkest thoughts and feelings. They are far more powerful when repressed, for they may erupt unpredictably in ways we cannot control. However much we may wish these feelings were not part of us, they will poison our lives until we acknowledge them and find ways to transform them completely.

We tie up much of our energy in holding qualities we consider blameful in check, or engaging in inner debates about how we 'really are'. This keeps our attention centered on ourselves, separating us from others. It becomes harder to see beyond the confines of self-interest. When we can catch glimpses of how we do this, we can recognize the defenses that prevent us from knowing the real nature of our emotions. Although we may not like what we see, we may sense for the first time that we could change our lives on a very deep level. Reflecting directly on what we see without excusing ourselves, we can begin to observe the tendencies we have been ignoring. Whatever we see gives us knowledge we can count upon to support our efforts to change.

Little by little, it is possible to become more objective. Even in the midst of emotion, we can watch ourselves as though we were actors in a grand drama, arguing with different images of ourselves. Each instance of more objective seeing helps decrease the heat of the moment; gradually we will be able to participate less in the drama. As we experience more directly what is happening, we can recognize the endless stories our minds spin as defenses and justifications, and see the underlying patterns they are trying to hide.

When we feel less pressured to interpret experiences to accord with our self-image, we can be more attentive to our deeper thoughts and feelings. Perhaps long after an unpleasant situation has passed, we feel a tightness in our stomachs or shoulders; what emotion are we holding? When we allow this tension to relax, what thoughts arise? Is resentment there, or anger? Is there fear? Touching the surface of the feeling lightly, we can watch the direction of our thoughts. Do the thoughts push the feeling down again or intensify it? We do not need to *act* on the thoughts or emotions, or feel guilt from anything that arises; we can simply observe the feelings and thoughts that move through our bodies and minds.

If we get caught up in the emotions and thoughts, we can also observe that. At what point did we begin participating instead of watching? What compelled us? Emotions that pull us very strongly into the drama they relate can sometimes be loosened up by changing our focus. Instead of focusing so heavily on the content of the drama, we can observe the structure of the emotion itself or the interactions between emotions, and watch their way of 'playing with us'. Perhaps we glimpse some unwanted quality in ourselves but instead of letting this knowledge 'sink in', we become emotional, and avoid confronting the truth by reverting to patterns of blaming ourselves. When we see what we are doing in a simple non-judgmental way, we can trace the patterns of emotions and thoughts much more clearly.

Watching our thoughts, deeply sensing our own feelings, we can be more at ease with whatever emerges within us. When we cease rejecting aspects of ourselves, we can open our hearts more fully and lightly touch painful places of negativity and confusion. Setting aside all thought of shoulds and woulds, we will find love and compassion arising in our hearts; we can direct these feelings toward ourselves, as though to a friend in need.

Once we know that love and compassion are already present within us, we will have the knowledge we need to open our hearts further. Whenever we feel old patterns returning, we can be more confident in our own inner strength and compassion, and allow whatever pain we experience to touch our hearts directly. Accepting whatever arises without fear or blame, we can sort out which images match what we truly are, which are false to our being, and which represent our deepest aspirations. Eventually we can go further, watching our words, our bodily movements, and our gestures, and bringing them into harmony with our inner aspirations. Comparing our words and our deeds, our images and our actions, we will find the inconsistencies we need to resolve.

SECTION SEVEN

Healing
Knowledge

CHAPTER 22: TRANSFORMING TENSION

CHAPTER 23: CONFLICT OF COMPETITION

CHAPTER 24: SEEING THROUGH PAIN

22

Transforming Tension

Our senses can be viewed as two-way channels,
capable of sensing inwardly as well as outwardly.

Our senses are naturally attuned to our surroundings, ready to resonate in response to any stimulation. Open to a constant play of movement and energy, our senses instantly grasp and transmit impressions of shapes and colors, movements, sounds, fragrances, tastes, and bodily sensations. Our minds, like the senses, are subtly tense even when relaxed; alert and active, they are continually responding to sense impressions. Fundamental tension exists in every living cell of our body. At a very basic level, tension seems to be part of our nature.

At the onset of the perceptual process, the mind grasps sensory impressions with lightning speed and sorts and processes them. Images are identified and labeled through a complex process that draws upon a wealth of memories and associations. Only then do our minds present us with sights, sounds, smells, tastes, sensations, and thoughts that we can cognize and respond to. What actually stimulates our conscious responses are the images and thoughts that emerge from this chain of inner activity.

The mind then continues to react to its own re-action. If we observe what is happening in our minds, we become aware of thought echoing thought as the mind comments on its own responses. In an instant we can be far removed from the immediacy of experience. While the echoes of one thought are still reverberating, our minds are processing ongoing stimuli from within our bodies and from the outside world, labeling and interpreting them in the same manner. Before we speak, thousands of impulses may have streamed through our minds. This excitable, highly reactive tendency of the mind renders us vulnerable to stress.

Even our accustomed activities stimulate countless internal reactions. Whenever the quantity or intensity of stimulations exceeds the capability of our minds and bodies to integrate them, residual tensions accumulate. As stimulation increases, our senses have less time to relax. They grasp faster, compelled to respond until the nervous system becomes overloaded. The mind in turn grasps faster to engage and sort out the barrage of impulses it is receiving. When overstimulated, the mind is likely to present us with confused interpretations of our experience. When its activity produces agitation in our bodies, we feel tense and anxious.

Long after the stimulations are over, tension remains in our body. If the tension goes unrecognized, or we have no effective ways to relax, it builds up, constricting the natural flow of our energy. When we become accustomed to tension, we may not notice that our senses are becoming numbed, our experience more tasteless and flat. Then we feel the need to heighten the intensity of stimulation.

Our very ability to enjoy an experience may come to depend on stretching our sensations to new heights. We can become so addicted to intensifying stimulation that we feel bored even in the midst of exciting events or acutely uncomfortable in the presence of people who are silent. When we are alone or have nothing specific to do, our bodies feel restless; our minds may sense this restlessness and dwell on thoughts that disturb us even more. Their endless interpretations provide us with many reasons for our discomfort, and stir up conflicting emotions. Emotional energy only increases our restlessness and provides our minds with still more fuel for interpretations. We might find ourselves too agitated to sleep or awakened frequently by disturbing dreams or thoughts.

Most people today have lived in a state of excitation and overstimulation since early childhood. Our fast-paced way of life bombards us with stimulation. Where in the course of a single day can we find more than a few brief moments that are free of mental, emotional, and sensory excitation? Even when we feel we are relaxing by reading, listening to the radio, or watching television, our emotions, desires, yearnings, anxieties, and fantasies are aroused by a continual stream of sights and sounds.

Our minds seem to thrive on excitement and encourage us to be continually thinking and doing. Excited, the mind tends to race and leap from thought to thought, skimming over the superficial levels of what is happening, but less able to derive meaning and satisfaction from what we are doing. Interpreting our experience through concepts that may have little to do with the real nature of our experience, we may tell ourselves we are feeling pleasure or learning something valuable when we may actually only be increasing the level of stimulation.

The faster thoughts and images arise, the more likely they are to become jumbled and confused. The complex feelings and emotions they evoke confuse us further, stimulating still more thoughts, feelings, and emotions in escalating cycles. Thoughts become blurred and indistinct, sometimes even incoherent, as our minds leap from subject to subject; our bodies respond with muscular tension and restlessness that heighten the level of agitation.

The greater our tension and anxiety, the more we feel impelled to act. We may be physically unable to sit quietly and allow body and mind to regain their balance and calm. In our excitement, we pour more of our energy into activity until our bodies and minds are exhausted; our bodies feel heavy and unresponsive, while our thoughts grow more complex and dense. If we have no way to break these cycles, we can reach a point where we feel paralyzed by tension that has nowhere to go. This tension is stored in our bodies and minds, creating the conditions for illness or despair.

To cope with stress and anxiety, we try to adjust our lifestyles according to the level of tension we find tolerable, and avoid situations that threaten to exceed our limits. We may find release in exercise, with alcohol, cigarettes, or drugs, with a good meal, or sexual activity. Periods of physical inactivity or prolonged sleep can relieve awareness of pressure; talking with friends gives us an outlet for tensions and confirms that others share our frustrations.

The ways we find to relieve tension may seem effective and even bring us great pleasure. We turn to them naturally whenever we begin to feel restless. As long as we can maintain an even balance between tension and relaxation, we may feel that tension is causing us no great difficulty. But do we ever feel fully rested from our efforts to relax? Or do our methods of relaxing create their own tensions? If these activities have actually relaxed us, why do we so often need to intensify them, or spend more time on them, or seek out new variations? It seems normal to wish to increase pleasure, but our efforts do not necessarily bring us the results we wish, particularly when we begin devoting more and more time to finding pleasure.

Any activity we enjoy, whether mental or physical, work or play, can itself become a source of dissatisfaction and anxiety. Even wholesome activities can become unhealthy when they take on a driving quality that intrudes on other aspects of our lives. Although we may have initially engaged in them for physical fitness or for pleasure, eventually they can occupy a much more central place in our lives.

Memories of pleasurable feelings, heightened by fantasies and notions of achievement, may keep us striving even when we are experiencing frustration or bodily pain. It becomes difficult to stop—something keeps pushing us to continue. As the pushing grows more demanding, our range of interests may narrow until we feel entirely dedicated and committed to a single activity. Our sense of purpose is convincing: We are determined to pursue this interest, although we may not know why; or perhaps we convince ourselves that it brings us great benefits. But our strongly focused minds can become oblivious to our own deeper feelings and the feelings of others who may feel neglected in the face of our preoccupation. Unable to reflect on where our interests are leading us, we can become trapped in activities that take much of our time and energy, crowding out other concerns that may have more long-range benefit to our lives.

Once we become strongly attached to improving our performance and feel the need for others to recognize that we are successful, we set ourselves up for greater pressure and the ever-present possibility of disappointment. With the increase of competitive pressures, pleasure tends to fade into a secondary goal.

Even if we have no inclination to build a particular activity into a major endeavor, our methods of relaxation can develop a driven quality that seems to provide a feeling of control over our bodies and minds, but actually contributes to stress and tension. Any mental or behavioral pattern can become a compulsive way of avoiding pressure, tension, or pain without actually resolving them. In the end, our activities may drain us of energy without providing us with the refreshment we seek.

Compelled to avoid pain, not knowing how to deal directly with pressure, we become runners in a race against tension. We hurry through each day, chasing after something that will bring us relief or trying to get away from something that will increase our tension. We cannot slow down and consider where we are going, or why we want to get there—we don't have time.

Like a machine that cannot be turned off, we keep on running. We run harder and faster, trying to keep up or get ahead, trying to reduce the pressure that seems to push us from behind. What can we do but run, run, run? We may even run physically in an effort to stay 'in shape' and relieve the tension and pressures we feel. Racing against time, we cannot escape the runner's dilemma—the more we run, the more we have to run. Only when we drive ourselves into deep physical exhaustion or emotional numbness do we find some relief from the terrible pressure of our lives. The sudden relief of tension may feel exhilarating, giving us a 'high' that can in turn become a goal, encouraging us to 'run' even harder.

Whether we numb our senses directly with drugs, alcohol, or intense overstimulation, or perpetuate cycles of heightening tension that end in exhaustion and collapse, either way of escaping pressure can be addicting. Our increasingly restless minds urge us on with memories of anticipation and pleasure, while forgetting the pain or numbness that was also part of the experience.

Is it possible for our minds to distinguish between real pleasure in experience and simple relief from tension? If we were truly relaxed and satisfied by our experiences, would we feel such a need to repeat the same experiences so often? If we have learned to interpret numbness as pleasure, what might our methods of increasing pleasure be doing to our minds and bodies? Underlying our activities there seems to be a discomfort, like a deep irritation we cannot completely relieve. We can satisfy ourselves temporarily by dulling or exhausting our senses, but we seem unable to relieve tension at its source.

When our ways of relieving tension are no longer satisfying or are becoming in turn new sources of stress, we grow more vulnerable to anxiety. The smallest disturbances in our routines can be very upsetting, and the slightest frustration can provoke us to emotional outbursts. Decisions are harder to make; we face sleepless nights more often, as we listen to our minds churning with inner dialogues. Exhausted and depleted, we cannot sustain confidence in ourselves or what we are doing, and suffer from the naggings of guilt and feelings of personal inadequacy. We find it difficult to get through the working day or to find comfort with families or friends.

In its most disturbing form, anxiety arises without warning. We may be going about our daily routine, even engaged in work we find enjoyable and creative, only to suddenly notice the same thoughts cycling over and over in our minds; we may be perspiring or nauseous. Time is passing; we may have a deadline to meet, yet we feel stuck and frozen, on the verge of real panic. The more energy we pour into what we are doing, and the more we think about what is happening, the more anxious and confused we become. If we cannot dispel these sensations, they can become overwhelming.

Once we have experienced extreme anxiety and know the panic that it can lead to, we may be deeply disturbed by the fear that it might return. All we associate with anxiety is suspect—the specific environment we were in when it struck, the type of work we were engaged in, even the people who happened to be around us. The need to somehow control this fear can lead us to fixate on certain behaviors that seem 'safe' or even to develop phobias we know are irrational, but cannot overcome. Being around other people may arouse nearly intolerable feelings of guilt or shame.

Because so many people suffer from anxiety today, we may give no thought to protecting ourselves until our anxiety surfaces in more extreme forms. However, if we understand how anxiety is rooted in tension, we can learn to avoid forms of behavior that encourage it. In strengthening our own internal resources, we can protect ourselves from all forms of stress.

Our methods of relaxation now emphasize releasing tension in ways that create more pressure or simply drain our energy and dull our senses and minds. It is possible that we could investigate the relationship of body and mind more fully, and find ways to dispel tension that would be more beneficial to our whole being. Then we could greatly increase our sensitivity to all forms of experience. Instead of 'exploding' the energy built up by tension, it is possible we could learn to tap and transform it.

We have far to go before we understand the interplay of the body, mind, and senses completely. Little is known about the relationships among bodily, mental, and emotional tensions. While there is much information about the physical aspect of our sensory organs and nervous systems, there has been little research into the inner operation of the senses and mind. Even the concepts we use to interpret our experience may be too fixed or limited to express the dynamic nature of the senses, body, and mind. By directly observing our own responses to tension and experimenting with new ways to defuse it, we can gain more pleasure from our experience as well as valuable insights into the intimate relationship of our own bodies and minds.

Our breath and heartbeat are natural monitors of tension: their rates tend to increase when we feel agitated and tense, and slow down as we relax. Because of this interconnection, we can use the rise and fall of the breath and the rhythm of our heartbeat to penetrate tension and anxiety. By simply focusing gently on breathing, we can slow the breath and allow it to find its own natural movement.

We can take a little quiet time to allow the natural rhythms and movements of our body and mind to relax the outer layers of tension. As our breathing softens and its rhythm smooths out, the mind becomes less crowded with thoughts and images, and the body begins to relax of its own accord. If we can sense the steady beating of the heart together with the flow of breath, we can feel a natural stability within our own body that will balance our tendency toward agitation.

When the body and mind are more relaxed, we might feel a softer, more subtle side of our senses. Although we usually use our senses as windows to the outside world, they may actually be two-way channels, capable of sensing inwardly as well as outwardly. We can try gently directing our senses inward. In releasing their fixation on external objects, we help them relax the grasping tendencies that keep them tight and tense. When they are more open and relaxed, they are more aware of whatever presents itself inside or outside of the body; the mind becomes less reactive and more quietly attentive. Then it is possible to simply see without looking *at* something, and to listen without listening *to* any particular sound. When sensations are not so tightly grasped, they arouse gentler feelings that encourage a smoother flow of mind and body energy.

Balancing in this neutral state, we can deal with tension directly. When we are quiet, we are more aware of the tightness in our bodies and minds, and we can use this awareness to tap the energy of tension. Bringing the attention lightly to sensations of tightness in the chest, we may find it possible to relieve pressure by imagining that each breath is expanding a space around the heart. The oppressive feeling can be opened up as though we were filling it full of air. With each outflow of breath, the tension can flow out into space. We can do this with other areas of tension as well, until our whole body feels more relaxed and open.

As the body releases accumulated tensions, feelings grow more direct and pleasurable. Our heartbeat slows, and both mental and physical agitation lighten; even our body temperature may subtly shift, regulating itself as the body becomes more balanced. With practice we can use the breath as a signal of the first vibrations of frustration or of any emotional disturbance. We can more easily find our balance before anxiety intensifies; we can lighten and expand any pressured feeling to protect both heart and mind from tension and stress.

After some practice, it is possible to relax further into the breath. With each exhalation, we can follow our breath outward, being particularly mindful of the point when the breath completely leaves the body, and allowing it to disperse into space. While we are focused on the space around us, the mind is alert and silent. Imagining ourselves protected from pressures by an egg-shaped capsule of silence that surrounds our body, we can expand this silence further and further into space with each exhalation.

When we remain quiet, mindful of breath in every moment, we can open a space between us and our thoughts. We might think of ourselves as observers of an interesting drama, able to see the colors and textures of our thoughts as they unfold, without feeling any obligation to respond. Relaxing our tendency to react to every thought and sensation helps to break the cycle of tensions. If we develop a more spacious, less pressured way of relating to our feelings and thoughts, we can restore our balance more quickly after any disturbance.

Seeing the relationship between tension and our reactive tendencies, we can understand how our habitual patterns of responding indiscriminately to stimulation perpetuate and intensify emotions, worries, and fears. Knowing that there is something we can do to relieve tension, we may be able to face our own emotions more directly, instead of reacting to them with further emotions. We might be able to watch how they manifest in our lives with a new interest and sense of balance, and free ourselves from the habit of self-blame that may be intensifying our problems.

Normally, we would have no way to unlock these deeply rooted patterns. But in taking care to quiet our senses, breath, and mind, we may find we have brief openings before we are totally caught up in predictable cycles. Quietly observing what is happening, we contact deeper responses that can cushion us from emotional excitement and help us to restore our sense of balance. Eventually, we can choose whether or not to respond.

Whenever we exercise choice by refraining from response or by responding in new ways, we gain strength and enlarge the space in which free choice is possible. Initially, our habitual responses may overpower our awareness, but our understanding of what is happening can encourage us to continue our observations and relieve feelings of helplessness and guilt. With patience, we can develop the ability to cut completely the force of even the strongest negative thoughts and emotions.

The key to natural protection from emotional stress and tension is mindfulness of the breath. Mindfulness is not forceful control, but an attentive awareness of what is occurring. When we remain quiet and observe the flow of the breath, the body and mind naturally release the energy stored in tension from its dense and solid forms. Liberated, this energy increases vitality and clarity, and strengthens our ability to defuse pressures. Instead of being caught up in a cycle of escalating pressure, we can develop an abiding peace and clarity that grow from within.

Relaxed and clear, our senses convey vivid impressions; our thoughts move slowly and cohesively, and our feelings have a rich and flowing texture. As relaxation deepens, we might even notice new vitality and new resonances within our bodies, as if we were responding to musical tones pulsing lightly within us. When we listen for this silent music, we touch our senses with greater awareness and join our mind and body in more harmonious interactions. Like perfect partners in a dance, mind and body, perfectly attuned, move freely and spontaneously with the rhythms of time in space.

As we understand ourselves more directly, we may find that our body and mind are capable of sustaining greater pleasure than we have ever experienced in our happiest moments. All of our capacities—perception, thought, feeling, and sensation—can be refined and developed in new ways that bring greater freedom and enjoyment in life. The energy now channeled into old patterns could be redirected in ways we have not yet discovered. With a more comprehensive knowledge, we can exercise mind and body to their full capacities and develop a positive, freer way of being that increases our appreciation of the countless dimensions of human life.

23

Conflict of Competition

*Measuring our lives against standards
set by others, we do not consider ourselves
intrinsically worthwhile, and our sense
of self-esteem is never secure.*

T he whole idea of competition belongs essentially
to the realm of contests, where we enter the arena
to win prizes and glory. The goal is not to produce
a fine product or skillfully perform a valuable service,
but to produce and perform better than someone else,
as determined by judges or well-established rules.
Athletes continually challenge world record-holders;
business people vie for record-breaking sales; intellec-
tuals and professionals aim for pacesetting breakthroughs. As goals are set ever higher, standards of
success rise, contributing to our sense of progress as
a society.

As the pace of the modern world quickens, the
tremendous pressure upon us is reflected, in part, by
the heightening of competition. Although competition has long been a part of human life, today it grows
fiercer; people feel more keenly the need to surpass

those around them in order to maintain their lifestyle and even their self-esteem.

Today, competitive attitudes are cultivated and rewarded in every area of endeavor. An aura of competition surrounds relationships among men and women in school, careers, and in the home, all the more so as traditional roles rapidly change. Few aspects of our lives are not affected by our desire to win in competition. We wish to be better than others not only in our jobs but also in our hobbies; we wish to have finer houses and cars, more attractive mates, and smarter children than our friends.

Competition affirms our sense of individual importance and enhances feelings of independence and self-reliance. Everyone wants to excel, to accomplish something spectacular. We aim for the most or the best of what life seems to offer. We strive to be the most attractive, the most intelligent, or the strongest. Our aspirations are stirred by visions of climbing the highest mountain, setting new records, and establishing new precedents; we enjoy developing our talents and testing ourselves against others. Life itself can become a challenging game in which we learn the rules of the roles we play and receive recognition for demonstrating our skills in those roles. When we become good at what we do, we gain a sense of accomplishment that can be truly exhilarating.

Competition begins in early childhood when we are compared to others in our physical growth, our looks, our skills, our attitudes, and our behavior. Such comparisons, based largely on circumstances beyond our control, seem to determine our worth, even to ourselves.

Once we begin competing, a momentum is established that carries us onward. As the 'best' are winnowed from the 'average' at each stage, the intensity of competition increases. If we do well enough in school, we move from the preliminaries to a more intense arena of apprenticeship or graduate study. If we qualify there, we pass on to the semi-finals of our career itself. But it seems there are no finals; one contest follows another as we progress in our career. Even when a clear winner does emerge, the stage has only been set for the next contest to begin.

Few can sustain competitive maneuvers all of their lives, and many are handicapped in their efforts to compete. Many people still bear the scars of self-doubts and feelings of inferiority originating in comparisons made during childhood and adolescence. A negative self-image developed in our early years can hamper us for the rest of our lives. Situations that challenge some can leave others cringing inside, unable to take advantage of opportunities for growth or to develop their talents and interests. Habits of self-deprecation and fear of failure can truly undermine our growth.

This kind of hurt is difficult to let go. If we cannot heal our feelings of inadequacy, we may spend much of our lives feeling useless and left out. How much needless suffering is endured in the name of competition? Have we no way to avoid wasting so much human potential?

Competition has side-effects even for those who do well under such pressure. In considering each new situation, we carefully weigh ourselves against the standards we must meet to succeed. If they seem too difficult, we may be deterred from following our natural inclination and talents. Succeeding at something tends to become more important than finding meaningful work.

Our lives unfold in a climate of tension: We must always do a little better to stay ahead; we must achieve a little more to protect our position. We may come to rely upon these pressures for sustaining our purpose and drive. But as the process gathers momentum and responsibilities accumulate, such pressures tend to create intense agitation and restrict creativity. We may feel compelled to cover up mistakes and excuse failures, spoiling the satisfaction of work well done.

As we become successful competitors, our actions may no longer satisfy us in themselves: Winning is the bottom line. We pressure ourselves to succeed so we can feel like the winner, whether we keep score by financial gains, status, or power and prestige. Attachment to winning also draws out our aggressive instincts and can cause us to lose touch with our sensitivity to others. We all know people whose drive to outstrip others leaves behind a trail of resentments, people for whom the rules of the game seem to justify any means to get ahead. Willing to live in a climate of hurt and distrust, they will risk anything in order to succeed in the present, confident that they can 'handle' what may arise in the future. As this sense of power becomes increasingly unbalanced, judgment suffers, and painful defeats are almost guaranteed.

Caught up in the momentum of competition, we may find it easier to act from expediency than from a long-range vision based on deeper values. Attainments that bring us speedy rewards or recognition have a strong appeal, for they relieve the immediate pressure upon us. We may feel we have no choice: Our profession or position demands that we demonstrate progress in specific ways in accord with fixed goals. But each new attainment may sustain us only briefly, while distracting us from more substantial accomplishments.

As one goal is reached, an initial rush of pleasure is followed by a period of uncertainty when our energy level may be somewhat depressed. Then we establish a new goal and motivate ourselves to meet the new challenge. As we restart ourselves again and again, our energy grows erratic, eventually wasting itself in the stopping and starting, and leaving us exhausted. We may reach a point where we lose our sense of direction or just cannot face another repetition of the cycle. Our vision may shorten so much that our goal is simply to get through the day.

As we grow older, those of us who have played the game well may feel secure in our position. But the greater our success, the more likely someone will find us an irresistible challenge. Security is likely to fade after we have reached and passed our prime. Aware that we are considered less desirable and useful with age, we experience any loss of attractiveness, skills, talents, or expertise with growing uneasiness, especially as we watch younger, more vigorous people prepare to take our place.

More vulnerable to old grudges, we may suffer the pain of being left behind while others take pleasure in our weakness. Yet our natural desire to preserve our self-esteem is strong, and to protect our position and reputation, we may become even more dedicated to playing the game. Taking our roles more seriously than ever, we may find our lives becoming more rigid and artificial. Even if the game becomes oppressive, we have little choice but to continue. Long after we tire of playing, the habit of trying to win and the fear of losing remain with us.

Measuring our progress in life against external standards, we do not consider ourselves intrinsically worthwhile, and our sense of self-esteem is never secure. Always on the defensive, grasping for what supports our position, we hesitate to trust ourselves or follow our own values. Without really wanting to, we may find ourselves 'going with the flow', unwilling to risk our position by standing up for what we believe in. We may be gaining our prestige, status, wealth, or power at the cost of our integrity.

When competition dominates our way of living, our whole sense of self-esteem can come to depend on meeting standards set by others. Often these measures have become so natural or seem so right to us, especially if we are successful, that it can be difficult to realize that we had no part in their creation. Some standards seem more objective than others, such as standards of accuracy or quality that reflect the reliability of our product or skill; here we receive feedback from our own results. But other standards are not necessarily inherent in the work itself.

Guidelines set by others can give us an external measure of how well we are doing, but cannot measure our sense of fulfillment, our enjoyment, or even necessarily how much we are learning or developing our skills. Once we have become dependent on measuring our success against such standards, we may lose touch with our own intrinsic worth. Even though we consider ourselves successful by society's standards, beneath our striving and aggressive veneer, we may feel increasingly uncertain.

Looking back over our lives in our later years, will we be satisfied with the legacy we are creating? Will others benefit from our reputation, our status, our prestige? How much good will come of our wealth? Perhaps we can leave an inheritance to our children and grandchildren, but in our hearts we know that financial or social attainments are ultimately a poor measure of our priceless energy and time.

Achievements such as athletic ability, wealth, prestige, power, and fame provide pleasure as ornaments to human life, and can be used in ways that benefit others. But when we come to depend upon anything that can be lost with time as the measure of our value as human beings, we create the conditions for regret later in our lives.

All that is really ours is in our heads and hearts. Our most precious and hard-won possession is our years of living, learning, and experiencing. No luxury can compare to the satisfaction that comes from a clear mind and a body vibrant with good feelings. When we develop a deep appreciation for the riches we bear within ourselves, we can draw upon an open storehouse of satisfaction in our later years. This is the only real support we can rely on as we pass from this life. If our life has been full and deeply satisfying, we can approach the end of our days with the sense of arriving at a well-earned rest. But if we have spent much of our time anxious and dissatisfied, dominated by roles, and out of touch with our own values, what emptiness might we feel as we approach our last days?

Yet most of us must live and work in the stressful realm of competition. How can we protect ourselves? We can begin by awakening a greater understanding of our own inner resources and by relaxing our dependency upon the judgments of others. We can learn to trust ourselves in new ways, so that whatever mistakes we may make will not catch us in the crossfire of excuses and blame that occur inevitably when we blindly follow models established by others. When we learn to trust ourselves, whatever we do will express a deep inner integrity that supports our sense of value and worth through the most difficult times, and paves the way to far greater accomplishment.

When we respect our own value, we become more aware of the value of others. We can view those we consider competitors more as fellow human beings who are challenging us to develop our talents fully and to perform at our best. In acknowledging their worth, we reaffirm confidence in our own worth also. Then it is possible to take our roles less seriously and play the game more lightly, helping ourselves and others to derive real enjoyment from what we do.

As our appreciation broadens to encompass all who have in some way contributed to our welfare, whether they be parents, teachers, friends, or even rivals, our sense of responsibility toward others grows deeper and stronger. Less directed to immediate gain, our vision naturally extends further into the future, enabling us to develop long-range goals. Sustained by vision, our energy flows more smoothly and is more directed. We do not become so excited about short-term gains, or so depressed about our failures or shortcomings. When we reach points that mark a certain level of achievement, we can simply take note of them and pass on, allowing the momentum of our energy to build with each accomplishment. Eventually the substantial results of our efforts will give us great satisfaction.

If we are disillusioned with the roles society offers us, and are unwilling or unable to play the competitive game, we can, instead, find roles that are uniquely our own and build within ourselves a new understanding of what it means to be a successful human being. Basing our lives on this knowledge, we can develop our inner resources to the fullest. Even if no one else supports us, even if we can see no material rewards in what we wish to do, we can develop our talents and abilities, and devote them to goals we consider worthwhile.

We might find that our most valuable contribution to society lies in following our own sense of what truly enriches human life. Whatever contributions we make to the welfare of others, whatever knowledge we can offer to uplift the quality of life will reflect back to us, enriching our own lives as well. Our time automatically becomes more valuable; we are worthwhile to ourselves, and we are useful to others. Based on a higher understanding of human value, our actions can heal the conflict inherent in competition.

We can clarify what we have learned to ourselves and pass on the benefits of our knowledge to others by acknowledging fully the pain and confusion that have led us to reconsider our old views. Where did we start? What steps did we take, within our hearts and minds, to change the course of our lives? What knowledge sustains and guides us? Our inner success will inspire others who feel caught up in frustration and pain, helping them find within themselves the knowledge they need to guide their own lives.

When our vision transcends self-interest, and we offer our time and energy to benefit others, we set ourselves free from the frustration and anxiety inherent in identifying ourselves personally with a goal. We are no longer compelled to vacillate between self-congratulation and feelings of inadequacy. Shifting from a personally oriented viewpoint to a more encompassing vision imparts unshakable strength and confidence.

When we feel inwardly free and balanced, inspired by a higher knowledge and vision, we can cooperate with others to achieve results far beyond what one individual could hope to accomplish. Cooperative actions performed for the benefit of all open up possibilities for unceasing satisfaction, setting in motion a willingness to share that could generate invaluable results far into the future.

24

Seeing Through Pain

*As we become more neutral observers of our pain,
we may be able to sense its cloud-like character.*

With all life, we share a vulnerability to pain. In fact, we are so accustomed to pain that it may go unnoticed unless our discomfort is prolonged or is unusually intense. From our birth to our death, it is unusual for a single day to pass without feeling some sort of pain. There are the common pains of minor burns, of headache, toothache, and indigestion; the more severe pains of arthritis, ulcers, and other chronic conditions; the pain of innumerable diseases and disabilities; the pain of worrying about vaguely disquieting sensations that mysteriously come and go.

Even if we are spared much physical pain, we cannot escape from the emotional suffering of anger, rejection, and jealousy in relationships; worry and fear about the welfare of our parents or children; anxiety about our jobs; uncertainty about the future. The list of emotional pains we commonly feel can go on and on. Pain is nearly a constant companion in our lives.

Although we can dismiss minor pains, stronger or more persistent pains are more difficult to tolerate.

The more vulnerable we are to pain, the more we feel the need for protection, but our attempts to protect ourselves are grounded in avoidance and are seldom satisfactory; they tend to dull our sensitivity and interfere with our enjoyment of life. While we can sometimes lessen pain's impact by numbing the senses, distracting ourselves, or trying to ignore it, we have no way to control its course and duration. We have no way to deal with pain directly. This is particularly true of emotional distress, which is even harder to treat than physical discomfort.

It seems important to see if we can respond to pain more constructively. Just as we can show a child how to rid himself of fear of the dark by calming him and encouraging him to see there is no real basis for fear, we can encourage ourselves to look more closely at the internal dynamic of pain, lightening our burden and freeing ourselves from fear.

When we look at pain closely, we can see that the basis for the fear of pain is a sense of separation between ourselves and everything else in our world. The stronger our sense of separation, the more we try to balance and control opposing forces in an effort to get what we want. The more we anticipate happiness, and the more energy we invest in controlling situations to accord with our desires, the more pain we experience when our expectations are disappointed, or when we find ourselves caught up in situations we are unable to control.

Our minds are continually balancing an intricate network of pressures that potentially threaten our sense of control and lead to pain: our drive to achieve versus our fear of failure; our ideals versus our capabilities; social obligations versus family duties; family duties versus work responsibilities; our desires versus the need for restraint. Our happiness may come to depend upon balancing these internal pressures while doing whatever we can to control conditions and events.

The need to control is reinforced by our conditioning. Social conventions set standards of behavior and politeness that demand restraint; our concern about our self-image forces us to adopt a certain style of expression. We engage in elaborate games that support our particular view of ourselves as well as the general appearance of independence and self-control. But in fact our sense of security depends upon mastering interlocking sets of manipulative patterns. We manipulate others, while others manipulate us, as we all vie for position, assert our will, resist attempts at domination, or search for ways to accommodate conflicting interests. Fear can arise whenever this balance is threatened, enmeshing us in anxiety or even arousing feelings of panic.

While our minds are preoccupied with maintaining balance, our senses are alert and naturally attracted to stimulation. Perceiving and responding, our senses lead our energy outward toward any situation, engaging our minds in perceptions before we are aware of what is happening. Going along with this current has become habitual; we engage and respond to stimulations automatically. By the time our minds interpret a sensation as pain, we are already involved, reacting to stimulation. Once our minds and senses are clinging to pain, we have lost the opportunity to protect ourselves. Unable to perceive this process at work, we know only that we are 'in pain'.

Thus, as familiar as we are with pain, it often catches us unawares. By labeling the sensation as pain and then responding, we also engage and marry it. Our attempts to reject it, to push it away, only distribute pain throughout the body and back to the senses. Where can these impulses go? Our senses have no way to release them; all they can do is recycle pain back to the mind, which grows increasingly agitated. More thoughts arise, stimulating the cycle again and intensifying the sensation of pain. We are then suffused with pain; we identify ourselves with it, become one with it. We have no choice but to cling to pain, as though we had grasped a high-voltage wire.

Tenacious and sometimes frightening in its intensity, pain appears, like a virus, to invade our bodies and minds from the outside. Sensing that we are an innocent bystander and a victim, we look for something or someone to blame, but this only agitates us more, intensifying pain and prolonging its duration. Certain thoughts or activities such as listening to music or reading can sometimes distract us from pain, but it tends to return when we stop. Trying to restrain our feelings only increases internal pressures and makes the pain worse.

When pain arises seemingly from nowhere, and there is nothing external we can blame, our logic forces us to turn blame on ourselves. Unable to relieve this kind of pressure, we may convince ourselves that there is no hope for relief and trap ourselves in a downward spiral of guilt and self-incrimination.

No matter how hard we try to avoid painful situations, powerful forces beyond our control affect us. There seems to be no way to avoid experiencing pain in our lives. We cannot dominate our environment, nor have we any power over time, which leads us inevitably into aging and death. No matter how strong or influential we are, we encounter situations we cannot control. We are caught in an impossible situation: We have no real control, yet our sense of well-being depends upon our ability to control. The more vigorously we insist upon control, the more vulnerable we are to frustration and pain. The fact that we have a human body subject to feelings, thoughts, memories, and emotions seems to condemn us to pain.

Where is there a safe refuge from pain? Even if our present circumstances are comfortable, in a flash a painful memory or the anticipation of an unpleasant situation can bring us emotional suffering. Knowing this serves to increase our fear of pain. Fear in itself is painful; it can become oppressive, numbing our senses and closing our hearts to others.

Though it seems we have no protection against the power of pain and fear, we can choose to look at pain differently and actually use fearful times or hurtful memories to break pain's hold. When we see that our efforts to push pain away do not bring us relief, why not reverse our responses and look directly at the pain itself? Relaxing into the sensations, letting them be, we can lighten their pressure and calm our minds. Once we cease thinking or talking about the pain, we remove the basis for identifying ourselves with it. We are no longer running away, but resting within the experience, observing what is happening.

When we are in pain, our body is likely to be tense and constricted, our breathing tight and forced. Relaxing this tension by straightening the back, expanding the chest, and loosening the stomach muscles, we can gain some immediate relief from pressure.

By watching the flow of the breath and allowing breathing to become smooth and regular, it is possible to open a space between ourselves and the pain. Within this space, we can flow into and then out of the pain we are experiencing. With each outward movement of breath we can sink into the feelings, lightly touching the pain we are feeling. With each intake, we can expand the space that cushions us from the pain's intensity. By doing this, we can view pain as separate from us, as an object that can be examined more dispassionately. From this perspective we can observe its ebb and flow.

If we maintain concentration on the breath, we might sense an inner movement subtly attracting our awareness back into the pain. We might feel our mind and senses reaching out to the sensation, but is it really necessary to respond? As an experiment, we can shift back and forth, alternating between paying attention to the breath and allowing thoughts to lightly touch the pain. Understanding the interactions of thought and pain may lessen the tension of fear and cast new light on the nature of our experience.

Seeing how easily the mind and senses engage pain, we can remain concentrated on the rhythm of breathing, while still being aware of the pain in a more gentle, open way. As we cease to respond to the impulses we interpret as pain, the sensation of pain may moderate and pass, allowing a more open, lighter state of mind to emerge.

With practice, it is possible to find a point of balance within this 'neutral seeing', resting within its openness, seeking neither to draw pain to us nor push it away. Neutral seeing allows light to penetrate the darkness created by internal pressures. It removes the sharpness of pain and stabilizes mental clarity, opening the way to further analysis. Eventually, it might be possible to see the whole dynamic of pain very clearly and to appreciate how we trick ourselves into engaging it by not recognizing the subtle interactions between our mind and senses.

As we become more neutral observers of our pain, we may be able to sense its cloud-like character. Clouds of confusion and pain envelop us, but are not actually connected to our being. We can move above them or below them, observing their shapes as if they were interesting forms in a clear sky. Only when we are in their midst do we become lost in their darkness. Using our intelligence to separate ourselves from pain, we can lighten our attachment to negative emotions and protect ourselves from suffering.

Watching the dynamic of pain, we can see that on a very basic level, our mind and senses respond to stimulations indiscriminately, naturally seeking out sensations; it is only later, when we identify and label the sensations as pleasure or pain that we consciously accept or avoid the experience. In a sense, any stimulation is like bait on a hook; by the time we feel the pangs of the hook, it is firmly implanted. The only effective way to deal with the situation is to see how the hook is constructed, and learn how to detach ourselves from it gently and compassionately. The more often we practice detaching ourselves from pain, the more skilled we become. Knowing that it is possible to deal directly with pain, we can free ourselves from the anxiety that intensifies and perpetuates it.

When we see how subtly we deceive ourselves into engaging and sustaining what we wish most to avoid, we can look more closely at other aspects of our experience. Perhaps similar patterns of internal manipulation are distorting our perception, making our responses to situations more negative than they have to be. Knowing that we do not have to identify so strongly with negative feelings—struggling against them or engaging in emotional dramas—we can examine all of our experience in a more objective light.

In time, we may begin to notice how negative emotions are linked together, as though they were the best of friends. When fear finds a way into our hearts, worry, anxiety, loneliness, and feelings of failure will soon show up as well, locking us into cycles of pressure and recrimination. Once our mind has become heavy and dark, the whole world begins to look black, and problems seem more solid and impenetrable. But we do have a choice: In responding to emotional urgings, we have invited this darkness into our minds; in detaching ourselves from negative emotions, we can lighten this darkness and free ourselves of an unwanted burden. When we acknowledge that we are responsible for our own pain, we have the key to unlock ineffective patterns of avoidance. With practice, we can replace restraint and fear of pain with compassion and understanding.

While we cannot predict what negative moods and attitudes will arise from one moment to the next, we can gain greater understanding of their origins and momentum, and learn to shorten their duration. Strengthening our awareness little by little, we can learn to let go of heavy, negative emotions and invite lighter, more positive feelings into our hearts. When we see that it is possible to be free of the fear of pain, we can take charge of our lives more effectively and find within all aspects of experience a pathway to self-knowledge.

SECTION EIGHT

Wealth
of
Knowledge

CHAPTER 25: IMAGES OF DESIRE

CHAPTER 26: TREASURY OF EXPERIENCE

CHAPTER 27: GLOBAL KNOWLEDGE

Images of Desire

We can wake up at any time,
simply by acknowledging what we know.

Centuries of poetry and song testify to the long-ing to love and be loved, to feel alive and free, to be at peace, to understand the meaning of life. Though these desires seem deeply a part of human beings, we do not often obtain what we wish for.

Each of us has personal images and ideas related to the desire for happiness. Like the details of a painting, such images combine to make up our whole picture of what we want. Some are images of how we would like to be, how we would like to look and act. Some are of our ideal mate. We have dreams of houses we want to live in, children we would like to have, businesses we wished we owned, bank accounts we think we need.

Our mind, like a masterful artist, assembles these images in different patterns and combinations, pre-senting us with finished pictures. When one of these images of perfection arises before the mind, we can feel our heart pulled toward it: "Yes, that is what I want. That would make me happy." So we follow the image, searching the world around us for something corresponding to our mental picture.

It is as though we desired a great and wonderful treasure. We are given old maps that seem to show the way—the path is laid out and the location of the treasure is pinpointed. So we start on our journey, comparing the landscape to the map, trying to orient ourselves. For a while we may feel we are on the right track, but eventually we find ourselves in the midst of a scene that was not on the map.

The images of happiness that guide us seem to build up over time, beginning in our childhood. Some we receive from our parents as we discover what makes them happy and what they want us to be. Television programs, songs, and books give us pictures of love and romance or exciting adventures. Smiling faces look out at us from posters, advertisements, and television, showing us how to be happy. We recognize the feeling: "Yes, that is how I want to look—this is what I must do to be loved. This object would bring me joy. That is the kind of person I want to meet."

As image upon image pour into our mind, they connect in elaborate patterns. Images of our early fantasies and ideals instilled in us by parents are interwoven with ideas learned from books or other sources. Sights, scents, sounds, sensations, and tastes associated with a pleasant memory can each evoke a feeling of delight. Combined with details of other memories or images, they can form composites that delight and bewitch us, luring us on.

This collection of images, each loaded with feeling, forms our idea of happiness. We imagine not in the abstract but in the concrete. Fame, love, success—as soon as the thought arises, a whole series of images may flash through our minds like episodes of a story.

Our minds seem to respond with great zest and energy to images. We can recall moments of pleasure and pain, and relive the joy or hurt associated with the memory. It is similar to the way we react to a movie. Although we know that the images are not real, we become absorbed in the drama and respond as though we were actually living the experiences. We find ourselves holding our breath in suspenseful moments or wiping tears from our eyes at a happy ending. Actors know this magical quality of the mind and use their own memories to evoke the feelings they want to portray.

Whenever a desirable image arises in our minds, we feel the longing connected with it, and our mind reaches out, expecting satisfaction. The image fascinates us and stirs us at the same time, increasing our longing. But the image is only an image; in itself it cannot satisfy us, only tempt us or whet our appetite. So we search our surroundings for something that will match the image.

The quest evoked by an image often has a thrilling quality as we anticipate our treasure just around the next corner. If we do not find it, we may settle for something close, though always holding back a part of our appreciation. Sometimes we think we have found it, and our energy surges toward the desired goal, object, or person. In time, however, our new love or possession and our image begin to slip apart as we notice qualities that do not fit with what we expected.

B y the time we are in our thirties, most of us have spent considerable effort trying to match situations and people to our desired images. But the match is never perfect or enduring, and the longing tends to persist. Somehow our minds are convinced our ideal exists—if we just look a little harder or longer, we shall find it.

Following dreams year after year, how many of us have found what we want? Some of us may have come very close, amazingly close: "If only I'd had a little more time, more money, or more persistence, it would have worked. This time it did not work out, but next time it will."

Because we have felt attracted to our images for so long, we easily mistake the desire they stimulate for spontaneous appreciation or love. But love and appreciation touch the living world with a gentle open hand, while desire reaches out and grasps objects forcibly, destroying the living presence.

Though we have invested so much time and energy in desire, do we ever question whether our images are leading us to the happiness we seek? If we look through our memories, even back into our childhood, can we find a time when we got exactly what we imagined—something that made us feel exactly the way we had expected, and lasted as long as we thought it would? Did our deepest moments of happiness come by chasing after an image or were they spontaneous or unexpected?

Our images are composites, created from many sources over time. What real object, person, or situation could match them completely? As we look at what is before us, we compare it with what we want to find: "This is not what I wanted, that is not appealing"—so we say, without letting what is present speak for itself. If our first impression seems to match our image, we grasp for it reflexively, ignoring the qualities that do not fit in with our expectation.

The process of judging based on our images drains the vitality and beauty from experience. Fascinated by the image of what we want and excited by the prospect of finding it, our mind does not have the open, receptive quality that would allow us to see what presents itself. Just as an agitated pool of water loses its reflective property, the mind stirred up by images loses its clarity and distorts what appears before it.

We have all had moments of deep quiet when we looked around with a fresh gaze, and the world seemed to come alive with color and vibrancy. Touching this precious aspect of experience filled our being with deep contentment and appreciation, renewing our body and mind. When we choose instead to filter our experience through the static images we have created, we cut ourselves off from the present moment, the source of true appreciation.

Fixated on our images, we come up empty-handed again and again. What we seek cannot be found, and what is present is overlooked. It is as though we wanted to satisfy our hunger with paintings of food. When the hunger continues unabated, we search our pantry for something that matches our paintings. But the more attracted we are to the picture, the less appealing the real food seems to be—none of it is quite right.

Comparing experience to our images, we are left unfulfilled. No matter how fine our image, the comparing degrades the real presence before us into a flat sensation. Unnourished, unsupported by our experience, we feel empty inside. Hungry for more, but not knowing how to get it, we grow agitated; when this hunger persists, we may feel deeply frustrated.

Agitation feeds on itself, evoking image after image that stimulates our hunger even more. This dramatic, colorful mental activity can become the whole of our inner life. Excited by our own creation, thrilled by our own emotions, we try to fill our emptiness with more and more stimulation.

Fascinated by the vibrations of desire, we lose our sensitivity to more subtle, lighter sensations. We come to require more and more intense stimulation to feel anything at all. Fueled by desires, our senses operate at so fast a rate that our perception distorts and blurs. It is as though we were traveling in a light plane powered with a jet engine, flying at many times its normal speed. The body shudders, and the scenery flies by so quickly that the instruments cannot register our position.

In this state of continual overdrive, the wanting mind moves so rapidly and erratically that it cannot make contact with anything substantial. Preoccupied by our own needs, we tend to see the world around us as nothing more than means to satisfy our hunger. Other human beings are used and discarded in the name of happiness; the wonders of nature become mere scenery in which we act out our fantasies. Without knowing what we are doing, we accustom both body and mind to ever increasing doses of excitement, tension, and stimulation in the effort to fill our emptiness. We become the willing victims of our own desires, ready to run our lives according to their dictates and requirements.

To obtain what we want from the world we must also measure up to other peoples' fantasies. Aware that our appearance and behavior are continually being judged and evaluated, we cultivate certain qualities, attitudes, and ways of dressing and talking to put forth an acceptable image. Our fear of rejection makes us vulnerable to manipulation. We buy all sorts of goods to improve our image; we seek advice on how to modify our behavior and even our thinking, feelings, and perceptions in order to present a desirable image.

Like a hungry guest at a banquet, we wish to fill our plate again and again, but are stopped by the disapproving glances from others. Our fear of rejection holds our own desires in check. We find ourselves torn between our wishes, which are stimulated by one set of images, and our fears, which are stimulated by another set. Although we try to control our responses, it seems we cannot choose not to respond, either to our desire or our fear. The images in our minds evoke our emotions automatically.

Tremendous tension can build up in our body and mind as we vacillate between one set of images and another. This tension further compels us to act—we must decide, we must do something. If our pent-up energy bursts out toward our image of desire, the relief we feel can convince us that we have gained contact with our genuine needs.

Although we follow our fabricated pictures faithfully, they betray us again and again. They promise us satisfaction, but they bring us frustration and pain. They cut off any experience too dynamic to be enclosed within them. Like the frames of a film, our images of desire repeat frozen scenes from old dramas; run one after another, they form a motion picture that never ends.

In the motion picture of our lives, the past is no more than a series of images, few of which evoke the pleasure of the images that arouse our desires in the present. What seems so important to us today may likewise mean little tomorrow; perhaps it will even be forgotten. Our present pleasures will soon be dream-like images we can hardly recall. Yet today's desires lead us from one day to the next, from one year to another, and from decade to decade. With each passing day, we create the conditions for the empty spaces we will find when we look back upon our lives in the future.

Of all the hours we spend in a day, we may remember only a few events, and even fewer of the thousands of thoughts that pass through our minds. Looking back over the past ten years, how much stands out as memorable? Whole weeks, perhaps months, may have vanished completely. How well can we recall the flavor of the experience we had yesterday, last month, or last year?

As we pull the dream-images of our hopes and wishes to us, we project ourselves into the future.

Eager to satisfy our desires more quickly, we leap over the present moment. Preoccupied with images and the chains of thought they produce, we lose track of time. But our bodies do not forget time; attuned to the living moment, they respond in harmony to its passing. Lines appear on our faces, deepen into creases, then into wrinkles and folds. Our skin loses its smoothness and luster, becoming spotty and loose; our eyes grow dim, and our ears lose their sensitivity to sound. It becomes harder to do things we once did with ease; our bones become more brittle; our joints stiffen and ache, restricting movement and creating a sense of frustration. Food loses its flavor; gums grow softer; teeth loosen. Our energy rises more slowly as sleep becomes less satisfying and dreams more disturbing.

Even in the midst of our chain of dreams, we sense we are moving closer to the time when the dream itself will end. Eventually this knowledge becomes oppressive, and we increasingly dislike reminders of our age. At some point we awaken to find that we are no longer the youthful person of our dream. Seeing reality more clearly, will we prefer death to living without the dream? When we can no longer ignore time, will our dream have been worth the dreaming? Will the emptiness and longing be too great to face?

We can wake up at any time, simply by acknowledging what we know: Time is passing, and time is our life. Awakening now, while we still have many productive years ahead of us, we can learn to truly enjoy life. Living in the clear light of reality, we can be wholly attuned to time, our life energy sustained by its dynamic momentum. Liberated from the compulsion of wanting and judging, our minds can be fresh and alive, open to experience. Clearer vision allows us to establish priorities more wisely and live in a way that will protect us from regret in our old age. Knowing what has real value, following our knowledge rather than our images, we can concentrate on bringing our most cherished wishes into being.

26

Treasury of Experience

*By observing our own experience, we can begin
this very instant to invite knowledge into our lives.*

O nce knowledge begins to bring deeper meaning
and beauty into our lives, the benefits of knowledge become apparent. At the beginning of our journey, however, we may sense the value of knowledge,
but still be unable to appreciate its full taste and
worth. Without realizing what we are missing, we may
settle for much less than we are capable of, especially when our old approach seems to be bringing happiness and a sense of value into our lives.

Our attitudes toward life can become such a part
of us that we cannot easily question whether they are
truly benefiting us, or whether they might be limiting
our freedom and satisfaction. Comfortable with our
old ways, we tend to shy away from investigating new
possibilities. Perhaps we are convinced that we are
getting the most we can expect from life. But it is
always possible to have second thoughts. An unexpected event, even a single question, can widen our

perspective and bring greater meaning and value to our lives.

In allowing ourselves the freedom to question and observe our experience, we may discover new approaches that will enrich our lives and prepare us for the inevitable changes that occur during life. Each questioning moment can lighten the hold of habitual ways of thinking and acting, opening up a little room for something new to happen.

Many different lifestyles offer ways to find meaning and value in life. We may gain our greatest pleasures from the excitement of new experiences; or from the pleasure of analyzing and understanding experience; or from moments of special beauty and insight. Goals and dreams can bring meaning into our everyday lives; or it may be memories that support our feelings of a life well lived. If we can investigate all these sources of meaning, we may find even richer meaning and value than we had dreamed possible. Perhaps we are settling for a few drops of nectar when we could have a whole cup.

Our lives and interests may have developed in such a way that we find our greatest pleasure in keeping active and busy. We may enjoy the excitement of new ideas and experiences, or perhaps we enjoy knowing that we are always doing something useful with our time. Our lives are full: We read books, develop hobbies, attend cultural events or perhaps do volunteer work; or we may just enjoy getting to know different people. If we can afford to, we may travel to different countries and explore the customs of different cultures. Even making plans can give us a sense of satisfaction as we anticipate the new activities of each day.

Although such a life may seem rich and rewarding, our movement from one thing to another can easily develop a restless quality. We may find it difficult to be alone or to have no specific plans for the day. We can actually feel guilty if we 'waste' any of our time, or if we are not filling our lives completely with worthwhile projects or activities. Or boredom may nag at us to find something more meaningful to do. In order to fend it off, we may even review the events of the day over and over in our minds, searching our memory for things we may have forgotten, or dredging up worries we had let go hours before.

When we feel driven to look for things to do, we might stop and ask ourselves why this is happening. If we need to keep searching out ways to fill our time, perhaps what we are doing is not fully satisfying. The pleasure our activities bring lasts only a short time; yet we seem to be depending upon this temporary satisfaction to keep us happy. When we feel moved to find something else to do, we might look more closely at the restless longing we feel. What is it we really want?

Instead of focusing our energy on the events and objects around us, we can take an entirely new approach to our daily lives. In the midst of each activity, we can add a new element: We can gently pay attention to how our senses are responding to every action and movement. We can open our ears to sound, and our eyes to the brilliant colors around us. We can sense the feel of everything we touch and even notice how our thoughts respond to different people. We may become aware of new shadings and nuances of experience, feelings and sensations that subtly rise and fall.

These inner movements are a direct response of our being to whatever is happening around us. Our ability to know, savor, and remember every detail of our experience is a unique human privilege. Observing our experience can become a field of interest that will never grow dull. Following the feeling tones that flow through the body, we contact a richer level of our own mind that can be a source of continual nourishment. As we touch our own feelings more directly, we can begin a journey in self-understanding that may prove more permanently satisfying than any activity we can now imagine.

Some of us may find meaning and value within an inner world; we travel from place to place within the mind instead of in the world around us. Each collection of thoughts and feelings, memories and fantasies is like a different neighborhood we can visit. Perhaps we have dreams of what we wish to make of our lives; we hold them before our minds, enjoying the feelings they bring us. Certain memories and special thoughts and feelings keep us company. When these feelings make us feel sensitive and alive, we know our lives are worthwhile.

Since our rich inner world gives us such pleasure, there seems no need to seek satisfaction outside it. To enjoy more of this pleasure, we may spend more of our energy on our inner world, while the outer world grows paler and duller. Our own realm of feeling and imagery is so deeply personal it may be difficult to communicate well with others. As we find ourselves becoming more isolated, we can even become accustomed to a kind of loneliness.

Perhaps before we become completely committed to our own images and dreams, we could question them more closely. What exactly do they offer us that we find so satisfying? The yearning we feel deep in our hearts arises when we imagine what we could become or what we could accomplish. But it is infused with a quality of sadness, almost of mourning. This bittersweet yearning makes us feel alive and caring, sensitive and idealistic. It seems like the 'juice' of life, a source of nourishment.

But why is there so much sadness connected to our dream? Why does the dream haunt us, making us feel somehow dissatisfied? Perhaps we are not hearing the full message of our hearts. Our goals arise before us as dreams, asking us to bring them into being. When we do not do this, our hearts feel a deep loss and disappointment. The higher and more impossible our dream, the more intense the sensation of yearning and sadness when we do not act to bring it into being. Yet we are so drawn to this sad yearning that the more intense it becomes, the harder it is for us to realize we are not actually hearing what our hearts are telling us. It is as though we were trying to satisfy our heart's hunger by relishing its pain.

If we continue to feed on our own yearning and sadness, we can never find fulfillment in our lives. When this yearning quality arises, we need to recognize the message of our heart: We are starving. We must act to accomplish our dream. Perhaps we feel we do not know how to bring our dream into reality. But we might ask our heart's advice. For so long our heart has been fed only dreams; its deepest desire may be to wake up. Awake, we can find a way to realize our highest aspirations.

Analyzing the world around us can provide another source of personal satisfaction. Our analysis, based on wide-ranging information and acute insight, can become very sharp and accurate: We may see clearly the complexities of the world situation, and be aware of the futility of proposed solutions to major problems. The more we see how human confusion perpetuates itself, the more critical we may feel.

The satisfaction we gain from being 'right' in our observations of the world may actually contribute to a sense of personal discouragement. Things look bad, even hopeless. Any effort we could make to change the world appears to be a waste of time that would only increase frustration. We see how blind people are to their own good, how selfish they are, and how reluctant to change. We may spread our discouragement to others by pointing out the futility of their plans and dreams. It is painful to be associated with the world we observe, so we hold ourselves aloof, even assuming indifference to wealth and recognition.

If we sense the possibility for some deeper happiness, we may dismiss it as just illusory. There may have been a time when we wished for more—perhaps we even tried actively to bring a vision of change into being—but that time is gone; our vision now seems a foolish dream, our early ideals out of touch with the reality of life. Why encourage others to accomplish what we attempted to do and failed? Why try to find a joy in living that we believe we cannot have? Such efforts seem completely unrealistic—a form of self-deception that we have seen through at the cost of much pain and do not wish to engage again.

When we feel that life is hard, we harden our hearts in response. We no longer feel we can give life another chance to disappoint us. It may seem that we have never been appreciated, that no one has ever really understood or deeply loved us. We may have difficulty appreciating others in turn or in communicating our feelings, for we cannot open our hearts without evoking the ache of old wounds that were never completely healed. In the process of trying to protect ourselves from disappointment, we have sealed ourselves off from the warmth and inherent wisdom of our own hearts. We may cling to our 'philosophy of life' with a kind of silent desperation. We are not really happy with it, but neither can we give it up.

Can we open our heart and make ourselves vulnerable once again? Can we give life, and ourselves, another chance? How others have regarded us in the past is not important; we deserve love, understanding, and appreciation, and we can give these to ourselves. Appreciation for our own capacity for feeling can help us to see beyond confusion and pain to true beauty and satisfaction. The language of the heart is compelling and has meaning for all human beings. It penetrates beneath the waves of self-deception, emotionality, and sentimentality to real depth of feeling. It depends not on words and concepts, but on genuine sensitivity to universal human needs and values.

266 Knowledge of Freedom

We might reopen our investigation of life and bring a new dimension to our intelligence, using it to note within ourselves the negative thoughts that prevent us from appreciating ourselves more fully. We are capable of responding to compassion and love as well as to pain; we can allow ourselves to experience both and find a new sense of self-appreciation in opening up the feelings in our hearts.

When we connect our senses and hearts with our heads, our vision becomes broader and more balanced: Our observation of life is not only sharp and clear, but vital and responsive. In allowing ourselves the opportunity to expand our knowledge in this way, we can transform our whole way of viewing ourselves and our world. Once our hearts begin to open, we can bring forth a generosity of spirit that is deeply satisfying in itself and grows as we share what we know with others.

We may find our satisfaction and purpose in life by aiming at a goal that seems worthwhile no matter what price we have to pay. Our dedication may take the form of high ideals, a great desire to be of service to the world, or even a desire to achieve status and wealth. Whatever our particular goal, we accept the sacrifices we must make to gain our ends. We may even feel that suffering expresses our caring, or that if the goal is too easy to reach, it is simply not worthwhile. We may actually value our goal even more because we have to make sacrifices to attain it.

Our aspiration can move us to wonderful accomplishments and bring our lives a strong sense of direction and purpose. But such single-mindedness may also reflect a narrowing of vision. Is it really necessary to endure so much? We seem to be training ourselves to be experts in suffering, 'conditioning' our bodies and minds to increasing levels of stress. Are we ready to risk bankrupting our lives for our goal?

But perhaps we are working for an ideal, sacrificing our personal comfort and welfare in the interests of others. We see those ahead of us as inspiring examples; we do not feel that we are acting selfishly. But why are we experiencing so much tension and stress? What is really more important to us, our feelings of accomplishment or the accomplishment itself? Are our ideals as high-minded as we thought? Do we have a need for recognition or a wish to be someone 'special' that is hiding behind a high purpose? Do we see others on the same path as supporting our own direction or as competition to be overcome?

When we pursue a goal for personal gain, competition and its pressure are inevitable. If we view those ahead of us as competition, we might reconsider how we feel about our goals. Perhaps if we begin to look carefully at our motivations, we might see our goals a little differently and could find more effective ways to attain them. We might be able to broaden our aim in ways that would orient us less toward competition and more toward cooperation.

Our stressful feelings may be showing us the direction to look: We could trace our feelings to their source and learn to transform their energy into meaningful accomplishment. With more knowledge of our mind and body, we could loosen suffering's hold on us. As we put less energy into tension and free up more energy for accomplishment, our sense of satisfaction will become richer and more enduring.

Feeling deeply satisfied with ourselves and our work is the most enduring accomplishment of all and the source of all other accomplishments. Whatever our endeavor, when we are fully honest about our goals and our expectations, our inner integrity will protect us from frustration and discouragement, and provide an unending source of creative energy. Whether we succeed or fail, we will be satisfied that we have done our best. Extending our vision beyond a self-centered purpose, we are capable of realizing the highest human aspirations. Such attainment is truly 'special', an inspiration to every human being who longs to be free of suffering and pain.

Meaning and value may appear to some of us to lie in moments of beauty, love, or openness that have given us glimpses of a finer way of being. In these precious moments, we felt intensely alive, sensed new possibilities, or had a new understanding. We realized then that there must be a way to experience deeper satisfaction in life.

Our efforts to recover this vibrant, open quality of appreciation seem wholehearted and genuine. Our goal is surely worthwhile, but we are still dissatisfied, for we are unable to sustain these moments. Without being aware of what is happening, we may be placing all our value on a few uplifting moments while impoverishing the rest of our life. We can easily become fascinated with our memories of these special times and spend much effort trying to recapture

unusual insights or feelings. Wishing so much to feel
or know some extraordinary state of mind, we become
like a hungry beggar holding tightly to a thimbleful
of nectar.

Why must we hold our tiny container so tightly?
It is not the thimble we want, but the nectar, which
we sense may be slipping from our grasp. In thinking
about beautiful experiences, interpreting them, talking
about them, and embellishing them with associations,
we are losing the flavor of the experience itself and
creating the need to revitalize it. What was ineffable
becomes concrete; the concepts we use are too frozen
to express vital meaning, and our memories are too
weak to restore the potency of the original experience.
When our need to recover a past experience is strong
and obsessive, the demand we make upon experience
narrows our attention to ourselves and our expectations. We measure our present experience against the
yardstick of memory, without letting the moment
reveal itself as it is.

Missing the richness of experience, we grow
hungrier and more anxious, and cling even more
tightly to our tiny measure of beauty and openness.
But what we need is a larger receptacle, one that allows
us to receive more juice from every experience, not
just those we fixate on as 'special'. Our own grasping
is tightening our minds and bodies, shrinking our
capacity to receive. If we can observe the way we are
cutting ourselves off from our own experience by
grasping, we can relax our desire to possess what
cannot be possessed. Opening widely to what is
happening here and now, we can expand our 'container', our capacity for appreciation, and respond to

every living moment as an unparalleled opportunity to receive the beauty and joy inherent in the unfolding of life itself.

E specially as we approach the end of our lives, memories of the past can be an abundant treasury of meaning and value. Looking back on happy moments, recalling the joy we felt with loved ones or the satisfaction of accomplishments, we can remind ourselves that we have lived a rich life. Memories seem to form the core of our lives; we may return to them again and again, for they seem more real and vital than our present experiences.

Although these images can bring us feelings of satisfaction, enjoying them is like licking the edge of a sharp knife spread with honey. Each time we recall our past happiness, we are reminded that the happiness has passed. We know those days are gone and will not come again. We may not wish to live in a world of memories, but can the present compare to the past when we were younger and had more vitality?

If we find ourselves wrapped up in memories of the past, we might check to be sure we are gaining more than feelings of sadness. Even if we receive great joy from our memories, they may be tricking us in a subtle way. It is easy to 'disappear' right into the picture of the past: We can almost feel the joy we felt then; we can almost reach out and touch old friends. But when we are absorbed in memory, the past—which is no more—feels more real than the present, where our life remains to be lived. As we grow older, our vitality naturally decreases, and with it the sensitivity of our senses; yet it may be that the present feels flat because we have lost contact with it.

If we can attune ourselves more closely to the reality before us now, the dynamic energy of the present moment will nourish us and renew our energy. By gently contacting each of our senses, we can intensify the sensations we are receiving. Focusing, for example, on our sense of sight, we can relax our eyes and touch shapes and forms lightly with our gaze. Each sight we see offers us a special delight we often miss when our minds are busy remembering. These richer feelings do not depend on the sharpness of our vision, but on the receptivity of our hearts and minds. Colors, sounds, and fragrances, rich textures and tastes are continual sources of vitality we can open like treasure chests. When we allow ourselves to respond to the immediacy of the present moment, the simplest experience evokes deep satisfaction.

Memories can also be used to bring more richness and vitality into the present if we change our response to them. As we remember, we can bring our attention to the feelings we are experiencing now. We can even invite a cherished memory to come into our minds, opening our hearts to it as if opening the door for an honored guest, allowing feelings of welcome and deep pleasure to spread throughout our bodies. How remarkable, this magical memory we have! When did the human mind discover it could recall experiences and evoke such deep feeling from the heart? How flexible memory is, turning from joy to sadness, sadness to love, in an inner symphony of textures and tones.

While we cannot always convey the flavor of a personal experience to others, when we use memories as touchstones to bring up feelings of joy and appreciation and let these feelings light up our hearts, we find that we can evoke similar responses in others. The events we are recalling are past, but our feelings are immediate, sources of vital energy that can bring us great and lasting pleasure.

When we experience love and caring, response to beauty, and the joy of sharing happiness with others, we share in a communion of deep feeling. Even when memories touch reservoirs of disappointment and sadness, we can remember that these feelings also are universal, understood by every human being. Gratitude and appreciation that we are alive, that we can feel and respond can be awakened at any moment in every human heart, helping to counteract pain and grief. This too is knowledge that can be communicated through our attitudes and actions. In embodying this understanding, we can uplift the hearts of others, and enrich every day of our lives with the warmth of intimacy and love.

The older we are, the larger the storehouse of life experiences we can recall and use to deepen our knowledge of the human spirit. In deepening our understanding, we touch a wellspring of warmth and gratitude that satisfies our inner needs and flows outward toward others. When we sense through our feelings a commonality with all human beings, feelings of loneliness lose their power. We naturally respond to friends who live in isolation and loneliness, lightening their burden and encouraging them to appreciate their lives in new ways.

Responding to feelings they know are real, the young will be drawn to us naturally, able to trust our openness and honesty. In expressing what we know to be true, we can help them to avoid difficulties and mistakes; we can help calm their fears and encourage their accomplishments.

The benefits our knowledge can bring to others and to ourselves will increase the meaning and value of our lives beyond measure. Knowing our own value, appreciating whatever life has brought us, we stand on a knowledge more precious than jewels, giving from the heart what we have experienced. When we give generously what we know, even death takes on a new meaning. Having learned what it means to live, we can carry gratitude for this knowledge with us to the end of our days.

Whatever our sources for meaning and value in our lives, we can expand them endlessly by grounding ourselves in knowledge. Every situation brings potential benefits; each moment can be laden with meaning. We can begin this instant to invite knowledge into our lives by observing our own experience. We do not need to wait for the right time, to prepare for some 'special moment' or to hold back from what life continually presents to us.

We may think that we lack knowledge, but there is no need for concern—in knowing we need greater knowledge, we automatically prepare an open place to receive it. As we maintain receptivity by observing and questioning our experience, knowledge will respond to our invitation as naturally as rain fills an open bowl.

As new insights come to us, there will inevitably be times when we cannot sustain a sense of progress and growth, and our receptivity seems to disappear. Then we might conclude that our simple questions and moments of 'breaking through' into a new understanding have little lasting value. Without being completely aware of how the process of opening unfolds in our lives, we can easily become discouraged and feel we have learned very little. Or perhaps in losing confidence in ourselves, we belittle our new knowledge by saying it is nothing new, just a variation on what we already understand. At these times, it is important to encourage ourselves to appreciate each aspect of the insight we have already gained, treasuring each step forward. Knowing that we cannot always sustain this new seeing is part of our knowledge as well.

As we see more clearly how growth manifests in our lives, we can share the benefits of our knowledge with others who are also feeling the need for greater meaning in their lives. In our modern world the isolation of individuals is very great. People live within their own patterns, moving toward private dreams and goals, while enduring what they feel is their own private pain. At any one moment, some of us feel confident and happy, others uncertain and confused, while we all have difficulties communicating with one another.

We are all at different stages of life, using different strategies and different views. These natural variations could help us balance and stabilize each other, if we only realized the difference that the smallest gift of understanding can make. Even a look, a gesture, a few kind words that let others know they are not alone can inspire them to discover within themselves the knowledge that can relieve their frustration and pain.

Knowledge is the most precious and powerful medicine, the best of all possessions, a treasure we will never lose. Outlasting all material or physical objects, more valuable than the purest gold, knowledge of our inner nature is a fountain of youth that rejuvenates the mind, bringing clarity and joy in living. As our mind distills knowledge from every experience and converts it to more enlightened action, our mind grows increasingly vital no matter how the body ages. Even when we pass from this life, the body of knowledge we have manifested in our views and actions will continue to grow; empowered by our life energy, it will help to sustain many future generations.

27

Global Knowledge

In thinking of what we can give back to the world,
we begin to take responsibility for being human.

Although our knowledge of the world seems to be rapidly expanding, our view seems to be becoming ever more short-sighted, oriented toward serving a self we do not understand. Lacking a deep understanding of our minds, we can never be fully aware of what actions are in our best interests, or take responsibility for the effects of our actions on others. Thus we cannot act with a vision grounded in knowledge of what is truly beneficial for us, our societies, and our world. Our best efforts may be ineffectual or even harmful; when we do not see clearly what we are doing in the present, we cannot shape our future with real confidence.

Our education prepares us to look forward to the future, but does not teach us the importance of being fully grounded in awareness of who we are and what we are doing here and now. We all have awareness, but we seldom recognize its full power; it is as if we had wings but had never learned to use them. Now we think we are doing well if we can leap to the other side of a small stream; we do not know that we have the capability to see to the farthest extent of the ocean and traverse its full expanse.

Our human awareness is so powerful that even if we tap only a small part of it we can accomplish more that we ever dreamt possible. Using our complete potential, we can soar to the height where our accomplishments have great and lasting value for both ourselves and for future generations. Vision set free from the self has no limits—it is able to draw fully upon the past, see clearly in the present, and range far into the future, with a scope that encompasses the entire world. Seeing a great field of possibilities for action, such vision finds meaning in bringing these possibilities into being.

Our perspective naturally widens when we shift our attention away from personal concerns and reflect on how our very being is sustained on this planet. Every moment of our lives, we depend on the air and the earth itself. Each day we benefit from the sunlight that warms our bodies and allows us to see; we cannot live without water for more than a few days. Each of these vital elements has been aeons in the making, during the formative stages of our galaxy and planet. Our human bodies have been gradually developed over several million years, during which each generation has passed along variations and changes to its descendants. Our language and images did not suddenly spring into being at our birth; centuries, even millenia of experience lie behind a single word. The experiences of countless human beings have contributed to our culture and the society in which we have made our home. We call upon vast resources at every instant of our lives.

We can see how much we are given by our world, but what are we giving in return? Will the planet be better for our sojourn on its surface, or worse? Many people today realize that we cannot continue to take so much from our world without considering the needs of future generations. While this view is a step forward, it is still oriented toward taking. From one perspective, we must take: All sentient beings take to sustain life and return only their bodies to the elements. But human beings have a higher consciousness and the knowledge to live their lives with a more balanced understanding of the relationship between human awareness and the future of life on our planet.

How can we realize the full benefits of being human if we do not use the knowledge we have? What use is our knowledge if we follow the patterns of more limited forms of life? Possessing greater capacity for understanding than other forms of life, we have a greater responsibility to consider what we can offer to life in return for its gifts to us.

In thinking of what we can give back to the world, we begin to take responsibility for being human and realize the enormous value of our individual lives. We see that we can offer the gifts of our energy, our awareness—our lives—to create a richer environment for those who follow us. Preoccupations and worries so important to the limited self melt into insignificance when our perspective on what it means to be human widens. Centered in a broad, open view, we can rely on our own inner resources to set long-range goals for our lives and plan a course of action to achieve them.

Although our vision is now very limited, we can use the resources we already have to heighten our awareness. Drawing on what we already know, we can project our vision as far as possible into the future and consider carefully what the results of our actions might be. Then we can think back, reviewing the past, reflecting on where similar actions have led us before, and questioning the cause of problems encountered in the past. What effects did such actions have on others in the past, and what effects will our present actions have on others in the future?

Thinking in this way, looking forward and backward, open to whatever we see, we gather together all the knowledge at our command. Strengthened with this knowledge, we can assess more wisely whether what we are doing is worth the expenditure of our time and energy. Once we have questioned our purpose carefully, we will see how one action builds upon the next; we will not lose energy and time in distraction or be diverted from our purpose. Periodically we can examine the results of our actions and readjust our course as necessary. Knowledge will grow with each reassessment, and our vision will become clearer.

This process is much like climbing a mountain. Without preparation, climbing even the smallest peak can be very dangerous. But when we take time to study the route and reassess it as we climb, we can proceed with safety and confidence. Eventually the summit will come into view, inspiring us to make even greater efforts.

When we are mindful of our goal and aware of the present moment, our concentration links our energy to the momentum of time, effortlessly sustaining us. Instead of interacting with surface appearances and superficial roles, we touch deeper dimensions of experience that return to us a rich and satisfying energy. Results grow steadily, as if we were tapping an inexhaustible source of power. Acting upon a personal commitment to offer something of value to the world, all we do emanates from a deep inner integrity and brings our whole being into a direct interaction with life.

Recognizing the value of our lives and taking complete responsibility for our actions, we begin to draw upon the full resources of our consciousness. When we learn how to use these resources, we awaken a far greater vision of what is possible for us to achieve. Linking vision to knowledge at each step of the way, we establish a momentum in our lives that heightens our interest and vitality, and culminates in global knowledge.

Global knowledge is the key to a fully-awakened consciousness, aware and fully concentrated on the present, responsive to the needs of all beings at all times. Acting in the light of global knowledge is like seeing clearly the highest peaks in the world and a direct route to the top; we can take every step with certainty, knowing that the higher we climb, the clearer our view will become—until it eventually opens out in all directions.

Able to see all the forces at work in our world, our consciousness could open up layers of time; the moment a thought crossed our minds, we would know exactly what action it would prompt, what effect our action would have on others, and the future results of that action. Rather than relying on the slow process of trial and error, we could immediately reject what we knew would not turn out well and concentrate on actions that would be more beneficial for ourselves and for others.

Can we imagine a world inhabited by millions who shared a vision of universal harmony and peace, and were able to unite their resources to bring this vision into being? We would have a world of wondrous beauty to pass on to generations of the future. Governed by a moral order based on global responsibility, the world would need no restrictive laws. Each individual, unique and free, would act in full knowledge of the results of his or her actions. With this understanding, we would not be likely to invite problems or suffering into our lives or into the lives of others. Everyone would contribute their genius with wisdom, mindful of the welfare of all that exists.

SECTION NINE

Inner
Knowledge

CHAPTER 28: LIMITS ON MEANING

CHAPTER 29: THE I AS KING

CHAPTER 30: THE ILLUSORY I

CHAPTER 31: TYRANNY OF THE I

Limits on Meaning

*Could our thoughts and actions be guided
by a more comprehensive and trustworthy
knowing intrinsic to our own being?*

We all live within an inner world of images, thoughts, and memories that shift continually, evoking a rich texture of feelings, emotions, and moods. Sometimes images arise vividly in our minds and spark a chain of thought; at other times we can sense our minds bringing an idea into focus. At first we may simply sense that we are seeing images or thinking thoughts, but soon thought becomes more substantial; we are aware of the actual words in our minds as we think or express them in speech or in writing.

The words expressing images and thoughts are concepts, linked together in strings that clarify their relationships. Concepts are the building blocks of our language, and their meanings are the substance of our knowledge. Many concepts we use today had their origin long ago. Throughout human history, one con-

cept has grown out of another, branching and proliferating like vines in a jungle.

Concepts may be simple identifiers like 'tree' and
'house' or more abstract notions like 'freedom', 'love',
or 'justice'. They are built up through a process of
distinctions, following a logical pattern that contrasts
'this' and 'not-this'. 'Green' is distinguished from
'not-green'; 'tree' is distinguished from all that is
'not-tree'. These distinctions depend upon each other
—'tall' takes its meaning in comparison with 'short',
'big' has meaning in comparison with 'small'.

As we continue to meet with new objects, we can
label them by distinguishing them from what we
know. An elephant seen for the first time is 'not-
anything-I-have-seen-before', 'not-dog', 'not-cat', and
so forth. Then we can adopt the name 'elephant'.
These simple distinctions form the foundation for
more complex concepts that draw upon the meanings
of many other concepts. 'Freedom' has meaning
because we can define what it means to be 'not-free'.
We can form an idea of 'love' by contrasting all we
associate with love with what is 'not-love'.

At some point in our childhood, we found ourselves thinking and speaking, using and reacting to
concepts. From parents, friends, and the other influences in our complex social conditioning, we absorbed
our basic conceptual framework. As infants, we were
fascinated by moving forms and patterns of light and
shadow; we learned to recognize our parents, as well
as to distinguish objects. We were already making
associations between what we saw, heard, smelled,
tasted, and sensed through our bodies. We may have

developed a sense that our associations had significance, but we had no words to express their meaning.

Listening to the spoken sounds around us, we learned to name the forms and qualities of our world. This process unfolded by trial and error; the words we first linked to the objects around us may not have always matched the words used by others: Two objects completely different in size and color were both named 'dog'; two others, nearly identical, were 'dog' and 'cat'. Corrected and recorrected many times, we shaped our early impressions to fit adult concepts and began to associate forms and sounds 'correctly'.

Eventually, we did not have to listen to the sound as sound—the sound touched our concepts immediately, and we 'heard meaning' directly. Concepts became a kind of shorthand, a convenient way to refer to familiar objects without having to describe precisely what we were seeing or exactly what we meant.

Simultaneously, we were taught how to react to these concepts: what we could and could not touch, what to value, what to desire, and what to reject; we even learned what to be happy and sad about. According to the customs of our culture, we were taught the proper way to categorize, use, and think about everything in our experience.

Gradually, many associations began to accumulate around concepts. They could touch memories and evoke complex reactions. We could, by uttering the word 'home', evoke a wealth of feelings and associations that gave this concept a special meaning to us. Perhaps many words took on a deep private significance, just as certain sights, fragrances, sounds, and sensations sometimes seemed to resonate with rich, unexplainable meaning.

But whatever had significance to us personally had to be expressed within the concepts available in our language. We had to accept the meanings we were given, and leave unspoken the meanings and feelings we could not communicate. The concepts we learned reflected back to us, and we began to think with the words of our language. The words that now form so spontaneously in our minds are all concepts transmitted to us by others. These concepts now condition how we view ourselves and our world, how we think, and how we respond to what happens around us. They create our everyday reality, and we use them to interpret all our experience.

Concepts begin as fluid and flexible, but become more fixed as we mature. When we are first learning a concept, such as 'space' or 'awareness', we are most receptive to nuances around it; we may play with it for a while, question it, and explore its possibilities. Once we feel we 'know' it, we tend to lose interest. Our willingness to reexamine, discard, or expand the scope of the concept decreases; the word is no longer alive, subject to modification in light of new knowledge, but frozen into an item of information that we possess. We rely on it automatically in our thinking, which becomes more a matter of recollection than a creative activity.

Relying exclusively on our conceptual patternings, we slowly constrict the natural openness of our minds. It becomes more difficult to perceive the subtle nuances of the changing moment. At the moment of perception, our minds grasp and interpret sensory information, and supply us with prepackaged concepts that have specific associations and emotional tones based on past experience. These associations arise simultaneously with the concept, projecting a past situation onto the present and conditioning how we view an experience. We do not necessarily respond to the immediate experience, but to the experience as it is filtered through concepts, memories, images, and associations.

Seeing a present situation as similar to a past one, we tend to react automatically, decreasing our ability to assess the present situation freshly. Bound to the past in this way, we cannot perceive the vast range of alternatives available in the present and so diminish our options for action. This tendency obscures awareness; losing touch with the open dynamic of the living moment, we live in a deadened world.

When concepts become this fixed in our consciousness, we can perceive nothing new. Unable to perceive the subtleties of each changing situation, we even repeat the same gestures and the same comments in situations that appear the same. When our minds become habituated to such automatic responses, they grow lazy and inattentive, especially in familiar surroundings. Our fixed views give us a sense of security. We feel we 'know' the objects in our world; we feel we 'know' people and other living beings. We count on things to stay the same and to fulfill our expectations of what they are supposed to be and do.

The more we reinforce this passivity by relying on deadened concepts, the more our minds resist reexamining what we know. As we force our experience into rigid molds, our inner world can become smaller and more limited, rather than enriched by our daily experiences. Confined to concepts that limit our expressions of feeling and insight, we can only duplicate the patterns we have learned, like our parents, grandparents, and their parents before them. All the knowledge we gain from our formal education and from our experience may only be an increasingly complex association of concepts that have little meaning to a human life. Such concepts are too frozen, too particularized, too distant from the realm of living things to express our deeper levels of experience.

Until we question, analyze, and reassess the concepts we use to express ourselves, we are restricted to only one set of interpretations for our experiences. Whether they accord with the reality of what is happening or bring us unnecessary pain, we leave ourselves no choice but to live in this limited realm. Even if our mental world is lonely, and we gain little pleasure from our experiences, our thoughts are familiar and give us an illusion of security and control that binds us to them. We may see no alternative to this way of understanding ourselves and our world. But when even such thoughts as these depend upon concepts we have never deeply examined, how would we know there are no other possibilities?

Can we even think about something for which we have no concept? If we had no concept of love, could we form expectations of what love is like, become disappointed when our experience did not match these expectations, or fantasize about people we love? If we had no notion of love, could we hate? What if we had no concept of 'I', or of ourselves as somehow separate from others? Then what would we love or hate? Could we become attached to people or things, experience insecurity, or fear rejection? If society could not present us with ideals that did not match the reality of our situation, would we feel guilty that we could not live up to them? How might the quality of our lives be different if we had no 'should' or 'would' in our language?

If we look carefully at our experience, we can see that many things that seem substantial and real are actually notions formed by our minds. Thinking about them and using them daily, we tend to forget that they are mental formulations and relate to them as real. Thus happiness, for example, is not inherent in the objects we desire, but grows out of the way we interpret a certain kind of excitement. However much we value happiness, it too is only a concept, a name that we learn to apply to certain types of situations or feelings.

Without our idea of happiness and the many related notions concerning what makes us happy, would we know if we were happy? Could we be unhappy? Would we have the same feelings if we lacked a word to express them? How could we spend time thinking about whether we were happy, or feel deprived if we were not?

It is nearly impossible for us to imagine what life would be like without such familiar concepts. We have come to trust our present conceptual patterning as a reasonably reliable reflection of truth, and see no reason to question it. But does our conceptual patterning increase our options for being and acting in the world, or is it too limited to serve our needs? Are our present concepts able to accommodate all the knowledge possible for us to gain, or have they become too rigid to sustain a more comprehensive perspective on knowledge?

When we depend automatically upon concepts, whether in thoughts, speech, or writing, we can actually decrease our ability to communicate. We all live in our own mental realm; our individual experiences have conditioned the specific connotations of the concepts we use. Although our mental worlds overlap those of others, they are never completely identical. Depending on knowledge filtered through concepts, we cannot wholly communicate our intended meaning; instead, we are subtly isolated from one another. Although we all use the same words daily, there is a gap in our communication that cannot be fully closed.

When we translate the concepts of one culture into those of another, this gap in communication is widened. The meaning of each concept may appear the same, but the connotations associated with it may vary greatly. Today, as English and other western languages are increasingly used in worldwide communication, the peoples of the world seem to be moving toward a shared body of concepts. Yet what is shared may only be superficial; the same words may have different meanings within different cultures. Even the structure of different languages may greatly influence the ability to express important nuances of meaning. Thus there is great potential for confusion and misunderstanding. We may unknowingly lose valuable knowledge in translation. Or the world's peoples may come to behave like partners in a bad relationship, exchanging talk and reassurances, but lacking a basis for real communication.

Are our current conceptual patterns necessarily the best basis for increasing our understanding of ourselves and our world? Have we explored the assumptions underlying our concepts? Had conditions in our past been different, other mental patterns might have evolved just as easily; then we would be living in another mental landscape, just as confident in our sense of reality as we are today. What we now consider to be unquestionable, self-evident truths might not even exist; we would have no way to think about them, yearn for them, suffer over them, or fight for them.

If we reflect on the nature of concepts and how uncritically we accept the reality they create, it may seem that we are caught in the midst of some elaborate computer program that is operating without our conscious decision. And yet we tend to feel that we are in charge of our thinking. Are we running the program or is the program running us? Can we separate ourselves from the program and allow our thoughts and actions to be informed by a more comprehensive and trustworthy knowing intrinsic to our own being?

In the light of greater understanding, could we retrain our minds into a more satisfying way of seeing? Is it possible to see through our conceptual patterning? Might there be a way we could open up our concepts and revitalize them with meanings that allow us to communicate our ideas more completely? Could we find concepts that are closer to the immediacy of our experience and more in tune with our insights and feelings?

There may be ways to glimpse a more subtle side of our consciousness that could allow us to examine the fixed patterns of our minds more clearly. When we relax the body, we can slow the flow of thoughts and images, and observe more directly the thought process itself.

Such relaxation need not involve any special technique. It is simply a matter of observing the thoughts that come, without comment or interpretations. When we try this way of observing the mind at work, what we see may not be quite what we expect—it may not appear to be very important. But over a period of time, we can begin to observe with an unforced, relaxed concentration that may be a new experience in itself. This way of looking inward might lead to important insights into the nature of thought, as well as a new awareness of the connections between thoughts and feelings.

Left to themselves, thoughts tend to carry on to a point where they pause, almost as if they have converged at a blank wall. We might have experienced such a pause when rigorously following a particular train of thought or when we found ourselves 'stuck' on a problem. At any time the mind may be silent for a moment. If this pause is noted, we usually consider that we have reached the end of a train of thought. If no new thoughts arise to continue it, we turn our attention to another subject.

But that seeming 'dead end' where thoughts melt into a single point could also be a gateway to new knowledge. Focusing on this point with a balanced concentration, we might see possibilities for a way of knowing that lies beyond our accustomed pattern of thinking.

If we can remain relaxed and aware, we might sense a feeling of brightness, as if light were shining through the silence. Our usual flow of thoughts and our habit of fixing attention on the content of thoughts give us few opportunities to sense the presence of light in our mental imagery. If we relax our hold on the content of thought and are attentive to the thoughts them-selves, we might sense thoughts arising from within this brightness just before they form into words.

The process may occur so fast that we immediately identify thoughts with words or perhaps whole strings of words that begin an inner dialogue. As more in-terpretations follow, involving combinations of con-cepts that evoke strong emotional tones, we may become aware of feeling burdened by a sense of heaviness that appears to be dark and serious. What thoughts contribute to this heaviness? What has happened to the qualities of openness and light with which the process began?

Perhaps as we ask these questions, the flow of thoughts again briefly pauses. But almost at once, a new flow of thoughts is in motion, lasting a long time or perhaps only a few moments before another sequence begins. Where are these strings of thoughts coming from? What happens when we take possession of the thoughts and consciously guide them in a specific direction?

Perhaps there does not seem to be a pause in the flow of thought: We are caught up in one sequence that has a theme or 'story line', when suddenly the content shifts, ànd we find ourselves in the middle of another story. How did we get from one story to the other? Does each one have a beginning and an end, or are they continuous? Do they overlap, influencing each other?

Questioning thoughts in this way, we can relax our fixed hold on the content of thought and gain new insights into our mental processes. Every thought is an opportunity to observe and learn from our mind. With experience, we can begin to see how thoughts can actually create confusion and prolong unpleasant states of mind. Eventually it will become more obvious how one thought generates another, and how the momentum of thoughts tends to build on itself, cycling and recycling impulses through the mind.

Just as a weaver creates a tapestry by establishing the basic threads of a fabric and embellishing it with pattern after pattern, our minds seem to weave thoughts and images in endless replications. When we catch the beginning of a thought, we can observe how it begins with a simple pattern that is open and spacious, growing more dense as images intertwine in ever more complex patterns.

Stimulating memories and associations that evoke universes of feelings and emotions, thoughts lose their openness as they proliferate and intermesh. Simultaneously, we can sense our critical faculties at work, labeling our experience as happiness, depression, ecstasy, boredom, or anger, as noble or blameworthy.

As each experience is sealed and witnessed by the mind, our thoughts about it become more substantial and 'real'; we then identify with the experience and react to it according to our conditioning. Out of all the possibilities for viewing a particular experience, we may choose to call it 'pleasure'. Then we project the experience outside of ourselves, and decide that we want to have that experience. Reaching out for things we associate with pleasure, we encounter our own image of what pleasure 'should be'. Grasping for an object, expecting to experience pleasure, and wanting to prolong it, we feel pleasure for only a short time. Almost immediately, we feel it slipping away.

Observing the ebb and flow of thoughts allows us to see how the mind attaches labels to perceptions, feelings, and emotions, and how it then produces commentary after commentary on what we are experiencing. Seeing these patterns of thoughts being woven together before our eyes, we may ask whether they actually create a solid cloth. Perhaps it is possible to view ourselves—not just our personality, appearance, and activities, but the very root of our being—in a different way. Such a fresh and open view could relieve the mind of the tendencies that freeze experience and make us vulnerable to confusion. Once we know it is possible to loosen the hold of concepts that entangle us in emotional pain, we have taken the first steps toward a new understanding that could transform the quality of all our experience.

With greater insight into who we are, what we are, why we perceive, feel, understand, and interpret in the manner we do, everything we know might be considered from an entirely new perspective. Then we could analyze our assumptions more deeply, deciding for ourselves what it is possible to change or not to change, which ways of thinking are healthy and valuable, and which involve us in needless suffering. As we continue to question, our thoughts may grow more vital and clear, opening up new possibilities for self-understanding and more control over the direction of our lives.

29

The I as King

*Like a great king protected
by his army, the 'I' is at home in its castle.*

Once our planet was a great kingdom at the center of the universe, encircled by the sun, the moon, and the stars that gave it light. Man, ruler of the earthly sphere, conceived the play of the cosmos as a performance enacted for his instruction, and read his destiny in the movements of stars and planets. Human movements were timed and guided by natural phenomena in an intimate drama of form and space, encompassed by divine presence.

In recent centuries, this view has changed. Earth has now taken its place in the vastness of space, a spinning body circling an average-sized star, which in turn is but one of millions of stars within one of many galaxies in our known universe. This view of the world was once considered revolutionary, but quickly became supported by an ever-growing accumulation of data, and has now been long accepted.

When the belief in the centricity of the earth gave way to this new view of the cosmos, the relationship between human beings and their universe changed. People began to lose their sense of felt participation with natural and divine forces. At the same time, new explanations of cause and effect created a new sense of order in the universe: The laws governing the natural order seemed no longer beyond human understanding, but discoverable by the intellect of man.

Although at first diminished by the revelation of the earth's relative insignificance in the cosmos, human beings eventually developed new confidence in their ability to gain supremacy over the known universe. The role of human being in the world began to seem even larger than before. New vistas opened for exploration by the human intellect. The heavens, once the realm of the divine, joined the natural world as the province of the human mind.

Despite a new vision of the vastness of the universe, the view that the cosmos exists for the benefit of man thus largely persists. But the sense of close interconnection between human beings and the rest of the cosmos has fallen into decline. Today a sense of the spiritual as a counterbalance to secular concerns no longer guides our vision, and human beings seem to stand apart from all that exists in the realm of nature as well.

As the range of human knowledge continues to expand to the far reaches of the universe, we may well marvel at the human mind and its capacity for knowledge. Were we to explore our mind with the same intensity that we have now explored the world around us, what new frontiers might we discover?

What interconnections between human being and other forms of life? Between form, being, space?

What do we now know about the nature of human being? Collectively, we have recorded histories of human activities, documented human ideas, and probed the origins of man. Still, there is little consensus as to what human being is. In one view, humanity began as a unique creation, endowed with a consciousness capable of knowing and responding to a creator; in another view, human being arose from a long chain of forms that began in a kind of primordial stew, sparked into life by chemical interactions. A combined view suggests that evolution gave rise to the specific human form, which at one point became uniquely able to understand its divine origins.

On one point everyone seems to agree: Human being is the most advanced form of life we know. Human being is still king, supreme among all living things, subject only—according to one's belief—to the will of a creator, the play of destiny, or the limitations of human intelligence.

Our quest for the origin of human being seems to end in belief or theory. We can believe in a creator, but how can we be certain? We can theorize about evolution, but our knowledge is incomplete and vanishes in the obscurity of time. Though science measures the brain capacity of early man, analyzes his bone structure, and studies his environment and culture, it can still only speculate as to how a truly human consciousness arose.

We cannot know the thoughts, feelings, or concepts of early man prior to written records. We cannot even be certain that our ancestors a thousand years ago knew their world as we know ours. How might the human mind have developed in the interim? What changes in perception or patterns of action might have occurred? What evolutionary development might even now be taking place?

Biological and medical sciences have analyzed the body in the same way that we have analyzed other objects in our world. In recent years, observation has reached more and more microscopic levels—we are now acquainted with the structure of genes and the metabolism of cells. We know how to alter heredity and can fertilize human cells in test tubes. Some day we may be able to construct a human cell and bring it to life, or foster embryos to maturity outside a mother's body.

But our technology has not brought us closer to understanding the nature of human being. Definitions of human life seem less certain than ever before. For example, a generation ago, human life was thought to persist as long as the heart continued beating. Now that hearts can be restarted, like automobile engines, or even created artificially, a living brain is considered the essential criterion for life. But even this definition is problematic, for we can sustain brains that show no sign of conscious activity.

What if the brain is functioning, but the body is dependent upon artificial stimulation? If the brain is impaired and the level of consciousness is dulled, at what point can we say human being no longer exists? Despite what we have learned about human biology, knowledge of our intrinsic nature remains elusive.

The mind is the last frontier in the study of man's uniqueness. But what is the human mind? Is it the brain, or located within the brain? Vital to human life, central to the functioning of the body, the brain seems to be our most distinguishing feature. But what makes the human brain human? We can trace the activities of the brain to some extent, but how does it learn and think? What exactly directs its functioning? Do all human brains function alike? If not, what makes one human brain think differently from another? Answers to some such questions are currently being sought in the study of neural patterns and brain biochemistry. Although certain connections have been discovered, our understanding seems far from complete.

Observation of human behavior has provided another approach. Over the past one hundred years, theories developed from such observation have given us numerous explanations of human behavior. Neuroses and instability are said to be due to family interactions or social conditions or to various combinations of cultural and biological factors. Yet our theories rely upon definitions of normal human needs, desires, and behaviors derived from social standards and conventions; since the full range of human consciousness has not yet been ascertained, we have defined 'normal' as equal to 'average'.

When deviations from standards of normality become social problems, or when human beings become unable to cope, therapy and drugs can 'normalize' their states of mind and enable them to return to society. But our knowledge and techniques appear insufficient: Psychological and emotional disorders seem to be increasing in number and variety. We continue to look for more effective ways of controlling abnormal behavior and dealing with symptoms of emotional dis-ease.

In spite of our research, human patterns of thought and action remain essentially unpredictable. We have no consensus on the specific causes of human actions; lacking this consensus, we find it difficult to determine who should be held responsible when actions cannot be controlled. Though we have studied behaviors and emotional patterns, examining the mind from the outside, our investigation of the self and mind is far from complete. Can we develop new forms of self-inquiry? Can we investigate more directly how the mind functions and how the self is established?

As individual human beings, what do we really know about ourselves? However we came into being, do we question the fact that we exist? Form, feelings, perceptions, conceptualizing abilities, and consciousness verify our existence as living beings. Our own experience appears to confirm our existence.

We appear to exist, but how do we *know* we exist? We think, we remember, we have a body, we have a mind, personality, and something we call 'I'; we have knowledge; we have skills; we have needs and wants; we have aspirations, hopes and dreams; we have emotions, views, and attitudes; we are happy, sad, loving, or angry. We are the center of our experience. We are the decision-maker, the judge of what has value. Can we even conceive of not existing?

When we say 'I' exist, what do we mean by 'I'? Do we mean the physical body, together with the senses that enable us to perceive our world and experience thoughts and feelings? But we tend to say "I have a body", not "I am a body"; 'I' exert control over 'it'. 'I' also have a mind, although it is open to question how much of this mind is always under 'my' control. What is this 'I' that organizes, thinks, experiences, and controls? Where is the personality that makes 'me' different from all other human beings, from all other forms of life, and from everything else in 'my' world?

Is 'I' 'my' individual, eternal soul that survives the death of the body? If so, why am 'I' so reluctant to let go of an aging, suffering body? Are we afraid of what might happen to this 'I' once it has lost the protection of the body? Are we concerned that this 'I' is not so substantial as we want to believe? If 'I' is the soul, how can it be eternal and unchanging, if at one point it feels strong and in control, and at another threatened with humiliation, embarrassment, or fear?

Is 'I' necessary for the body to function? We have no proof that this is so. In fact, the body may well act more efficiently without the interference of 'I'. 'I' seems to have little control over metabolic processes and much of the nervous system; heartbeat and breath, though most vital to our life, do not require monitoring by 'I'. Direct human responses to emergencies are often most effective when we are not conscious of an 'I' at work. Perhaps we know of impossible feats performed under duress, as when a mother has lifted a car to free a child trapped under it. In such cases, it seems we can act before the 'I' has a chance to think: "'I' cannot do this." What is it that responds in these instances? Perhaps our notion of 'I' is insufficient to describe the whole of our being.

What do we really know about this 'I' that is so pervasive, that owns our bodies, feelings, perceptions, ideas, concepts, and possibly souls? Can we set aside all our assumptions of what 'I' might refer to and ask it to prove its existence? Can we ask it "What are you?" and receive any answer other than "I am"?

We can question every other kind of knowledge, including the nature, even the existence of a divine creator, but we are curiously unable to question this 'I'. 'It' just is—impenetrable, mysteriously inaccessible, unseen. Like a great king protected by his army, the 'I' is at home in its castle. The supremely confident 'I' can well afford to disregard our questions.

What would happen if we decided to consider ourselves separate from this 'I' for a time; if we issued a challenge to the 'I'? For example, when 'I' responds to a desire, we could say no. What happens? Does the desire intensify? What thoughts arise? What anxieties or emotions? Can we maintain our decision, or do we feel driven to respond? How many reasons arise to convince us that we have to respond? What images come to mind, what fears of loss? If we can remain unmoving, perhaps we will note a shifting quality to the thoughts and feelings that play on our desires, uncertainties, and fears. Is there an 'I' directing this inner scenario?

At times when we feel hurt or insecure, and our confidence is shattered, we can again set ourselves apart and simply watch what arises. When 'I' wants reassurance, we can try depriving it as if it were a child that needed to learn a very important lesson. Whatever happens, we can just be quiet, without response, and simply watch the 'I'. Listen to it rationalize what happened; note the blame it assigns, the threats, the 'second thoughts', the feelings of guilt and fear; listen to it pick and nag for company; listen to it cajole with promises of a good time; listen to it pity itself; note the sad mourning for what could have been; feel its rage. In this shifting, chaotic inner realm, where is our solid, stable 'I'?

If we have been able to remain quiet and watch the thoughts that arise, we may have observed that it is possible to separate part of ourselves from what is happening. We can simply observe our thoughts, feelings, mental imagery, and urgings; we do not have to act on them. Who is this observer? Who is exerting influence over whether 'we' respond? Perhaps we are more complex beings than we thought.

30

The Illusory I

*Questioning the 'I', ego, self-image,
or any other label we associate with ourselves,
we can track dissatisfaction to its source.*

When we look at any experience, we can note the sights, sounds, bodily sensations, smells, tastes, and mental imagery that flood our senses and stimulate our bodies. If we resist these inner invitations to respond and simply sit with our experience, we can look beneath the surface, watching vague sensations and feelings arise, solidify, pass through differing intensities, and subside. As long as we remain detached, we can observe the ebb and flow of inner responses.

Careful observation reveals an alert, poised quality, a kind of expectancy or readiness. If we balance ourselves in this quality, we can sense a subtle tension supporting it, or feel the vibrations of our senses powering this readiness.

Although apparently still, the mind in its readiness is already reaching out and inviting stimulation. Like a frog sitting motionless until a movement within its range stimulates a lightning flicker of its tongue, our minds are prepared for instant response.

Out of the vast play of energy internal and external to our bodies, our physical senses select certain data that enter the range of their perception and feed these impressions to our minds for response. At once the mind reacts to organize, process, and interpret the sensory data. Contrasts of light, sound, odor, taste, bodily sensations, and mental activity are instantly integrated, and the appropriate bodily responses are activated.

At this level of response, our senses react automatically. For example, the pupils of our eyes contract automatically to regulate light. There is no opportunity to think about what is happening or make conscious decisions about what to do. Our energy is caught up in the momentum of experiencing.

The stimulation of the senses and the momentum of our internal responses are dramatic and powerful; this interaction activates the most basic levels of our consciousness, evoking images, sounds, smells, tastes, sensations, and thoughts, together with feelings, memories, and associations rich in tones and textures.

Immediately there is a sense of engagement, a reaching out to grasp, prolong, or manipulate the constantly changing thoughts, images, or sensations. The moment thoughts and feelings arise, something engages the feeling and urges us to act. The experience is happening; therefore it must have an owner— someone to cognize it, relish it, or reject it. Because experience is, 'I' am. Because 'I' am, 'I' must be experiencing some 'thing'. But where was 'I' in the earliest stages of the experience?

In the case of a visual perception, the process seems to begin with an experience of seeing. There is something large and solid 'out there'. It is a tree. Then what is 'in here' that is seeing this tree? It is 'me'. I am seeing a tree. There is seeing, there is a tree that can be seen, and there is the one seeing the tree. If there is the experience of seeing, and if there is something giving rise to this seeing, then there must be someone *doing* the seeing.

If 'I' responds, then it must respond to the arising thought or image; thus, the thought or image is the subject, effecting a result upon the object, 'I'. Or is the thought or image the object, because it is not part of 'I'? 'I' am central, 'I' identify, 'I' name, 'I' am the subject. 'I' see the tree, the tree doesn't see me!

Our primary experience is one of responding to a situation that presents itself—a simple movement of energy. Initially there is only an interaction of our senses with a situation; only secondarily does the experience become polarized into subject and object— a relationship between two things, such as a tree or a thought and ourselves.

Only when we identify something like a thought or a tree does the issue of subject and object arise at all; even then the thought or tree is actually cognized before we can know: "'I' am having a thought." Habitually we refer to ourselves as the subject or owner of the experience: "'I' am having a thought" or "'I' see a tree." But really it seems that the thought itself is the subject, producing the idea of 'I' as a response. When we reverse this situation linguistically, we condition the way we view our reality, turning it upside down.

But the 'I' is not satisfied with itself as an object, an entity that receives incoming data and responds. The 'I' wants to be subject, the owner of experience, and to dictate the terms of response. In staking out this position, 'I' seems to have no competitor within our bodies and minds; its assertions go unchallenged, and it establishes itself as governor or king. Sensing that there is a controller, we create a viewpoint that we find stable and satisfying, an 'I' that stands apart from our experience and our physical form, yet directs them. We become able to identify ourselves, our experience, and 'other' things as 'I', 'me', and 'mine'.

How accurate is this picture? The 'I' has incomplete information as to exactly what is occurring; the sense of 'I' arises after the momentum of perception and integration is underway. The perceptual process flashes to its conclusion far too quickly for 'I' to comprehend fully the welter of sensory stimulations, memories, associations, and feelings. All that the 'I' can evaluate, judge, and know is the integrated image presented to it.

Because of the limitations of our physical senses, even the image recognized by the 'I' is not entirely true to the external object at any point in time. What we consciously perceive as a stable object is an after-image, a composite of information filtered through our senses. Although the after-image seems concrete and real, it is only a momentary stabilization that approximates what is 'out there', no more substantial than a dream image that arises without external stimulation.

Because everything involved in the process of perception—the stimulus, our sensations, our perceptions and thoughts—is in motion, the moment we become aware of and name our experience, the actual experience has passed. Although it takes time for light to reflect off objects, time for our senses to respond, time for experience to be identified and owned by the 'I', the process occurs far too rapidly for our untrained observation to detect.

When we see a star, we are not seeing the star as it is at this moment, but as it existed perhaps millions of years ago. For all we know, the star may no longer exist. In the same way, there is a gap between our actual experience and our identification of it; what we are experiencing at this very moment is already past.

Because the interval between the experience and our identification of it is so brief, we tend to confuse the fleeting experience with the label we assign it. Overlooking the living moment and riveting our attention to the concept, we miss aspects of experience that are not already cognized and labeled. We live our lives through a fixed repertoire of responses, unable to appreciate the fluid, dynamic nature of our experience.

The 'I' may continue to grasp at a memory of the experience, but it cannot prolong the living, changing moment. We cannot relive precisely the same experience any more than we can relive moments from our childhood. Prolonging the sensation or savoring the same sensation under similar conditions is no more possible than drawing the same water twice from a moving river. While our minds participate directly in the living reality of movement and change, the 'I' is frozen into a realm of fixed concepts, dead to the nuances of experience, naturally threatened by manifestations of change.

Once an experience is appropriated by a feeling of 'I', the experience ceases to simply be; it can now be thought about, evaluated, and judged, joined with memories of past experiences and complicated by conditioned associations. All of these factors become instantly integrated; then, since 'I' own this complex integration of thoughts, feelings, memories, associations, and so forth, 'I' need to act on it—to change it, use it, accept it, reject it, control it.

Like an executive responsible for the welfare of a corporation, the 'I' takes charge of the situation and must respond. When sensations produce discomfort, there is no longer a simple experience of discomfort, but the notion: "'I' am uncomfortable; 'I' have to do something about it." If the experience is pleasant, there is not simply pleasure, but the concept: "'I' am happy; 'I' want to continue being happy."

The 'I' dictates that one experience is desirable and another is to be rejected solely in terms of whether the experience supports or threatens the 'I'. Picking and choosing in this way seems to guarantee dissatisfaction in our lives, for we control neither the circumstances that give rise to each experience nor our emotional responses.

We should not fall into the trap of thinking that the 'I' is just an idea that can be tossed aside once it is acknowledged. If the 'I' is simply an idea, it is one of the most powerfully supported ideas ever created. It has shaped the lives of human beings more than all the greatest rulers of the world combined, and it continues to dominate all our life experiences.

Since the 'I' appropriates our experience and freezes it, it is tempting to consider the 'I' or the ego as an enemy. We could end our inquiry there, projecting all our difficulties onto this mysterious entity. Or we might go one step further and say that projections of this sort are just another of the 'I's many devices to deceive us; relieved at having found a scapegoat, we might never reflect upon who it is that is doing the projecting.

Instead of trying to outwit the 'I', perhaps we can truly acknowledge the reality of our situation: the confusion and lack of awareness that lock us into repeating patterns of action ending in frustration and dissatisfaction. The forces that make up our world—historical, biological, and mental—work together to solidify everything in our experience into a dense and static realm of concepts; we assign different labels, such as pain, tension, and 'I', to the ever-changing nuances of experience. But we can open the wider world of our consciousness by questioning any one of these labels.

In questioning the 'I', ego, self-image, or any other label we associate with ourselves, we can track the roots of dissatisfaction to their source. If we knew that such questioning would give us the opportunity to rid ourselves of all the lingering unpleasantness of life, we would certainly begin at once. Or would we? Since the notion of 'I' is so intimately identified with our total being, examining it closely may make us feel threatened. Questioning the 'I' is like questioning our own identity—as if we began to suspect that all our life until now had been a dream from which we were about to waken.

We might discover that, in establishing the concept of 'I' and allowing that concept to shape our view of the world, we have entered into an illusory partnership with an entity that has no existence of its own. Reinforced in our concepts and linguistic patterns, the 'I' has become solid and real, a stable entity in a changing world. Although our bodies grow to maturity, flourish, and age, our notion of 'I' undergoes very little change during our lifetimes.

Because we identify this 'I' as a solid, unchanging entity, it carries a strong emotional tone and an extensive set of associations and assumptions. Most importantly, this 'I' is a person: not just any person, but 'this person—me'. Experience is 'my experience', and very important to what 'I' think I am, or what 'I' want to feel.

By accepting our understanding of 'I' uncritically, we may be causing ourselves unnecessary difficulties and cutting ourselves off from more liberating ways of being. Although seeing the 'I' directly, without its seductive guises, is an unsettling experience, it can be the beginning of true inner freedom. Questioning the 'I' strengthens us to face ourselves honestly and wakes us up to our intrinsic human worth. Is it a risk we are willing to take?

31

Tyranny of the I

*Because we have confused ourselves with 'I',
we cannot appreciate our own real nature
or intimately experience the world we live in.*

When the notion arises: "I am having this experience, this experience is mine; I see this object, this object relates to me," the 'I' is taking possession of our bodies and our experience. It is reaching out to extend its dominion in all directions.

Once ownership is established, the 'ego/I/self' structure alters our perception of ourselves and our world to suit its own requirements for security. Like water bending beams of light, it shapes our concepts, views, and attitudes to protect itself against exposure and loss. The 'I' requires stability and security, and fills us with fear when we are faced with reminders of impermanence.

In direct contradiction to our own knowledge of impermanence, we consider everything touching on the 'I'—our thoughts, feelings, emotions, bodies—as solid, real, and enduring. Change and impermanence become enemies to be fought, denied, or avoided. We become divided against ourselves, torn between our inner awareness and the everyday 'reality' we create.

Once we establish ourselves as a subject and take possession of our experience—exerting our will to control its outcome to our satisfaction—we set ourselves up for suffering. We make a contract with ourselves, committing ourselves to ignore the implications of impermanence in our lives. Based on an illusion, this contract is inherently untenable; it can be sustained only through continual reinforcement and reassurances, and protected at the expense of our vital energy.

The terms of this contract manifest as control. The demands of the 'I' drive our lives as if it were an actual person dictating what we will perceive, what we will think, how we will feel and react. The 'I' has needs, and demands satisfaction. Learned behavior covers the 'I's stridency in layer after layer of conformity to the standards expected by parents and society, but its needs do not change. It craves attention, approval, reassurance, possessions, and power. Inflaming desires and warping our judgment, it drives us relentlessly to seek what it wants.

The 'I' must be made to feel worthwhile and important. It must be defended from reminders that it is precarious and vulnerable. Like a vine grafted onto our consciousness, it extends its tendrils everywhere. Our identity, our confidence, our feelings of value and worth are inextricably intermeshed with the 'I'; our whole being has become identified with this 'I'. When it is securely in control, we feel in control and are comfortable; when it is threatened, we feel endangered and become fearful.

Because all of our experience is evaluated and judged by this 'I', we feel pain when it feels insecure, and act instantaneously to protect it. Even when we sense we have made a mistake, we find it difficult to acknowledge mistakes directly and take full responsibility for our actions. Compelled to cushion the 'I' from pain, we make socially acceptable apologies we do not really mean, or defend the 'I' by blaming others.

If these efforts are not successful, we can go instantly to the other extreme, demeaning ourselves by telling others how weak and helpless we are. Either way, we protect the 'I' from the need to change. If we cannot protect the 'I' sufficiently, it turns against us. We find our confidence shattered, tormented by self-doubts and self-recriminations, while the 'I' regains its sense of power at our expense.

Fed by power and control, the 'I' cares nothing for our inner well-being. It cuts us off from our real feelings and makes it impossible for us to see clearly what is beneficial for growth. We cannot listen to wise advice without becoming defensive or offended; we cannot accept knowledge that questions the 'I's control. The 'I' will even say, "I have no ego."

Judging only by its own needs for protection and control, the 'I' can override deeper sensibilities and concern for the welfare of others. Unrestrained by awareness of the natural dignity and value of others, the 'I' tends to dominate an ever-widening territory. When the 'I's demands are given free rein, we can unwittingly become as selfish and demanding as a child, forcing others to meet our desires.

Our most valuable human capacity, the ability to love and respond, is distorted by the 'I', which recognizes only its own needs and provides us with a set of false ideas: Through the veil of self-centered concerns, we equate domination, dependency, and control with real caring and responsibility, and blind ourselves to the conflicts we are creating in the lives of those we love.

Because we are not free of the 'I's influence, all of our relationships, even our closest friendships, involve unspoken 'pacts' to reinforce each other's self-image. If this pact is broken for any reason, the other will feel slighted or threatened. We may allow others to express negative views and opinions of us in the light of apparently honest evaluations of our actions; but if they penetrate too deeply into our self-image, the 'I' senses an attack on its preserve and has to protect itself or retaliate in some way.

In passionately charged interdependent relationships, we may sense the 'I's insecurity as fear of rejection or abandonment, and may express this fear in resentment, jealousy, or angry attempts to reestablish control of the other's attitude or activities. Real panic may hide behind demands for attention and profuse expressions of caring. Insecurity and fears can spark cycles of rage, verbal or physical violence, fear of loss, profound regrets, and reconciliations, until one partner or the other becomes exhausted.

Although not always reaching such extremes, love intertwined with the needs of the 'I' cannot be restful and openly appreciative; the 'I' plants the seeds for resentment and hostility even between responsible and caring people. Although we all desire to love and be loved, a relationship with an independent being who cannot be somehow controlled is intolerable to the 'I'.

The 'I's demand for domination conditions us to an attitude of ownership. The 'I' urges us to purchase, control, protect, and use objects for our pleasure. Much as the 'I' takes possession of our bodies, thoughts, feelings, and emotions, it extends dominion to our possessions; it leads us to think of what we own as an extension of ourselves.

Possessions that are personal expressions of our identity, such as cars and houses, become the focus of intense emotions—rage at their theft or loss has driven human beings to violent actions. Their aging and deterioration remind us uncomfortably of our own mortality, and we may seek renewal in their replacement and remodeling.

Intensely attached to possessions and suffering constant anxiety from fear of losing them, we may put ourselves in debt to accumulate more, and still not be at peace. The 'I' is watchful, looking everywhere, envious of those who have what we lack, torturing us with wanting and frustration. Even in the face of death, the 'I' will not relax its control: We make wills that disperse possessions according to its desires; we plan and purchase funeral arrangements, mausoleums, burial plots, and the engraving for headstones at its command.

Extending its dominion to all forms of life, the 'I' leads us to think that the beings who share this planet with us are subject to our use and control. At times in human history, it has been possible to own people as serfs or slaves with no concern for their suffering; women have been bought and sold as wives or servants, their living conditions, lives, and deaths completely controlled by others. Today, animals are thoughtlessly exploited for human use, as companions, breeding stock, clothing, food, and subjects for medical experimentation. For centuries, many people would not acknowledge that animals, or even some groups of human beings, actually suffered pain.

By virtue of our intelligence and ability to dominate the planet, we have come to view the earth itself as existing for our benefit, subject only to the conflicting claims of our own kind. Do we consider, as we use the land we depend upon for food and homes, that we may have a moral responsibility to preserve its value for future generations? For other beings?

When the 'I' wants and cannot have what it wants directly, it may be charming and seductive; frustrated, it may become resentful or strike out in anger; failing to gain its ends, it may explode through the facade of control. If humiliated, the 'I' retaliates instantly to cover up its vulnerability, excusing itself for failure, providing justifications for its rage, and blaming things outside its control for its frustration.

Unless we have studied its ways and have insight into how it works, when the 'I' is threatened, we cannot avoid feeling emotionally upset. If the blow to the 'I' is substantial, we may have to endure hours, even days, of internal dialogues as it convinces itself that it is back in control.

Strangely enough, although we seek satisfaction, happiness and pleasure last only a short time, whereas self-doubts, emotional pain, and anger may remain with us for days or even weeks. Sometimes we relive painful situations again and again, feeding resentment, hatred, or jealousy, ignoring whatever enjoyment the present moment could offer us. Such feelings may take up a substantial part of our lives, coloring our actions in the present and planting the seeds of difficulties in the future.

Why should one kind of experience be so transitory and the other so pervasive, particularly when we prefer the feeling tone of pleasure to the feeling tone of dissatisfaction? Why are the emotional states we wish most to avoid the ones most easily prolonged? Why can't we let go of frustration and pain?

We would not willingly live with another person who tormented us in this way. Perhaps we need to ask ourselves what is causing this pain, and whether it need be endured. Are we harboring an unnecessary and undesirable visitor?

What do we gain from our contract with the 'I'? The costs are undeniable: We take on its insecurities as our own and drain our vital energies to maintain its sense of control and well-being. Afraid of the pervasive pain that a threatened 'I' can inflict, we allow it to manipulate and warp our true feelings and altruistic motivations. To avoid internal distress, we provide rationalizations, reassurances of stability and self-worth. Or else we hesitate to take risks that are necessary for self-growth, and settle for far less than we are capable of achieving. We conceal our failure or errors even from ourselves, although they may manifest as doubt or guilt. We repress emotions unacceptable to our self-image, hiding them under a veneer of calm. Committed to the 'I', we become strangers to ourselves.

What is our reward for such diligent service? We are forced into a defensive stance: Everything that happens is a possible threat to our feelings of self-worth. Whether we mask this defensiveness with a patronizing attitude, with self-righteousness, or with passivity, we 'protect' our 'I', cushioning it from direct contact with experience.

Erected like shields between ourselves and others, our protective barriers become automatic. They become the 'I's bodyguards. We are committed to this defensiveness early in life, and often view our protective barriers as integral aspects of our personality. After years of sustaining them, it is difficult to conceive of other ways of being and acting, no matter how much difficulty they cause us. But in erecting these barriers around the 'I', we subtly set ourselves apart from those around us.

Protected by its retinue, the 'I' can deceive us, sometimes subtly, sometimes to an extreme degree, into acting against the interests of others, even those we deeply love. It causes us to act against our environment, and to act against our own best interests. Eventually we may find ourselves isolated and lonely, even in the midst of family or friends, feeling hungry for more meaningful relationships, but unable to give or receive true love and affection.

Because we have confused ourselves with 'I', we cannot appreciate our own real nature or intimately experience the world we live in. Although we yearn for meaning and value in our lives, we do not know where to find them. Instead of interacting with experience directly, we perceive all that happens just as an audience watches a drama played for its benefit. We have become habituated to the role of viewer, detached from the whole. All we know is grounded in illusions established by 'I', made ever more solid, believable, and real by repetition and accumulation.

Judging, controlling, and manipulating for its own benefit, the 'I' blinds us to the creative unfolding of our experience. Firmly established in the control booth, the 'I' makes sure that we watch the image and keeps us from the reality. The ultimate falsifier, the supreme teller of fairy tales and lies, the 'I' perpetuates itself by separating human being from life.

SECTION TEN

Knowledge
of
Mind

32

Maneuvers of Mind

Looking at the human predicament,
we may not know whether to laugh or cry.

As far back as we can trace the dynamic of our perceptual processes, our mental energy has been attracted to objects—not only the physical objects discerned by the senses, but also the thoughts, concepts, associations, and memories that form our knowledge of ourselves and our surroundings. In a sense, we can think about the world we live in as the creation of our own minds.

Caught up in the dynamic of perception and yet unable to see how it works, we naturally embrace the version of reality created by our thoughts and concepts as being unquestionably real. We learn to link our hopes for fulfillment to illusory images and ideals, and look for satisfaction outside ourselves. As confusion leads to confusion, we are never able to satisfy the wanting that lies at the heart of our creation. We commit ourselves to repeating the same patterns over and over again: We seek, we are eventually disappointed, and so we seek again.

It seems there would be great value in thinking about our lives in a new way. But what is happening in our minds as we read and reflect on the ideas written here? What is going on even as our eyes pick up stimuli from the page, and our minds sort and integrate these impulses into concepts and words? Are we stepping out from our accustomed way of knowing, or are ideas only pointing to ideas, building new variations of old patterns? As we read, are we picking and choosing what fits with what we already understand?

It is tempting to think that somehow we can escape from the momentum of our thoughts, but isn't that just another thought? And where does it lead us? Whatever we say to ourselves, aren't we simply re-peating the same patterns? How can we ever escape from the domain of the 'I'? Who would be escaping?

Even if we wish to free ourselves from the frozen concepts of the past, isn't this thought or desire dependent on words and concepts? Even the finest thoughts we have—thoughts of awakened mind, of awareness, of enlightenment—are names and concepts interpreted and judged by the mind. Not knowing who we are, unable to see where we are going, we seem to live at the mercy of our creation. How can we know what we want—how can we trust that what we are looking for even exists?

Although our way of being seems not to be ours by choice, who is participating in these patterns, if not ourselves? There is no one else to blame—we are the supporters and reinforcers of our 'reality', our inherited creation. We run the show; we are producer, sponsor, manager, player, audience. This is our drama, our tragedy. We may smile or laugh from time to time, but our comedies are brief interludes in the larger drama of our lives. We have programmed ourselves for tragedy: We play all the parts and weep at the end. We no longer know the play is a play, for we have become part of our creation.

Tricked by the movement of our own minds, how many times have we spun variations on the same drama, thinking we are beginning another new journey or adventure? But how many times have we simply repeated the same old patterns, with much the same conclusions?

How can there be any alternatives, when every thought and idea leads on to the next until we no longer know where or how we began? If we try to break out of a well-established pattern, what internal dialogues do we hear?

"You can't get out—there's no way out. There's nothing you can do."

"It's so damn discouraging—I never get what I want. I'm so depressed. There *must* be another way."

"No way. There's no way. It's all set up this way. Nothing will change it. You have to keep on going like this—you have no choice."

"Can it really be true?"

"Oh yes—it's always been this way."

"Then there is nothing I can do. I have to stay the way I am because there is no other choice. Yes, this is all I know; this is all I can do. Especially after twenty years—why think of changing now?"

"Oh yes, keep it up. I strongly recommend it."

Holding tightly to discouragement, confusion, and disappointment, we remain loyal to our part in the play, an innocent victim sentenced to frustration and dissatisfaction. How obedient we are! Each day we turn up for work, ready for the next episode. No matter what comes our way, we play our part: Our entrance cue is "I want;" our exit line is an expression of frustration and pain. Obligated to our own action, we keep going on—after all, having put this much into it, could we just walk away?

Every day we witness the shared confusion of humankind. All day long, we 'watch' dramas like our own, as our families, co-workers, friends, and neighbors play out the continuing story of their lives. Communication networks have spread across our globe like a vast array of nerve cells, connecting millions of people together. We watch each other, we tell each other our dramas, we ask for more: "What's new?" The old news has left us confused, uncertain. What will happen today?

Sometimes the news-story continues in episodes, night after night. Each evening we hear the updated version, the latest comments, the most recent expert opinion on 'what it all means' or even what actually happened. Commentaries themselves become news. We perpetuate this self-operating illusion-machine by tuning in, by believing it, by acting upon it, by being confused by it. Reports presented to us in words backed by images become instant unassailable 'facts'. "I saw it on TV."

Every waking moment, our inner 'news program' runs on and on. We never tire of listening to our internal newscaster reporting and making commentaries on the drama of our lives. Strangely, naively, once we have heard a 'report', we believe our own words.

When we stand back a little and imagine the huge drama of wanting and frustration going on all over the planet, isn't it amazing? Imagine all the people in all the cultures and climates of the world, each person with individual habit patterns, backgrounds, and moods, completely focusing their life energy on the fulfillment of their wants. Will they find what they seek? Will they be satisfied?

Here is someone who wants money; there is one who wants power; over there is one who wishes only for love. There are countless variations in the pattern, but each one plays his part totally, dedicating his whole life to the fulfillment of wants and desires. Wherever we look, throughout the world, aren't we all participating in the same sort of drama? Looking at our human predicament, we may not know whether to laugh or cry.

Envisioning the rest of our lives, what do we see? How long will we carry on with our searching and wanting? How much time will we spend dissatisfied and restless? How many hours will we have of fear, worry, anxiety, and loneliness? How many hours of happiness?

Having made ourselves into seekers who can never realize our dreams, we seem to have sealed ourselves into our creation with whispered messages only we can hear: "I have to have . . .", "I'll never be happy because . . .", "Wouldn't it be wonderful if . . .", "If only I had . . .", "I can't do anything about it. It's hopeless. I can never do anything else." Both fool and fooler, duper and duped, we whisper secretly to ourselves: "This isn't what I want, but somehow, somewhere, it must exist. I have to find it!" As images dance into our minds, inviting us to follow, we embrace them like a lover and go where they lead, until we are left empty-handed once again.

Faithfully, we listen to the catalogue of disappointments. We accept the suffering, take it as our own. Isn't this our duty—isn't this what it means to be responsible?

But do we need to hold so tightly to our drama of dissatisfaction? Why bring home to our hearts the subtle disappointments, the doubts that plague us? Why put our precious energy at the disposal of the 'I', protecting its sophisticated structure of lies? Do we need to invest our lives in shapes and forms that have no lasting meaning, building more and more elaborate sandcastles by the sea? Must we continue to be so gullible? Even if thinking in this new way turns out to be another sort of game, isn't the only honest view a frank admission that we would rather be free from frustration and pain?

Perhaps we can draw the line. Perhaps the time has come to leave the stage and get on with our lives: "Enough is enough! For a long time I have taken part in this drama, not even knowing I was suffering. Convinced that this was my duty, I have accepted what was brought to me by my senses, my most intimate friends and neighbors. I thought my job was to hold on stubbornly; I have been blindly faithful, totally committed. I was tricked, and I have given away my life. I have nothing left I can call my own. Not even my words belong to me. I have utterly lost my freedom. No more for me, thank you! That's enough!"

When we see how deceived we have been, how much of our life has been wasted, we may fall into deep hopelessness and even think of 'leaving the stage' by taking our lives. But isn't this just another trick of the 'I' to prevent us from making our lives worthwhile?

If we can see the patterns that hold us hostage, it may occur to us that in the very act of seeing, we have touched a deep source of knowing. What is this new seeing and new knowing? Where does it come from? Is it different from thinking? Is it just another trick of the 'I'?

Seeing clearly our human predicament, we may discover a deep certainty that we do not know what to do. If we can rest within the 'not-knowing', without judgments or evaluations, we may be able to play a little with our situation. How do we know we don't know? What knowledge do we draw upon to tell ourselves, from the bottom of our hearts, that we do not know? Do we know more than we know?

Observing the activity of our minds in a quiet, relaxed way, we find that thoughts soon sweep us up in the old drama. It all happens so quickly we cannot seem to track the movements in our minds. For one thousandth of a second we may glimpse a pause, but it is hard to experience the transition from one story to another. We seem to jump like a grasshopper from the middle of one set of images to another, and once our energy is bonded to the contents of the images, it is difficult to see anything else.

But perhaps we can be strongly involved in our images and at the same time step back a little, watching in a loose way. Even when the characters, images, and language all mix together and become so real we cannot help but take them seriously, we may still be able to watch and observe. As the images shift and change, they may seem to be illuminated—what is this 'light' that allows us to see our dreams and memories? Or perhaps the images themselves are somehow imprinted on a transparent field of light energy.

Thoughts and images seem to shoot into our awareness from nowhere, already linked together into a complete scenario. But this may be misleading. If we could see the smaller units that make up our stories, would we take the drama itself so seriously?

If all of our dramas are happening within the mind, we may want to ask: Then who is creating the suffering and who is receiving it? It seems that the 'I' is part of the story, not its creator. If there is no one creating or receiving suffering, then where is the substance of the mind's activity? What is the nature of our human mind?

There seems to be much to learn about the active light energy of our minds. By observing our experience, we begin to see through the interlocking thoughts and images that make up our familiar world. We open a wholly new perspective. Self-observation strengthens awareness, which supports the growth of insight and heightens the clarity of observation. The positive feedback from this process is rewarding in itself and encourages our continued efforts.

As awareness grows, our thought patterns can become our partners and our friends. When we experience pain or discomfort, we can consult with our own intelligence to find a way to release ourselves from the pain. If we find ourselves holding on stubbornly to frustration or dissatisfaction, we can question ourselves more closely. Where can the holding on itself take place, if not in our own thoughts?

33

Directionality of Consciousness

Led by thoughts and images
away from our vital center, we have
no place of rest, we have no real home.

Our eyes are windows to a spacious view of land and sky, filled with colors and patterns; our ears detect the songs of birds, subtle rustlings of movement, the tones of the human voice. We smell the varied fragrances in our world and join the sensitivity of nose and tongue to savor tastes. We are responsive to touch and texture, capable of experiencing a wide range of sensations. Our senses vibrate, our minds receive impulses and sort and translate them into impressions and images. Patterns of light and shadow are interpreted as the end of one form and the beginning of another, and sounds, odors, tastes, and textures are then integrated with each form. Through all of our senses, the cognitive aspect of our consciousness continually interacts with our surroundings, shaping thoughts into complex mental patternings that we express in our speech and language.

At some point in the past, human beings began to recognize contrasts of light and shadow as discrete forms that could be named. Contrasting, identifying, and naming forms, they created a world of interdependent polarities: big and small, hard and soft, male and female. Although all such distinctions, as well as the labels applied to them, were a creation of the human mind and varied in character from culture to culture, they eventually took on greater substance, and came to be viewed as actually solid and real.

From this single seed, rooted in the perceptual process, human beings created the self and its world. They became the perceivers who experienced their surroundings as an objective realm. Looking within, they could reflect upon contrasts perceived in their own inner states, and give names to feelings and emotions. Thus they were able to distinguish between likes and dislikes, pleasure and pain; they could remember and reflect upon their sensations. Using names, human beings could evaluate their experience and express preferences and opinions.

Gradually names took on more meaning through associations with other names; concepts became more complex. Eventually, the basis was established for more sophisticated abstract thinking. From this long chain of development, molded by language, culture, and environment, our present mental patterns have evolved over many thousands of years.

Throughout human history, the object-oriented part of our consciousness has received continual reinforcement. Deep channels have been carved in our minds, directing our mental energy away from the open dimension of consciousness into the realm of objects. With each thought or sensation, our minds now flash with the speed of an electric current to engage the apparently objective world. From birth, we are conditioned by these patterns of perception, thought, and responses.

We automatically employ these patterns to interpret and respond to objects and situations. This one way of responding is all we know: Like a train following a track, we seem predestined to follow the route laid down in the course of our evolution. Although we may be convinced that we are thinking and acting from choice, we are actually conditioned to a sense of separation and to the pushes and pulls of polarities. We are bound to evaluate and react to everything in terms of likes and dislikes, desirable and not desirable, good and bad.

Committed to a view based upon duality, and confined to the conceptual structures that emerged from this view, we cannot conceive of the possibility of having a more open patterning for our thoughts and actions. There is little in our way of life even to make us query our patterns of perception and thought, or reflect upon the deeper implications of how we view ourselves and our world.

At the same time, the force of attraction to the objective world has grown more intense than ever before. Modern societies have given birth to countless new technologies, setting in motion a new kind of evolution powered by the ingenuity of our rational minds. Although our scientific and technological evolution is a recent development in our planetary history, its force has significantly increased the natural momentum of change.

Today, the primary thrust of our creativity seems directed toward improving our physical well-being through broadening the scope of technology. Even now, each new advance strengthens our dependency on technology, giving us little choice but to support its growth. But are we directing this growth with wisdom, to enhance all aspects of human life? Or will its development crowd out human values and draw us into an artificial and dehumanizing way of life?

Already our modern way of life depends upon complex networks made possible by modern technology. Each aspect of our society, such as education, finance, and transportation, has its own elaborate network supported by sophisticated machinery. These networks themselves are becoming more closely linked together as overarching communications and information networks are developed.

Machines are deeply interwoven into the fabric of social and private life. A large percentage of our time and energy is now devoted to running and maintaining these machines and systems. This trend can only accelerate as modern nations strive to stay up-to-date in order to maintain leadership in an increasingly competitive world.

Huge quantities of information must continually be processed to keep our societies running smoothly, and we need increasing numbers of machines to perform these functions efficiently. Mirroring and extending various functions of the human mind, computers can be developed to support even more complex systems than we have at present. Our dependency upon computers is rapidly increasing; in the future, they may be essential for the functioning of nearly every aspect of our societies.

In years to come, we may see increasing cooperation between human beings and computers. We already know that computers are potentially powerful educational devices. We also envision developing artificial intelligence that will duplicate the rational functions of the mind; we may be able to supply this artificial intelligence with instruments far more sensitive than our own sensory organs. Soon computers will be programming each other, adding a new level of technological sophistication.

Computers that can make rudimentary projections and decisions free us to concentrate on more important aspects of the decision-making process. But when computers are able to make decisions more efficiently and predictably than human beings, we may find it expedient to give them control over more complicated decisions, even those that affect human lives. While such a shift could eliminate the factor of human bias or error, the role of human being as decision-maker and controller would be seriously challenged. Will the time come when we feel it expedient to relinquish what has always been a purely human prerogative?

As the world grows more chaotic and confusing, might we come to be more and more attracted to the computer's rational predictability? Could some of us even begin to identify more with computerized intelligence than with our fellow man? Might we eventually begin to evaluate our own intelligence by comparing ourselves to computers?

What do we really know about this human mind, which now seems to be on the verge of duplicating itself artificially? What role will we, as living beings, play in the future, if our rational, logical, and decisive abilities, our most highly valued assets, are superseded by a more advanced model? Are we thinking ahead, and guiding ourselves in the direction we wish, or are we caught up in a momentum that is leading us in tightening circles, narrowing our vision and limiting our options for the future?

Answers to such questions must be grounded on the most complete knowledge of human being possible. Before we are swept into a future that might not turn out as we wish, we need to look closely at our present situation and begin a process of examining the very basis of our knowledge—our human consciousness and the nature of our minds.

In reflecting on the complexities of the mind, it might be helpful to think of our ordinary consciousness as a ship, with the rational, judgmental mind as its captain, charting the course that our lives will follow. Our senses and nervous systems, as well as the integrative and cognitive centers of our mind, all have their own networks that channel power throughout the entire ship. Yet they also work together, coordinated by mind.

The intricate power system of our mind-ship involves countless interactions that stimulate the energy of our consciousness, evoking waves of power that enter our cognition with great force as thought explodes into images. These images multiply, reflect, merge, and divide into more images that continue the same interactions. Engaging each other and feeding back countless replications, the shifting images structure themselves into more definite patterns. These patterns of images are also in motion, reflecting, dividing, and reforming in innumerable combinations. All this activity is encompassed within thought, as if thought itself were a sphere of faceted prisms, each having the depth and brilliance of a diamond.

Discrete thoughts spin out of this sphere, arranging themselves in the linear progression of a chain of related thoughts. These in turn interact and proliferate in a complex inner dynamic that includes bursts of sensory impressions, perceptions, memories, associations, and interpretations, flowing together and responding to each other incessantly.

Even before we glimpse the arising thought, the process is nearly complete, arousing feelings and emotions that channel more energy into the cycles of patterning. This entire system is preprogrammed to fire automatically with the onset of the perceptual process.

Our mind-ship floats on an ocean of emotions, sometimes encountering fair weather, at other times riding out storms. The ocean, in flux with the shifting current of desire, is seldom calm; guiding the ship through uncertain waters, the captain makes the decisions that determine our course.

But can we rely upon our captain to guide us wisely? On one level we think we know our own minds. We train their rational capabilities and use them to bring a cohesive order to our lives. We can test the sensitivity of our senses and track their corresponding centers in our brain; we can trace the perceptual process, define our integrative and analytic abilities, and measure them according to our set of definitions. But can such methods reveal our full human capacity?

The more closely we look at the nature of the mind, the less confident we become. We consider the mind to be the arbiter of our knowledge. All that constitutes our reality is cognized by mind. Mind tells us what is knowable and what is unknowable: Our questions arise in mind and are answered in mind. Mind measures, mind interprets, mind carries on dialogue with mind, mind evaluates and judges, mind decides.

When we investigate the nature of our inner realm of feelings, emotions, thoughts, memories, associations, and concepts, we find that mind is the arbiter of our experience as well. But if we try to investigate the field behind our perceptions and thoughts, mind is curiously silent. It seems that mind can measure only within patterns of thoughts and concepts; mind has no measurements for mind.

Is the rational mind truly in command of our whole being? How is it influenced by emotions, feelings, and the fluctuating receptivities of our senses? What is the real nature of thought? Are there other aspects of our consciousness we do not fully understand? How would we know if there were? What happens to our consciousness when we sleep, when we spend hours unaware that we are thinking? Do we really know who we are, and if not, can we know where we are going?

Can we trust our minds to discern the true from the apparent, or to distinguish real values from the superficial? Even when we think we are being rational or reasonable, is this always the case? Our position may seem reasonable on the surface, yet be grounded on false assumptions. If we are skilled, we can justify nearly any position we care to adopt. Even unconsciously, we might shift from position to position at different times, automatically adjusting 'facts' to suit our purposes. Just as we tend to be taken in by outward appearances, we tend to accept logical arguments as persuasive without examining their underlying assumptions too closely. We may regard the written word even more uncritically than spoken language. Like the thoughts that preceded them, words tend to be 'believable' when presented 'rationally'—we forget that both words and logic are constructs of the human mind.

Perceptions are instantly named and labeled by the mind, giving rise to thoughts and ideas that create a particular version of reality. Our sense of 'reality' is especially strong when we are caught up in a strong emotion such as anger. We assert, we deny, we reject, all based on what we 'know' to be right. Yet the next moment we could feel warm and loving. Then our reality might be very different; the reasons for our anger would no longer be compelling; we might later deny our previous anger. Was one 'reality' less real than the other? What kind of thread linked these two 'realities'? We could probably establish a connection that would seem very plausible. Are such connections valid, or are they assumptions? Are they true in themselves, or are they what we want to believe is true? How do we know?

The 'shaping' of our reality can be seen most clearly in circumstances when we feel a need to 'cover' for ourselves. We seldom need to lie—there are usually many 'half truths' that will serve to protect us. In one sense, none of our answers need be wrong, although all may be deceptive. We easily lose sight of the subtle ways we hide the full truth from ourselves and others. Once we have explained our actions, and the other person has accepted our reasons, our own minds may take them as complete truth. Words give our reasons solidity; once the words are spoken, we can easily convince ourselves that they are true. We have no protection from such deceptions arising from the flickering quality of our own minds. Our 'reality' may be more 'flexible' and unstable than we realize.

This flickering quality seems to pervade our experience. For example, we value our right to 'change our mind', but is this 'change' based on new knowledge we have fully investigated? Or does it reflect instead a shift of interest or motivation? How stable is our grasp on what has value and is worth pursuing? How can we trust our minds, when they can 'change', be changed, or influenced so easily?

Lacking greater knowledge of the workings of our own minds, we feed our consciousness a mixed diet of the true and the false, the real and the artificial, beginning with the thoughts that arise in our minds. When we believe in the reality of the thoughts and images created by the sweeping momentum of cognition, we fuse our awareness to illusion and plant the seeds of self-deception. Each time perceptions arise, more thoughts are created, and the process of fusing our awareness to the illusion recurs.

Our consciousness becomes attuned to this on-going process; the seeds planted earlier take root and grow. The pristine quality of perception decreases; a restless quality permeates all our experience, conditioning our view of ourselves and our surroundings. Reaching out for contact with the real, we meet with the superficial, the temporary, and the artificial.

Because our consciousness is so strongly fixated on the objective pole of our experience, looking within and studying ourselves closely becomes very difficult. For all our knowledge of the observable world and our ingenuity in manipulating our environment, we know little about our own nature.

In the context of our own experience we know that our consciousness is more than our rational mind. We have a whole inner realm of responses; we experience love and appreciation, and feel joy when we open our hearts to others. Our feelings of well-being arise from a source within us we do not fully understand. We know of intuition and inspiration, but have no way to explain them; we know of creativity, but cannot arouse it by an act of reason or will. We can respond to a sense of wonder and power that transcends our sense of self, and can exercise compassion for fellow human beings.

These seem to be universal human responses to living in a world inherently beautiful, changing from moment to moment in an unfolding that is always new. But our responses to our living, changing world are interpreted and judged by the part of our minds that tells us what to desire, what to reject, and what will 'make' us happy, as if we had no means of 'being' happy within ourselves. We apply labels that are not intrinsically our own, but grow out of our cultural conditioning. Since this conditioned aspect of mind cannot penetrate the barriers of the perceptual process, it cannot know the heart of our being, the part of ourselves that responds to the true and the real. When knowledge of human being does not penetrate beyond our physiology and the more observable aspects of our consciousness, how can we even think about our full human birthright or open new possibilities for growth?

Our consciousness is naturally receptive and can be sustained by an inflow of appreciation and joy. But like a great lake, it can become depleted when its energy flows only in an outward direction. When our consciousness is continually preoccupied and pressured, filled with thoughts, desires, and anticipations, we leave no open space for revitalization. Eventually, our consciousness becomes tired. Our senses, inadequately supported by our awareness, become numb and dull, requiring ever more intense forms of external stimulation.

Our present way of living and being in our world cannot prevent this from happening. However many facts we have at our command, and however well we learn to manipulate information, our use of mind is not dynamic enough to awaken the full power of our consciousness.

For all our effort to satisfy the natural human desire for a healthier and happier life, there are signs that a deep hunger is growing within our most prosperous societies. Needs and desires seem to be increasing rather than decreasing. As we move into the future, devising new applications for our knowledge and producing an endless stream of new products, we seem forced to go faster, driven by a restless wanting that will not be stilled. In a sense, our creativity is being channeled into imagining new products and bringing them into being, so that we can then desire our new creations.

Our lives now move quickly, carrying us on a wave of wanting, allowing us little time to deeply enjoy any one experience. While a feast of products and pleasures is spread before us, we have time only to sample and move on, following the images of our desires from place to place. We are always in motion; led by thoughts and images away from our vital center, we have no place of rest; we have no real home.

34

Unbounded Mind

*The energy of human consciousness
may share an affinity with light
that we do not yet understand.*

At this critical time, when the pace of change may be exceeding our ability to direct it with wisdom, our alternatives are rapidly diminishing. The knowledge we apply now will decide whether human being is dominated or liberated by all we are bringing into being. We face the need to create a new vision for humanity, a vision that will uplift peoples of all nations and provide the foundation for a new understanding of peace and prosperity.

Inspiration to create and sustain an expanded vision of human being can only arise from greater knowledge of human consciousness. Yet in concentrating on the aspects of the mind that can be evaluated and analyzed, we may have come to assume that we cannot know our consciousness. How can we so easily assume this when we use our minds continuously? We live within our own consciousness: It is our life, our home, the essence of our human being. Saying we cannot know our consciousness is like saying that we cannot see our lips moving when we talk. From one perspective, this may be true, but the solution is to look into a mirror. We may simply not yet have discovered the mirror that will reveal the true nature of our consciousness.

Perhaps this mirror lies within our consciousness itself. Behind or around our thoughts we may sense a reflective field or a crystalline mirror-like quality. Perhaps the objective world is mirrored in our mind more completely than we know. If we developed the means to examine our minds more directly, using the discoveries we make about the nature of physical realities as indications of what we might find within, we might discover an entirely new way to view ourselves and our relationship to our world.

During the last several centuries we have used scientific methods to explore the world around us. Looking to the heavens, we discovered that the sun was not the center, but a part of a great galaxy, one of many. Now there are speculations that our galaxy might be part of a still larger system. Investigating solid forms, we found they were composed of molecules; going deeper, we found molecules were composed of atoms; going still farther, we found electrons, protons, and eventually even stranger particles that vacillate between matter and energy.

In each case, we have found nothing flat, linear, or static. From the smallest to the largest units of matter, the physical universe seems to exhibit repeating patterns. Entities revolve around each other, spinning in cycles; matter becomes energy, energy matter.

Space is vibrant with dynamic interactions that convert ultimately into light.

Might our minds follow similar patterns? Are thoughts complex patternings of energy? Is our consciousness related to fundamental physical forces? These questions are now only speculations, for we have not developed the means to examine the full spectrum of human consciousness at this fundamental level.

In the past, when we felt the pressing need for greater knowledge, we have made strenuous efforts to develop better means of observation. Perhaps we can apply this same sense of urgency to understanding human beings, and develop ways to research our consciousness more deeply. As a starting point for research, we could begin with what resources we have: our senses, perceptual processes, and our analytic abilities. We have used our senses to gain knowledge about the physical world; perhaps we can also use them in other ways. We might be able to use our vision to 'look within' in more than a metaphorical sense; we might also be able to direct our other senses inward as well.

'Sensing within', we may find that our senses have a subtle aspect related to a broader awareness. Normally, we say that our senses are 'aware of' something, inferring a relationship between ourselves and what we are seeing. It might also be possible to simply 'be aware' without reference to who is aware of what, shifting emphasis to 'inside' the experience. There might be 'seeing' or 'hearing' in greater depth and fullness than we now know. But until we have more direct experience, we have no words to express the difference between our customary understanding of awareness and awareness that goes beyond a subject experiencing an object.

Learning to 'read the language' of our more subtle perceptual abilities, we might find a fascinating realm that we have overlooked. Through sustained observation and analysis, we could expand our conceptual structures to embrace new knowledge of human consciousness. Once our perspective on human consciousness began to change, every new discovery concerning our physical world could inspire us to look within, balancing our knowledge of the observable world with knowledge of the observer.

The ancient maps defined the edges of a flat world where dragons awaited those who ventured beyond the limits of the known. The view that the measurable aspects of our consciousness are all we can know may be as limiting in our time as was the flat world view in ages past. With a greater vision of human destiny and the courage to traverse our mental realms, what might we find? How far could we go if we were not stopped by our conventional understanding? If we were willing to face our dragons directly?

Constricted by the pressures mounting on all sides, human beings are confined ever more closely to the channels of knowledge established long ago. The pressure itself makes it nearly impossible to see that our lives are essentially recyclings from the past. Weary of this endless repetition, our consciousness may be growing old and tired, darkening under the burden of stagnation and pressure. Lacking a means of replenishment, our collective mental vitality may be winding down in entropic cycles. Should this be happening, we may soon become locked into our present patterning. Then it would be much more difficult to renew human consciousness; future generations would have no choice but to repeat the same patterns in ever-tightening cycles.

Yet now, in this moment, we have a priceless opportunity to awaken the full resources of our consciousness and reinvigorate our minds. How can we conceive of the dynamic power of our consciousness, which has sustained itself for a million years of human evolution? The energy of human consciousness may share an affinity with light that we do not yet understand. Turning toward that light, we might find it the source of all our inspiration and creativity.

With more mental energy, we could rise above the turbulence of confusion and desire that clouds our vision, and view human potentialities in a far brighter light. Tapping even a part of our awareness, we gave rise to our present creation. If we can find ways to awaken the full power of awareness, we could enter a new phase of human evolution and revitalize ourselves and our world.

35

Knowledge of Freedom

*The magical play of the mind contains
all possibilities for growth and change.*

I t seems we have come full circle. Is this the end
of our journey? Did we begin with speculation
about our past, only to end with speculation about our
future? What new knowledge have we gained?

Perhaps we are now aware of how little we really
know. We have seen that the world around us, even
the all-encompassing universe, plays out its role in the
drama of birth and death, creation and destruction. In
our mind's eye, we can imagine the life of our sun and
earth beginning in a swirling cloud of elements. We
might imagine even earlier beginnings, moving back
to a mysterious point in time that preceded the very
formation of the universe. Beyond this point it is difficult to even imagine. Behind each beginning, we touch
upon a realm of complete uncertainty.

If we consider the future of our world, we arrive at
a similar point of unknowing. We assume that some
day our sun will grow old and die, collapsing into

nothingness. All life on our planet will certainly be extinguished. It seems that even the universe must eventually come to an end. Will even space and time cease to be? Our earth, our galaxy, the universe—all seem to arise and disappear from an unknown point of potentiality, which our knowledge, limited to a fixed spectrum of existence, does not reveal.

When we consider the origins and destiny of human beings, we are again at a loss. Our origins are uncertain, and our future is completely unknown. As we travel back in time, the thread of understanding that links us to the beginnings of human being grows ever more tenuous. What circumstances brought forth a mind that could think, form associations, and re-member? What gave rise to the fine-tuned hearing and voice that made speech possible? What motivated human beings to develop language?

We are even uncertain about the chain of events that brought human beings to this point in space and time. One event has led to another, somehow leading to the present, as civilizations and nations have come and gone. Who could have predicted, five hundred years ago, how human beings would live today? Who could have known then what this country would turn out to be? With all the different possibilities that now exist, who can say how the world will be in another five hundred years?

Imagining the beginning of our own life, we are caught in the same uncertainty. We emerge out of nowhere—from some space and time we cannot comprehend. Eventually our body will dissolve back into the elements, but what will become of the energy that activates our body and mind? What is the destiny of our consciousness? This remains as mysterious as the time before our birth.

Bounded by uncertainties, we live out our lives in an unceasing stream of change. Nothing stands still, within or without; we and everything in our world pulse with the heartbeat of time. Our seemingly solid bodies encase whirling galaxies of particles that mirror the nature of all existence. Every form, every cell, every particle of our being and of the world around us is continually becoming something else, eternally free of a fixed place in the known or of a resting place in the future. Like a river, change carries all existence in a continuous stream.

Even our seemingly stable lives are swept along by change: As our day unfolds, our senses resonate to the world about us; images and thoughts pass through our minds, our breath flows in and out, supporting our speech and action. Our hearts beat in pace with our movements and emotions. Moment by moment, we live amidst a continual flow of perception, thought, and emotion, patterns arising and subsiding in seem- ingly unending repetitions. Each moment arises as an uncertainty, an unknown as vast as the moment before the universe came into being, as deeply sig- nificant and full of potential as the moment before our own birth. How can human beings endure living in such pervasive uncertainty?

Existing in a perpetual state of unknowing, we seek stability nearly reflexively. We view our lives as having a beginning, a duration, and an ending: a story written in time. We experience ourselves as moving through time as an actor moves across a stage, playing out scene after scene. We live out the story of our lives, thinking we are moving forward as we attempt to realize our dreams: what we desire for ourselves and for future generations. Yet it seems we are replaying the same story again and again.

Within this story, we see only the end result of changes. We look, and we see the same images, the same forms, the same people day after day. We walk through the same routines, say the same words, make the same gestures, respond according to the same patterns year after year. Desire, pleasure, boredom, excitement, disappointment, new desire, anticipation, frustration—interwoven patterns, reinforced by memories and associations, enchain us; we have no way to break free and see ourselves as we are. Our awareness is hypnotized by sameness and repetition.

From the moment we engage a thought, we repeat ancient patternings of naming, freezing into concepts the living reality before us. Out of an infinitude of potentialities, we shape distinct entities by labeling, delineating, measuring, defining, and particularizing. How could we even function if we had to rename everything each instant? Dividing time into separate moments and space into solid forms, we cognize 'real things' moving through time as well as space.

We set up unquestionable rules to define 'real things', and we find ourselves in a realm of things that we 'know'. We 'know' what happiness is, or freedom; we 'know' what we mean when we say 'mind'. We 'know' what suffering is, and we 'know' who we are. When we gather together all of the names we 'know', we have our body of knowledge, which we use to live in our world. Even knowledge becomes a 'thing' that we particularize into endlessly finer distinctions.

Wherever we look in our language, we can see the emphasis on the concrete and the real. We give substance to intangible ideas, such as freedom and progress, and to our process words, such as movement and change. We can make things even more solid by saying: "This is." "This is not." "We are."

We step into the 'real' and deadened world of things when we say "I am." Ignoring the changing open field of potentialities, we make ourselves separate, lonely beings existing in a world of frozen, separate things. We are locked into a definition of 'real' that we cannot change without calling our very existence into question. We cling to these notions of existence; we support this view with our life itself, believing in 'I am' as our most certain fact of all. It gives us a place, a position, just as everything we can name has a position. But what do we know of its substance—what is the nature of our being?

Denying the nature of our vibrant world, we have no freedom from the things we 'know'. We have no freedom from the things we name, the things we can see and feel, the things which arouse our desires and aversions. We are not free from wanting, from frustration, from anxiety; we have no freedom from loneliness, anger, guilt, or regret. We have no freedom from our own thoughts.

Knowing all this, we gain some insight into our situation: We have been deceived by untold ages of conditioning into accepting a view of life that binds us to repeating patterns, limits our freedom, and perpetuates suffering. We can see how our very senses present us with fixed things, oblivious to the changing flow of life. We can begin to see how our thoughts and desires lure us into repeating the same dramas until we run out of time, and our stories come to an end in old age and death.

We may see the futility of repeating the same themes; we may want to be free. But where is the knowledge broad enough to free us? Our present way of knowing expands only in specific directions; following old patterns, we are moving inexorably toward greater specialization. Confining knowledge into ever smaller and more isolated compartments, we are losing sight of the knowledge that gives meaning to human life. Our knowledge is like a great cone that opens on a wide vista. The further we extend ourselves along its surface, the broader our vision appears to grow, and the more we may feel we have unlimited potential for extending its range. Yet limiting ourselves to the surface of the cone, we are susceptible to 'tunnel vision'.

Can our present way of understanding ourselves and our world ever provide us with real freedom? How can we trust our knowledge when it continually tells us stories to make us think we are already free? Although our lives are permeated with deep suffering and insecurity, we deny our unknowing; we reject the uncertainty that would compel us to begin our search for knowledge and freedom. Even if we try to forge an opening in the pattern, the mind shifts the focus of attention back to words: Instead of freedom, we are given words which justify our pain, and thoughts that confine us to the patterns which perpetuate our suffering. But words do not set us free. They lull us with reasons for our suffering, reasons for our limitations, for our wanting, hatreds, aggressions, and violence toward ourselves and everything in our world. Our words are leading us in circles, while we think they are pointing the way to freedom.

When we see the full implications of continuing as we are and ask "What can we do?," our thoughts instantly display an array of solutions, but they all involve us again in the same patterns. Our fixed notions of ourselves and what we are capable of becoming shut the door of possibilities for what we can experience, know, and do. Our words, our language, and our thoughts have locked the door and concealed the key. Within our inner prison, our choices are limited, and freedom is an empty word.

It seems we will not accidentally escape from this prison of our way of knowing. Its walls are held in place by our sense of separation, our short-sighted actions, and our inability to see beyond our own self-interest. Our habitual patterning exerts a force upon the mind like a magnetic attraction, drawing the mind to 'solid' images, objects, and thoughts, and binding it to this solid realm. Even if we see the patterns and try to break free, we are drawn back into the patterns almost reflexively.

But now more than ever we need to wake up and recognize the limitations of our knowledge, not only for ourselves, but for the future of all human beings. During the last few decades, we have begun to direct our knowledge into channels which are pathways to destruction, endangering the survival of all forms of life on our planet.

How can we free ourselves from this prison when the patterns bind us so tightly? Although it may be hard to recognize and hard to use, the key to unlock the prison door lies within us. The knowledge that binds us can also be the knowledge that opens the path to freedom. We already have a wealth of such knowledge: We know the extent of our limitations; we know the ever-tightening cycles of wanting and frustration that constrict our vision; we know the hopelessness of continuing as we are. Now we need to take the next step, and set our knowledge free.

Grounding ourselves in the knowledge we have, we can awaken determination to never again be caught up in duplication. This determination *is* the confidence we need to break free of the patterns that bind us. With each effort we loosen the hold of habitual responses and experience a new inflow of knowledge. Although our initial efforts may not succeed, we can encourage ourselves, knowing that knowledge will support us. When we back determination with new knowledge and apply it immediately in our lives, we gain strength from each experience. Remembering and acting upon all we know, we refine our knowledge continually. In time, we can build up a dynamic momentum that will completely overcome the force of our patterning.

Although our present knowledge is limited, it has also created much beauty. It has given us powerful tools to enhance human life: Everything we need for an unparalleled renaissance of human well-being is in place. The whole field of our consciousness lies before us, awaiting exploration. Our knowledge is like a nugget of unwrought gold; on the anvil of our questioning mind we can work it into a golden sphere of unequaled beauty.

Once we know how to recognize the face of knowledge, we will find knowledge everywhere. Observing, analyzing, and applying what we learn, we can open our minds to knowledge every moment of our lives. The whole pattern of human life, in all of its variations, can be unfolded for us to study and appreciate. Even the experience of others can become a source of knowledge: Those older than we are show us where our lives are leading; those younger can remind us where we have been.

After we have loosened the confining patterns of our thinking, we can find a way to open the walls of the cone, and see the full sphere of potentiality afforded us by time and knowledge. All that now seems so crowded and solid—our physical world, our complexities, thoughts, feelings, emotions—can open into a realm of infinite possibilities. Freed from the enervation of repetition, we can find our way to freedom and invite greater knowledge into our world.

Open to the flow of experience and the rhythms of time, we can free ourselves of frustration and pain, and live with a mind that is free. Relying upon our inherent receptivity to knowledge, we can create a new model of freedom and project its image so powerfully that it can overcome the divisive forces at work in the world.

Perhaps eventually we could open wide the eyes of mind, and stretch the limits of our imagination, returning to the zero point of human consciousness, the point of all potentiality. What vistas might we see, if we were to understand the full power of the human mind? The human consciousness may prove the most inspiring frontier in our history, an endless wellspring of knowledge, and our means of liberation from all limitations. Every situation, every thought or concept that appears to be stagnant could be a vehicle to a greater knowing. Even pain and confusion can be our doorways to knowledge.

By opening up the closed aspects of our experience to the greater knowing inherent within our minds, we can enter into a love affair with knowledge. With knowledge as our greatest friend, our supporter, and our witness, we can free ourselves from all limitations. We need never reduce the quality of experience to something that is 'known'. We can appreciate each moment with interest and wonder, in tune with an unfolding that is always new.

This freedom belongs naturally to the mind. Shifting and unbounded, the mind, like a vast ocean, has great depth and restorative power. Waves arise on the surface, taking myriad forms—high peaks and white foam, gentle ripples and bubbles, sprays of tiny drops. The boundaries of the droplet or the wave are not rigid; each form is continually changing, ever becoming new in a dynamic continuum of infinite potential. Waves arise 'into existence', endure in a changing fluid form, and disappear. Yet every form is water, fluid and transparent, unfixed and ungraspable. Within each tiny droplet is contained the deepest secrets of the ocean.

This magical play of the mind contains all possibilities for growth and change; its very nature is flexible and free. So free perhaps, that we become confused and hasten to stabilize ourselves and our world. But even our solid realm holds a potential that is truly unlimited. Every entity contains worlds within worlds, pulsating with life.

No position we take will imprison us forever, although no position will ever be able to encompass the natural flexibility and potential of the mind. Yet we can learn to move through experience like a fish through water, an accomplished dancer, or an eagle soaring in the sky. We can pass from understanding to understanding, deepening and broadening our vision until we reach a freedom from all fixed positions, a transparent clarity based on freedom itself.

Viewing freedom as intrinsic to our being, we discover that our lives are what we make them. All options are open, our choices unlimited. When we have knowledge, space grants us unbounded opportunity, and time presents us with infinite possibilities for change.

Index

experience (*continued*)
  quality of, 212, 213
  sharing of, 233

family, 48, 50, 105, 139
fantasy world, 95, 117, 134, 250, 252, 255
fear, 21, 94, 116, 142, 151, 172, 175, 177, 179, 182, 200, 227, 230, 235, 237
  of failure, 237
feeling, 224, 262, 263, 293, 308
fire, 8, 13
fishes, 7
free enterprise, 45, 46
freedom, xix-xxi, 26, 42ff, 100, 260, 361ff
  attitudes towards, xiii
  individual, 43, 46, 105, 281, 337
  inner, 161, 317
  limitations on, xx, 363-365
  mental, 162
  of religious belief, 43
  of speech, 43, 50
  of thought, 43, 48
  protection of, xix, 43
  side-effects of, 48
frustration, 32, 45, 51, 69, 70, 93, 104, 127, 166, 176, 177, 256, 322, 336, 366
  relief of, 221
fulfillment, 139, 142, 230
future, 17, 19, 50, 71, 281, 345, 351, 358
  knowledge of, 163

gaps, 37, 112
goals, 53, 112, 139, 229, 234, 263, 274
  long-range, 232
Golden Gate Bridge, 31
good intentions, 61, 62, 71
government, 49
'greater good', 46
Greece, 12
gridlock, 73
growth, stages of, 169ff, 184
guilt, 95, 127, 133, 165, 176, 218, 219, 238

happiness, 144, 165-166
health, 111
heart, protection of, 221
heartbeat, 220, 221
helplessness, 171, 180
hope, 62, 141
hopelessness, 69
Huang-po Valley, 10,
human beings, 7-15, 277, 303, 353, 359
  destiny of, 163
  history of, 26
  nature of, 303-304
  origins of, 163, 303
  sense organs of, 7

Other Dharma Publishing Books

Time, Space, and Knowledge: A New Vision of Reality by Tarthang Tulku. Thirty-five exercises and a rigorous philosophical text reveal ever more brilliant times, spaces, and knowledges.

Dimensions of Thought, Volumes I and II produced under the direction of Tarthang Tulku. Explorations of the Time-Space-Knowledge vision by scholars and practitioners from all walks of life.

Gesture of Balance by Tarthang Tulku. The Nyingma method of meditation wherein all life experience is meditation.

Openness Mind by Tarthang Tulku. The sequel to *Gesture of Balance*, with more advanced meditation practices.

Hidden Mind of Freedom by Tarthang Tulku. A guide to self-understanding based upon articles published in *Crystal Mirror* and *Gesar* Magazine over a nine-year period.

Kum Nye Relaxation, Parts 1 and 2 by Tarthang Tulku. Over 200 exercises for discovering the relaxing energies within our bodies and senses.

Skillful Means by Tarthang Tulku. A manual for making work a source of unlimited fulfillment.

Crystal Mirror Series edited by Tarthang Tulku. Introductory exploration of the various aspects of Tibetan philosophy, history, psychology, art, and culture. Seven volumes currently available.

If you order Dharma books directly from the publisher, it will help us to make more such books available. Write for a free catalog and new book announcements.

Dharma Publishing   2425 Hillside Avenue
Berkeley, California 94704   USA

The symbol in ancient Lantsa script on the preceding page spells the Sanskrit word *Jayantu*. It signifies victory and expresses the wish that all people be truly free.